Primitive Baptists of the Wiregrass South

UNIVERSITY PRESS OF FLORIDA

Florida A&M University, Tallahassee
Florida Atlantic University, Boca Raton
Florida Gulf Coast University, Ft. Myers
Florida International University, Miami
Florida State University, Tallahassee
New College of Florida, Sarasota
University of Central Florida, Orlando
University of Florida, Gainesville
University of North Florida, Jacksonville
University of South Florida, Tampa
University of West Florida, Pensacola

Primitive Baptists of the Wiregrass South

1815 to the Present

John G. Crowley

University Press of Florida
Gainesville · Tallahassee · Tampa · Boca Raton
Pensacola · Orlando · Miami · Jacksonville · Fort Myers · Sarasota

Printed in the United States of America on acid-free paper

First cloth printing, 1998
First paperback printing, 2013

Library of Congress Cataloging-in-Publication Data

Crowley, John G. 1955–
Primitive Baptists of the wiregrass south : 1815 to the present /
John G. Crowley
p. cm.
Includes bibliographical references and index.
ISBN 978-0-8130-1640-5 (cloth: alk. paper)
ISBN 978-0-8130-4468-2 (pbk.)
1. Primitive Baptists—Georgia—History.
2. Primitive Baptists—Florida—History. I. Title.
BX6385.G4C76 1998
286'.4—dc21 98-39624

The University Press of Florida is the scholarly publishing agency for the State University System of Florida, comprising Florida A&M University, Florida Atlantic University, Florida Gulf Coast University, Florida International University, Florida State University, New College of Florida, University of Central Florida, University of Florida, University of North Florida, University of South Florida, and University of West Florida.

University Press of Florida
15 Northwest 15th Street
Gainesville, FL 32611-2079
http://www.upf.com

Dedicated to the memory of my beloved mother,
Lillian Esther Redding Crowley (1909–1996),
always a pillar of strength and a fountain of wisdom to me.
A descendant of many generations of Primitive Baptists,
she exemplified all that is good about them.

We are travelling home to God,
In the way the fathers trod;
They are happy now, and we
Soon their happiness shall see

—*Primitive Hymns,* no. 201, v. 2

CONTENTS

ILLUSTRATIONS

PREFACE

Travelers in rural South Georgia and Florida occasionally notice small, severe chapels in remote areas, often without a sign giving the name and denominational affiliation of the church. These are the meetinghouses of the Primitive Baptists, and many newcomers to the region live virtually in the shadow of their houses of worship and seldom learn anything of them.

The Primitive Baptists are a small denomination with their main strength in the southeastern United States. Their distinctive characteristic is an intense conservatism that has won them the nickname "Hardshell" and a fearsome reputation for gloomy austerity. As with many such epithets, Primitive Baptists may call themselves Hardshells but do not care for others to address them so.

The real life of the denomination occurs mainly in local churches and associational bodies, since it has no hierarchy or common headquarters. Focus on a local or regional group of Primitive Baptists reveals the influence of powerful personalities and social movements better than would a study of larger scope. Other than the writer's master's thesis, little, if anything, has appeared on the particular group of Primitive Baptists covered here.

In much of South Georgia and Florida, however, these people represented a significant religious force until well into the twentieth century. The Wiregrass and pine barrens regions of the southern coastal plains constitute an area historically understudied, and the early prevalence and long continuance of the Primitive Baptist faith in these regions represent an important and neglected facet of the culture. Those who settled the Wiregrass and flatwoods regions of South Georgia and Florida were largely stock drovers. These folk reflected a distinct culture in which the Primitive Baptist denomination figured prominently. Georgia Antimissionism took its first rise in this region, and the denomination remained numerically supreme in many areas until after the Civil War and strong until long after the turn of the twentieth century. After the Second World War and the decline of southern rural communities, Primitive Baptists entered a period of sharp decline in numbers.

The Primitive church still survives best in those regions where its attendant culture ran deepest.

Casual observers often dismissed the Wiregrass people as backward and illiterate. The often complex doctrinal and disciplinary issues handled by Primitive churches and associations show that the unprepossessing dwellers in the "cow counties" of the coastal plain carried on a surprising intellectual activity. Often, their controversies seem to have been exacerbated by social forces, which their separatist ideology addressed by transmuting them into ecclesiastical terms. Thus, the Missionary Controversy represents their reaction to the forces of the Jacksonian era and to the entry into the region of a second wave of settlers with more money and social standing than the original pioneers. Civil War, Reconstruction, Progressivism, the Depression, and the Cold War era all influenced the Primitives, but on their own terms, in conflicts having little apparent relationship to the greater world.

The Primitive Baptist groups central to this volume are the Ochlocknee Association, with its antecedents, filiates, correspondents, and schismatic offshoots, covering most of southern Georgia and Florida. These Primitive Baptists displayed most of the trends affecting the denomination throughout its history but also show several aspects unique to the region, particularly the formation of splinter groups of conservatives, locally confined, principally in the Okefenokee Basin and adjacent regions.

I had the tremendous advantage of coming from a family traditionally identified with the denomination, although as for many such children, my instruction in the faith followed no forced or formal pattern. A regular attendant of the Primitive Baptist churches in North Florida and South Georgia from 1969 onward, I obtained material sufficient for many books, both from the rich oral tradition of the church and from its voluminous and carefully preserved records. Much of this material appears in the endnotes.

A transfer of membership to another denomination, followed by a period of no formal religious allegiance, provided me with much needed perspective, tempering the intitiate's knowledge with the outsider's detachment. In the following pages I hope to provide a loving, sometimes astringent, but I hope fair assessment of the Primitive faith, as a contribution to southern social history and an act of gratitude to the church that contributed much to my personal formation, and as an offering to my ancestral shades.

The number of people who have helped me in this work is legion. Foremost are my late mother and her sisters, the late Sarah Mae Redding Parrish (1908–98) and Julia Nell Redding Parrish, who first introduced me to my ancestral religion, whose keen memories and brilliant insights into that faith greatly guided me. Over the years a great number of Primitive Baptists living and dead, far too many to name without leaving some out, taught me much about their denomination. Always when I needed access to rare records, photographs, and personal recollections, they helped without stint or complaint. The generosity of my beloved cousin, Dean Day Smith, made possible both the completion of my education and the writing of this book. I thank the members of my Florida State University Ph.D. committee: Dr. Joe M. Richardson, Dr. Peter P. Garretson, Dr. Maxine D. Jones, Dr. William W. Rogers, and Dr. Walter L. Moore. I also wish to single out Dr. Lamar Pearson of Valdosta State University, whose advice, encouragement, and motivational counsel throughout have been invaluable.

→ 1 ←

"The Rock Whence Ye Are Hewn"

Origins of Southern Primitive Baptist Doctrine and Practice

The 1838 Circular Address of the Suwannee River Baptist Association declared that

> shortly after the ascension of Christ, . . . persecution arose so high against the Church that it had to flee to the wilderness, where the Lord had a place prepared for her, even in the Valley of Piedmont, and other places, where they wandered about in Sheep-skins and Goat-skins. Though they were not known under the title of Baptist, yet their enemies acknowledged that they practiced and believed, as the Scriptures tolerate us to believe. There they staid preaching, believing and practicing, as they had received it from the Apostles, till the Reformation; then they came forth with the same Gospel Doctrine that we find in the Scriptures. So we can say the origin of the Baptist can be traced back to Christ and John, and that no other denomination can trace theirs further back than to the Pope; and we are bold to say that the Baptist Church of Christ never came out of, nor went into, what some call the Holy Catholic Church of Rome.[1]

Most Primitive Baptists still believe that their churches have an unbroken succession of identical belief and practice going back to apostolic times. Most historians of religion, however, believe Primitive Baptist doctrine originated in the so-called "Hyper-Calvinism" of the English Independents and Particular Baptists and that their church discipline and liturgy derived from the union of the Regular and Separate Baptists.

Early Baptists in the South fell into two major groups, the Particular or Regular Baptists and the Separate Baptists. The Particular Baptists took their title from their belief in particular redemption, or limited atonement: the belief that Christ died to atone for sins of the elect only. With the rise of the Separate Baptists in the 1750s, the older Particular churches called themselves Regular Baptists. The greatest single influence on the development of the American Particular Baptists was the Philadelphia Association, founded in 1707. Centrally located in an area with many Baptists, the Philadelphia organization served as a model for later Baptist associations.[2]

Associationalism played a tremendous role in Primitive Baptist history. It originated early among the English Particular Baptists. By 1644, seven Particular Baptist churches existed in and around London. In that year, they met and produced a Calvinistic confession of faith.[3] In 1653, English Particular Baptist soldiers, settled in Ireland, formed a church union based on the military "associations" that emerged during the English Civil War. The Irish Association called for the formation of similar groups among other Particular Baptists and for such groups to maintain denominational unity by corresponding. Such associations were widespread by 1660, and the pattern then established remains in use among Primitive Baptists today.[4]

Although the Particular Baptists found great utility in associations, they also feared the hierarchical potential of these bodies. At a 1677 general meeting in London, the delegates were careful to state that "these messengers assembled, are not entrusted with any Church-power so called; or with any jurisdiction over the Churches themselves, to exercise any censures either over any Churches or Persons, or to impose their determination on the Churches, or Officers."[5]

In 1750, the Philadelphia Association published an essay on associational power. It declared the Apostolic Council in Acts 15 the biblical basis for associations. The exposition expressed the ambiguous standing of associations among a people devoted to the sovereignty of the individual church. Associational members did not think the association a "superior judicature." Churches had the right to "exercise every part of gospel discipline and church government, independent of any other church or assembly whatever." However, associations had power to drop disorderly churches from fellowship and to advise their member churches to do the same.[6]

The Philadelphia Association soon adopted the early British Baptist practice of interassociational correspondence, an important instrument of unity in a denomination with no real hierarchy or center. In 1761, the Philadelphia Association voted to revive annual correspondence to "the Board of Particular Baptist ministers in London . . . as a part of that community, in the British dominions, (whereof you have in some sort the superintendence)."[7] By 1766, the Phildelphia Association corresponded with other American associations, and later it exchanged printed copies of its minutes with them.[8] This practice remains an important aspect of associational life among Primitive Baptists.

Associations on the Philadelphia model appeared in the South in 1751, with the organization of the Charleston Baptist Association. Oliver Hart, a young minister from the Philadelphia Association who had recently relocated to South Carolina, promoted the formation of an association. Charleston, Ashley River, and Welsh Neck churches formed the association, with the church at Euhaw joining soon afterward.[9]

In eastern North Carolina, General Baptists, the ancestors of the later southern wing of the Freewill Baptists, organized churches in the 1720s and 1730s. These large, loosely organized congregations, easy in discipline, required no account of conversion from candidates for baptism and soon got the attention of Particular Baptists. In the 1750s both the Charleston Association and the Philadelphia Association sent ministers into North Carolina to reorganize these churches on the Particular Baptist plan. John Gano, one of these ministers, attended a meeting of North Carolina preachers and preached from the text "Jesus I know, and Paul I know, but who are ye?"[10] He and his companions then went to work, leaving the North Carolina Baptists scarcely recognizable. They reduced one General Baptist church from one hundred members to the five who convinced the visitors that they were genuinely born again. They sifted twelve out of another fellowship of more than two hundred members.[11] One General Baptist preacher's "experience" did not pass muster with the Philadelphia preachers. Crestfallen, he told an inquiring neighbor, "The Lord have mercy upon you, for this Northern minister put a *mene tekel* upon me."[12]

In 1765, these eastern North Carolina churches formed the Kehukee Association.[13] This body played a pivotal role in the history of the Primitive Baptists. From Freewill Baptists, the Kehukeeites developed into thoroughgoing predestinarians, later leading the southern Primitives in opposition to missions.[14]

As the name indicated, a strong Calvinism characterized Regular/Particular Baptist belief. During the seventeenth and eighteenth centuries, however, Calvinism underwent several developments that resulted in shadings of opinion among both British and American Calvinistic Baptists. In the eighteenth century, the doctrine later stigmatized as Hyper-Calvinism emerged, which greatly exalted predestination and minimized human ability.[15]

In 1689, the English Particular Baptists adopted the Westminster Presbyterian Confession—later to be known as the London Confession—with a few changes in regard to church organization, baptism, and civil authority in religious questions. The Philadelphia Association formally adopted it in

1742; it thus also came to be called the Philadelphia Confession, and its High Calvinism became the doctrinal standard of the Particular Baptists. The Charleston and Kehukee associations adopted the Philadelphia Confession at their organization.[16]

In the late 1600s, some English theologians began to take higher ground on predestination. Joseph Hussey (1660–1726) first clearly stated the stronger Calvinist position. Ordained an Independent minister in 1688, Hussey preached the duty of all persons to believe. In 1707, however, he published *God's Operations of Grace but No Offers of His Grace.* As the title suggests, Hussey argued in this work that the doctrine of unconditional election made appeals to all persons absurd. The sovereign operations of God ought to be preached to sinners, but not offers of grace on conditions. Hussey stigmatized preachers who combined offers of salvation with divine sovereignty as "half-hearted Calvinists."[17] This position became that of the English Strict Baptists and the American Primitive Baptists in the next century. Hussey's *Operations* was being offered for sale by a Primitive Baptist publisher as late as 1978.[18]

The greatest Baptist theologian of the eighteenth century, John Gill (1697–1771), firmly advocated the no offers position. Brilliant, though largely self-educated, Gill joined the Particular Baptists in 1716 and received ordination in 1720. He published, among many other writings, a voluminous commentary on the Bible, a *Body of Divinity,* and *The Cause of God and Truth,* written in reply to the Arminian Daniel Whitby. The Primitive Baptist historian Sylvester Hassell hailed Gill as "the soundest, the most learned, and the most able Baptist theologian since the death of the Apostle John . . . the only man that ever hunted and drove out Arminianism from the explanation of every verse in the Bible, from the beginning of Genesis to the end of Revelation."[19]

In the *Body of Divinity,* completed shortly before his death, Gill wrote at length on preaching to the unregenerate.

> [The gospel] is not a call to them to regenerate and convert themselves . . . which is the pure work of the Spirit of God . . . nor to any spiritual vital acts, which they are incapable of, being natural men and dead in trespasses and sins. Nor is the gospel-ministry an offer of Christ, and of his grace and salvation by him, which are not in the power of the ministers of it to give, nor of carnal men to receive; the gospel is not an offer, but a preaching of Christ crucified, a proclamation of the unsearchable riches of his grace. . . . Yet there is something which the ministry of the word, and the call by it, have to do with unregenerate sinners: . . . the fullness, freeness, and suitableness of this salvation, are

> to be preached before them; and the whole to be left, to the Spirit of God, to make application of it as he shall think fit.[20]

Gill and the other anti-offer Calvinists were widely read. The Philadelphia Association recommended his commentary to its ministers as late as 1807.[21] David Benedict recalled that in his youth (c. 1810), "our old Baptist divines . . . were generally strong Calvinists as to their doctrinal creed, and but few of them felt at liberty to call upon sinners in plain terms to repent and believe the Gospel, on account of their inability to do so without Divine assistance. Rousing appeals to . . . consciences on the subject of . . . conversion did not constitute a part of their public address."[22]

Gill's Calvinism never completely dominated Particular Baptist thought in England or America. In the 1730s, a controversy arose among the English Particular Baptists over "whether saving faith in Christ is a duty required by the moral law of all those who live under the Gospel revelation?" Abraham Taylor, a former General Baptist, and others maintained that it was, while Gill and several other ministers maintained the opposite. Those on the negative side of the "Modern Question," as the controversy came to be called, made a distinction between "evangelical" faith and repentance, which came from God alone, a gift rather than a duty, and a "legal" faith and repentance, which unregenerates could perform and which obtained for them some benefits, though not eternal salvation.[23] This controversy laid the foundation for a reaction against anti-offer Calvinism among English Baptists in the late 1700s.

The Separate Baptists emerged from the Great Awakening, the evangelical revival that swept Britain and America in the mid 1700s. The Separates spread throughout the lower South after 1755, and for several years their relations with the older Particulars were strained. The southern Separates arose from the labors of Shubal Stearns and his brother-in-law, Daniel Marshall. Stearns and Marshall, originally Connecticut Congregationalists, experienced conversion under George Whitfield's preaching during the Great Awakening and, like many of his other converts, felt the Congregational churches to be dead, formal, and unspiritual.[24] Whitfield's followers, called "New Lights," frequently withdrew from the parish churches to form "separate" congregations with stricter church discipline. These Separate congregations allowed preaching by men who had not received collegiate training and also demanded an account of a conversion experience as a prerequisite for membership, a practice that had fallen into disuse in many Congregational churches. With their insistence on a converted church membership, and with the example of the numerous Baptists of Rhode Island near at hand, many of the Separate New Lights embraced believer's baptism and became Baptists.[25] So many New Lights turned Baptist that Whitfield supposedly remarked, "My chickens have turned to ducks."[26] Stearns joined the Baptists and was ordained by them in 1751, in Tolland, Connecticut. He and the Separates "had strong faith in the immediate teachings of the Spirit." Guided, as they thought, by divine revelation, Stearns soon moved to Virginia and joined the Opeckon Baptist Church, then a member of the Philadelphia Association. Here Daniel Marshall joined him, having previously attempted, under a similar divine impulse, to serve as an independent evangelist among the Iroquois, until his labors were interrupted by the outbreak of the French and Indian War. Marshall converted to Baptist views and joined the Opeckon Church.[27]

Some of Stearns's friends located in central North Carolina where they found a vast religious destitution. They wrote to Stearns and Marshall, inviting the two to move to North Carolina. In November 1755, on Sandy Creek in central North Carolina, Stearns and Marshall and others, mostly their friends and relatives and numbering altogether sixteen, constituted Sandy Creek Baptist Church, the first Separate Baptist church in the South.[28]

North Carolina provided South Georgia with many of its early settlers. The early Tarheels were not a very prepossessing group of people, if most reports can be trusted. The most venomous and extended portrait of Carolina backwoods delinquency comes from the acidulous Anglican parson Charles Woodmason, whose inexhaustible well of vituperation poured forth streams of invective against the manners and morals of the frontiersmen. Preaching on Granny Quarter Creek, he saw "such a pack [as] I never met with—Neither English, Scots Irish, or Carolinian by Birth—Neither of one Church or other or of any denomination by Profession, not having . . . ever seen a Minister—heard or read a chapter in the Scriptures, or heard a sermon in their days. . . . They are the lowest pack of Wretches my Eyes ever saw . . . as wild as the very Deer."[29]

The simple, highly emotional preaching of the Separate Baptists enjoyed great success among these people. In a short time, more Separate Baptist churches sprang up in central North Carolina, with preachers venturing into Virginia and South Carolina. Eventually, Baptists emanating from Sandy Creek evangelized from the Atlantic to the Mississippi.[30]

The older Particular Baptists hardly knew what to make of the Separates. When Sandy Creek Church asked a South Carolina Regular Baptist preacher to assist in the ordination of Daniel Marshall, that preacher replied that "he held no fellowship with Stearns's party; that he believed them to be a disorderly set; suffering women to pray in public, and permitting every ignorant man to preach that chose; and that they encouraged noise and confusion in their meetings." Finally, Henry Leadbetter, a South Carolina Regular Baptist preacher and another brother-in-law of Marshall's, came and assisted in the ordination.[31] It was at about this time that the Particular Baptists in the South began calling themselves "Regular" Baptists, to distinguish themselves from the "disorderly" Separates.[32] Not all Regulars looked down on them. John Gano, a minister of the Phildelphia Association, visited the Separate Baptists and reported them to be "rather immethodical" but basically sound.[33] Prejudice existed on both sides. Stearns was friendly toward Gano, but the other Separate preachers regarded Gano with suspicion and did not admit him to their associational meeting. Stearns prevailed on them at least to allow Gano to preach. Although he did not preach with "*New-Light* tones and gestures," he so impressed the Separates that they warmed to him.[34]

If they appeared "immethodical" to a fellow Baptist, to parson Woodmason they appeared stark mad. He described at a Separate Baptist communion service

> one fellow mounted on a Bench with the Bread, and bawling *See the Body of Christ,* Another with the Cup running around, and bellowing—*Who cleanses his Soul with the Blood of Christ,* and a thousand other Extravagancies—One on his knees in a posture of Prayer—Others singing—some howling—These Ranting—Those Crying—Others dancing, Skipping, Laughing and rejoycing. Here two or 3 Women falling on their Backs, kicking up their Heels, exposing their Nakedness to all Bystanders and others sitting Pensive, in deep Melancholy lost in Abstraction, like Statues, quite insensible—and when Rous'd by the Spectators from their Pretended Reveries Transports, and indecent Postures and actions declaring they knew nought of the matter. That their Souls had taken flight to Heav'n, and they knew nothing of what they said or did.[35]

The Particular Baptists required a relation of a convert's conversion experience. However, they either did not evaluate it as strictly as did the Separates or they employed different criteria. In 1753, the Philadelphia Association declared that "it appears to us, both from scripture and experience, that true saving faith may subsist where there is not assurance of faith," and that therefore "a person sound in judgement, professing his faith of reliance on Christ for mercy and salvation, acompanied with a gospel conversation, ought to be baptized."[36] The Separates, fresh from the crucible of the Great Awakening, condemned this moderate admission policy. They demanded that their converts should "feel conviction and conversion; and . . . be able to ascertain the time and place of one's conversion."[37] The Sandy Creek Association refused communion with the Kehukee Association because, among other things, the Kehukee Regulars "did not require strictly from those who applied for baptism an experience of grace."[38] Rather than the solemn, rational, theologically exact train of convictions of sin, awakenings of faith, and so forth demanded by the Puritan tradition, the Separate experience of grace more often consisted of dramatic visions and dreams. Some South Georgia Primitives still incline to the view that one who has not had a dream, heard a voice, or seen a vision has no business applying for membership.[39] The public relation of these things gave considerable amusement and often aroused the contempt of those representatives of the rational faith of the Anglican establishment. Woodmason reviewed the practice with his usual charity. "But another vile Matter that does and must give Offence to all Sober Minds Is, what they call their *Experiences*. . . . To see a sett of Mongrels under Pretext of Religion, Sit, and hear for Hours together a string of Vile, cook'd up, Silly and Senseless Lyes, What they know to be such, . . . must grieve, and give great Offence to ev'ry one that has the Honour of Christianity at Heart."[40]

Doctrinally the Separates were mildly Calvinistic, if not Arminian in some cases. Woodmason chortled over their schisms and doctrinal disputes. "They don't all agree in one Tune. For one sings this Doctrine, and the next something different—So that Peoples Brains are turn'd and bewilder'd." He mocked their consequent divisiveness in a description that to this day sometimes fits Baptists: "Then again to see them Divide and Sub divide, Split into Parties—Rail at and excommunicate one another—Turn out of one meeting and receive into another—And a Gang of them getting together and gabbling one after the other (and sometimes disputing against each other) on abstruse Theological Questions . . . such as the greatest Metaph[ys]icians and Learned Scholars never yet could define, or agree on—To hear Ignorant Wretches, who can not write . . . discussing such Knotty Points for the Edification of their Auditors . . . must give High offence to all Intelligent and rational Minds."[41]

The most serious point of dispute among the Separate Baptists concerned the extent of the atonement. This was later one of the principal points dividing the Primitive and Missionary Baptists. In 1775, the Rapidann Separate Baptist Association in Virginia nearly divided over the question of the extent of the atonement. Eventually a majority of the association declared in favor of the High Calvinist doctrine of limited atonement. Faced with a division, however, both parties agreed to an uneasy compromise, the "Arminian" or general atonement party accepting the doctrine of "particular election of grace, still retaining our liberty in regard to construction."[42] This tolerance had fairly well evaporated fifty years later when the Missionary Controversy reached its height. The Regulars regarded such variation in sentiment with extreme distaste. In 1752, the Philadelphia Association concluded that members denying unconditional election, original sin, and final perseverance were not "true members of our churches . . . be their conversation outward what it will."[43]

Woodmason shared with many other persons down to the present an annoyance with the peculiar manner in which the Separate preachers delivered their extemporaneous sermons, which they believed directly inspired. When preaching, they chanted their sermons in what Woodmason described as a "squeaking, untuneable, unintelligible Jargon. Neither Verse or Prose, Singing or Speaking. And when one of them lately was reprimanded for this, and asked—Whether he sung, or spake, He answered in this blasphemous Strain *It is not I that speak—but the Spirit of God that dwelleth in me.*"[44] Many later Primitive Baptist preachers in South Georgia and Florida preached in this manner. Although the Separate Baptists primarily believed in "inspired" preaching, the Regular Baptists considered some divine assistance neccesary to preach acceptably. When, in 1771, the young Edmund Botsford once failed miserably in trying to preach, an older minister told him, "I thought that perhaps, Botsford might be one of those preachers, who can preach when they please; but I now perceive that Botsford cannot always preach just when Botsford pleases; I am therefore encouraged to hope that he may be called of God."[45]

Both Separate and Regular Baptists loved singing as much as their contemporary descendants do. John Leland noted that some native Virginian hymns had "more divinity in them, than poetry or grammar; and some I have heard have but little of either." He noted that during the Great Awakening in that state "singing was more blessed among the people than the preaching."[46] Separate Baptist singing may have been more alluring than that of Regulars. A Philadelphia Presbyterian complained in 1763 that both Presbyterians and Regular Baptists "droll'ed out" their singing and sounded like "the Braying of Asses."[47] By 1792, the English Particular Baptist John Rippon's *Selection* circulated among American Baptists. This prototype of early Baptist hymnals consisted of 588 hymns, without any musical notation and arranged according to subject. A casual perusal of its contents reveals at least one hundred hymns still in use among the Primitive Baptists in South Georgia and Florida. In the preface, Rippon argued against the universal Baptist practice of ministers "reading line by line" or "lining out" one or two lines at a time as a hymn was sung, a practice that allowed a congregation to have only one hymnbook and also enabled illiterate members to sing. He quotes Isaac Watts's criticism of the slow and monotonous style of singing among the dissenters. By the late seventeenth century, however, "lining" hymns had become a "matter of scruple to some people, and to remove an old custom, *though a bad one,* is like removing the ancient landmarks."[48] Among several of the more conservative Primitive Baptists in South Georgia, lining is still considered one of the ancient landmarks. I attended a recent association in that area which only narrowly averted a potentially divisive resolution critical of ministers who had commenced leaving off the old practice. Also, the more conservative the faction, the slower and more minor keyed their singing.

Early Baptists sang with no accompaniment other than the lines being chanted by the "singing clerk" or "tune h'ister."[49] The melodies usually came from the local ballad-singing tradition. For instance, they sang the hymn *Wondrous Love* to the tune of the pirate ballad *Captain Kidd.*[50] David Benedict recalled that in his youth in the early 1800s, the Baptists "would as soon have tolerated the Pope of Rome in their pulpits as an organ in their galleries."[51] Other Calvinists, particularly Scottish Presbyterians, also despised organs as the "kist o' whistles," or the "devil's bagpipes." The early Methodists followed suit. Wesley claimed to have "no objection to instruments of music in our chapels, provided they are neither *heard nor seen.*" When a Presbyterian church finally installed an organ, an elderly clergyman refused to pray, saying "Call on the machine! If it can sing and play to the glory of God, it can pray to the glory of God also. Call on the machine!"[52] The great majority of Primitive Baptists today remain adamant against the use of musical instruments in worship.

The Separate Baptists maintained a strict church discipline, which extended even to matters of clothing. One reason the North Carolina Separates long objected to a union with the Regulars was that the latter were "too superfluous in dress."[53] Plain apparel and "preciseness" of speech caused them to be compared to the Quakers.[54] John Leland compared them to Cromwell's Roundheads. "They were distinguished from others, merely by their decoration. Where all were of one mind no evil ensued; but where some did not choose to dock and strip, and churches made it a matter of discipline, it made great confusion." According to Leland, the hardships of the Revolution reduced everyone to plainness. By 1790, "those who behave well, wear what they please, and meet with no reproof."[55]

The Separates strove to model all their religious practices exclusively on the Bible. The spirit that prompted them survived among the later Primitive Baptists in their insistence on a "thus saith the Lord" for any new religious practice and in their generally scrupulous tendencies.[56] They particularly horrified Regular Baptists by allowing "private members and women to speak in their assemblies under a persuasion of their being under a divine impulse."[57] Most Separate Baptist preachers had little learning, and indeed, as their reception of John Gano indicated, they exhibited some suspicion of learned ministers. As late as 1813, Benedict reported that critics believed the Virginia Baptists held "as an established maxim, that human learning is of no use." Even the Regular Baptists regarded education as something of a frill at best. Wood Furman noted a prevalent belief in the Charleston Association that "scripture example, and doctrine [are] against the education of ministers."[58]

The Separate preachers made up for lack of worldly learning with zeal. Daniel Marshall, the Separate Baptist Apostle of Georgia, typified the preachers of his order, being "not possessed of great talents" but "indefatigable in his labours."[59] Many preachers pastored several churches.[60] Few Baptist ministers, either Regular or Separate, received much in the way of financial support. Early Baptist preachers cursed the Congregational and Anglican establishments as hirelings until they were often embarrassed to solicit support for themselves. On those occasions when they did say something on the subject, they often collided with the apocryphal deacon who said, "The Lord keep thee humble, we'll keep thee poor." One minister, forced to relocate in order to earn a living, reportedly told his congregation, "You love the gospel—but you love your money better." Well after 1800, one Virginia minister observed that "the support of preachers in Virginia is extremely precarious. By most it is viewed as a matter of alms, and of course only afforded to the needy. I doubt whether there is one who averages 300 dollars per annum, and perhaps not ten, who get 150 regularly. Some of the most popular and laborious preachers in the State often pass more than twelve months, without receiving a cent for their publick services. No man dare preach about it. He is at once defamed as a money hunter." Many Baptist preachers, however, having been in the vanguard of pioneer expansion into new areas, obtained and improved vast tracts of land, which afforded them comfortable livings.[61] John Leland compared certain Baptist preachers "to the ass . . . loaded with figs, and feeding upon thistles."[62] While some ministers grumbled about such neglect, others encouraged it. Elijah Craig, one of the early Virginia Baptist preachers imprisoned by the colonial authorities, later emigrated to Kentucky. There he published a book arguing that the Bible forbade preachers receiving any money for their services. Benedict noted that a person "acquainted with the negligent spirit and parsimonious maxims of the Kentucky Baptists . . . would be led to think that the author intended ironically to reprove the churches, rather than censure the avarice of their ministers."[63]

Baptist meetinghouses usually matched their rough and ready preaching. Commenting in 1813 on the overwhelmingly rural meetinghouses of the Virginia Baptists, Benedict described them as the "small, unsightly, and inconvenient things in which they now assemble."[64] Twenty-six years before, Wood Furman criticized South Carolina Baptists for worshipping in "mean and contemptible" meetinghouses while living in comfortable dwellings.[65]

The Separate Baptists, did more in a generation toward extending the Baptist faith than the Particular/Regulars had done in the preceding century. Although suspicious of the doctrinal latitude among the Separates, the Regulars admired their strict discipline and remarkable growth and eventually sought union with them. In 1787, the Regulars and Separates in Virginia achieved a union after some protracted discussion. The chief hindrance to union by 1787 lay in the indefinite doctrinal views of the Separates. They had never published a confession of faith and held in their communion many members considered Arminians. They finally achieved union by adopting the Philadelphia Confession but "to prevent [it] from usurping a tyrannical power over the conscience of any, we do not mean, that every person is bound to the strict observance of everything therin contained; yet that it holds forth the essential truths of the gospel, and that the doctrine of salvation by Christ, and free and unmerited grace alone, ought to be believed by every Christian, and maintained by every minister of the gospel."[66]

In South Carolina, the Separates began to dominate the backcountry after 1760. In 1789, their principal association entered into correspondence with the Charleston Association and dropped the title "Separate."[67]

After the unification, the southern Baptists entered a forty-year period of fairly broad toleration of doctrinal differences. John Leland, leaving Virginia in 1791, commented on the mixed doctrinal character of the Baptists. "Some [plead] for predestination, and others for universal provision. It is true that the schemes of both parties cannot be right; and yet both parties may be right in their aims. . . . The preaching that has been most blessed of God . . . is *the doctrine of sovereign grace . . . mixed with a little of what is called Arminianism.* These two propositions can be tolerably well reconciled together, but . . . men often spend too much time in explaining away one or the other."[68]

This oil-and-water mixture of sentiments lasted only as long as the force of its original blending. After the Revolution the Baptists emerged from obscurity and became a major denomination. There being no further need to present a united front in the face of oppression and scorn, their divisive tendencies soon enjoyed full rein.

Separate Baptists settling north of Augusta provided the major impetus for Baptist expansion into Georgia. Daniel Marshall founded the Kiokee Baptist Church in 1772, and the fellowship established several branches, some of which later became independent churches. Marshall encouraged many young men to exercise as preachers, and, under his leadership, Kiokee Church ordained a number of Baptist ministers who later became prominent.[69]

The Regular and Separate Baptists never formally divided or united in Georgia. While most Baptists in pre-Revolutionary Georgia were Separates, Edmund Botsford, a young Regular Baptist minister from South Carolina, alone represented that wing of the denomination, preaching to a handful of Regular Baptists in Lower Georgia. The Lutherans, Anglicans, and Presbyterians already established on the coast regarded even the relatively sedate Regular Baptists with apprehension. When Botsford applied for permission to use the Lutheran Church at Ebenezer, the shrewd German deacon there at first refused, saying, "Tese Paptists are a very pad people; they pegin shlow at forst, py and py all men follow dem." Had the deacon lived much longer, he would have seen himself proven a prophet.[70]

Daniel Marshall moved to Georgia about the time that Botsford began preaching in the colony. Unlike his younger compatriots, he often ignored the Regular/Separate distinction and immediately asked Botsford to preach at Kiokee. Having heard him, Marshall shook hands with him and said, "I can call thee brother, and give thee the right hand of fellowship, for somehow I never heard *convarsion* better explained in my life." This handshake largely accomplished the union of Regulars and Separates in Georgia.[71] In 1784, the year Daniel Marshall died, several Baptist churches in the Augusta area organized the Georgia Baptist Association, which grew rapidly. In 1786 it had ten churches with 518 members. By 1790, it had 2,877 members in thirty-four churches.

The early Georgia Baptists tolerated a fairly wide range of theological opinion, although their tolerance had definite limits. Jesse Mercer, arguing against the exclusive high-Calvinism gaining ground among the Primitive Baptists in the 1830s, recalled the doctrinal variety extant fifty years earlier:

> It seems to be taken for granted that all those venerable fathers, who founded the Baptist Denomination in this state, were as stern calvinistic preachers as are the opposers of the *new plans*. But this is altogether a mistake. Some of them were so—seemed set for the defense of

> the gospel. Of these, Silas Mercer [Jesse Mercer's father] and Jeptha Vining were the chief. Abraham Marshall [Daniel Marshall's son] was never considered a *predestinarian* preacher. To use his own figure; he used to say, 'he was *short legged* and could not wade in such deep water.' He, with several others, was considered sound in the faith, although *low calvinists.* Peter Smith and some others were thought rather *Arminian;* some *quite* so. But no division was thought of till Jeremiah Walker adopted and preached openly the doctrine of *final apostacy.* Then a division ensued; but soon after the death of Mr. W., the breach was healed.[72]

Jesse Mercer, born in eastern North Carolina, grew up as an Anglican in the territory of the strongly predestinarian Kehukee Association. James Hervey's *Theron and Aspasio,* a theological dialogue, converted him to Calvinism, and he subsequently joined the Baptists about 1775.[73] Hervey submitted the manuscript to John Gill with instructions to note "whatever he saw unevangelical in doctrine, inconclusive in argument, obscure, ambiguous, or improper in expression."[74] Under such tutelage, small wonder that Mercer seemed "set." In 1787, he wrote: "We are fully convinced that Salvation is all of grace, or all of works; for they cannot be mixed in this business. . . . Therefore, we believe it to be the duty of every Gospel minister, to insist upon this soul comforting, God honoring doctrine of Predestination, as the very foundation of our faith. We cannot see how the plan of salvation can be supported without it. And we believe it to be a doctrine which God generally owns and blesses to the conviction and conversion of sinners, and comforting of his saints. . . . Since it has been so clearly preached in our parts, and insisted on, the work of the Lord seems to flourish in a more powerful manner than before. . . . And sinners are made to tremble under a sense of their lost and undone estate."[75]

Jeptha Vining, the other champion of Calvinism among the early Georgia Baptists, first appeared as a minister from Lynche's Creek Church to the Charleston Association in 1755. He moved to Georgia during or after the Revolution and settled on Rocky Comfort Creek. Here he helped organize several churches. Mercer wrote of him:

> Mr. Vining was a firm believer in the Calvinistic doctrines, and of course constantly defended them—such as Election, Predestination, Effectual Calling, and the Final Perseverance of the Saints through grace to eternal glory. These were his constant and favorite topics. It has been, we know, the opinion of many, that the preaching of these doctrines, is not favorable to the conversion of sinners; but the reverse

> of this was manifested in the ministry of Mr. Vining. He preached the doctrine of election without reserve—it was his theme—and yet few have been more successful in the conversion of sinners to God, and in promoting practical Godliness in the churches.[76]

The Methodists found the Baptists with a virtual monopoly of preaching in the Georgia backcountry. Georgia Methodists soon increased to the point that they concerned the Baptists. The 1788 session of the Georgia Association wrestled with several questions inspired by the interlopers.[77] The association that year refused to debate the question "Is the want of saving faith in Jesus Christ, properly called the damning sin of unbelief?" They perhaps feared that debate of such a fundamental issue between moderates and Hyper-Calvinists might have gotten out of hand. In 1790, the association received a letter from Samuel Harris, a famous Virginia Separate Baptist preacher, "noticing that we are poor, dirty creatures, by nature . . . also, exhorting us not to fall out concerning God's decrees." The same year, however, the association adopted its first articles of faith, the fourth and sixth of which stated:

> We believe in the everlasting love of God to his people, and the eternal election of a definite number of the human race, to grace and glory: and that there was a covenant of grace or redemption made between the Father and the Son, before the world began, in which their salvation is secure, and that they in particular are redeemed.
>
> We believe that all those who were chosen in Christ, will effectually be called, regenerated, converted and sanctified, and supported by the spirit and power of God, so that they shall persevere in grace, and not one of them be finally lost.[78]

Baptists reacted to competition from the Arminian Methodists by placing more emphasis on their predestinarian views, as opposed to the free will doctrine insisted on by their rivals. Benedict noted a few years later that "there are but few congregations of any denomination in the State, besides the Baptists and Methodists: both of these are very numerous; and we are sorry to say, that instead of striving to walk together as far as they are agreed, many of them on both sides spend too much time in disputing about Calvin and Wesley, perseverance and falling from grace."[79]

In 1793, the size of the Georgia Association prompted a division into upper and lower districts, the upper district retaining the associational name. At the new association's organizational meeting in 1794, the new body chose the name Hephzibah, meaning "My delight is in her." Eighteen churches entered the new organization. The few Baptist churches in southern Georgia belonged to this association.[80] Many of the Baptist settlers of other parts of South Georgia originated among the churches in that area.

The Hephzibah Association's early history had little to distinguish it. Benedict, in 1813, could write only that "this body contains but few preachers in proportion to the number of churches, and all we can say of them is, that they are a plain, laborious, and pious set of men, who labour six days in the week for the support of their families, and the seventh for the good of souls."[81] Beginning in the early 1800s, the ministers itinerated by pairs in areas destitute of preaching, after they "laid by" their crops in July. During this period between cultivation and harvest, both the preachers and the people had the leisure to travel to meetings.[82] By 1814, this association contained twenty-seven churches with a total of 1,422 members. Only five of these were in the Wiregrass and flatwoods regions of lower Georgia, where most early settlers of South Georgia originated.[83]

In the long-settled coastal region of Georgia, the Baptists came early but arrived late. Various Baptist groups attempted organization there for many years before churches actually emerged from their efforts.

In 1802, the black and white churches of Savannah and the Newington Church formed the Savannah Baptist Association. From its commencement, the Savannah Association conveyed an impression of more openness and polish than did other Georgia Baptists. On Sunday evening, during their constitutional meeting, they heard "admirable social music by the Savannah Harmonic Society." The association officially endorsed the "excellent" London Confession, indicating a strong Regular Baptist influence.[84] They did, however, enter into their minutes their conviction that the reference in the confession to "elect infants" did not imply, in their judgment, the existence of reprobate infants.[85] Many churches in adjacent areas of South Carolina united with the Savannah Association. Beginning in 1807, its name became the Savannah River Association, presumably because so many of its churches were then located outside the immediate neighborhood of Savannah. By 1817, this association had grown to thirty-three churches with 5,771 members. Of this membership, the First and Second "Colored" churches in Savannah and the Great Ogeechee "Colored" Church comprised 2,743 of the total. In that year, the association divided, with the South Carolina churches retaining the original name and those in Georgia taking the name Sunbury Association.[86]

The Great Awakening produced the Separate Baptists and the Baptist expansion throughout the southern backcountry. The Second Great Awakening, or Great Revival, provided the impetus for Baptist expansion into South Georgia and Florida. It also produced a spirit of reform and improvement, which eventually resulted in the Primitive Baptist Schism. The Great Revival commenced in Kentucky about 1799, and spread from there to many parts of the United States. In a few years, about ten thousand joined Baptist churches in Kentucky alone. Attended by strange physical phenomena, the Revival often degenerated into exhibitions of such "exercises" as the "jerks," "barking," and the "rolling excercise." Benedict notes "these *rolling* disciples often met with mud in their way, and got up from their devotions in a sorrowful plight." Benedict tried to believe such things were rare among the Baptists, or at least were not encouraged.[87]

The revival burned until it reached the Atlantic. With a curious combination of Baptist fervor and Savannahian snobbishness, the 1803 Savannah Association noted that "thousands of the fallen race of Adam, have recently experienced converting grace, submitted to sacred ordinances, after the example of the glorious head of the church, and crowded his temple gates. The unbelieving, the rebellious, if not convinced, and reclaimed, are astonished, and confounded, to hear numbers of both sexes, and of the first respectability, evincing that religion is no cunningly devised fable, by publicly declaring the great things God has done for their souls."[88]

→ 2 ←

"This Wilderness Counterey"

The Baptist Expansion into South Georgia and Florida

The Baptist cause in lower Georgia grew as the frontier expanded. Settlement after the Revolution increased most rapidly in the upper part of the state. The pine barrens, flatwoods, or Wiregrass country, the region between the coast and the piedmont, attracted settlers slowly. Cessions of territory by the Creeks in 1773, 1790, 1802, 1804, 1814, and 1818 gradually opened the region.[1] The treaty of Moultrie Creek in 1823 made easier occupation of the Florida interior north of Ocala. A subsequent treaty in 1832 eliminated the Indian title to the rest of the state.[2] However, Osceola, Coacoochee, and several thousand belligerent Seminoles made their disapprobation of removal long and widely felt in Georgia and Florida, by Baptists as well as others.

The land itself seldom elicited praise from those who crossed it headed for more promising places. Captain Basil Hall described the area as "almost everywhere consisting of sand, feebly held together with a short wiregrass, shaded by . . . endless forest. The poverty of the soil, and the difficulty of procuring water, will, in all likelihood, condemn the greater part of them to perpetual sterility."[3] Members of a Georgia legislative committee sent to view the stretch of pine woods acquired by the Indian cessions of 1814 and 1818 considered it "unwise to spend the people's money trying to develop a country which God Almighty himself had left in an unfinished condition."[4] Wiregrass terrain covered an even greater area in Florida. Most of Florida, classed as flatwoods, or "high pine," was similar to lower Georgia.[5]

Surveyors laid off Wayne County, and huge Appling and Irwin counties, comprising most of southeast Georgia, in 490-acre lots. The only other region surveyed into such large tracts was part of mountainous Rabun County in northeast Georgia, a commentary on the contemporary valuation of mountain and pine barrens lands. Even so, the cost of the title to a lot in those counties started at eighteen dollars in 1820, but due to poor demand, the price had to be dropped to twelve dollars in 1823, eight in 1826, six in 1830, and five in 1831. Finally, in 1841, an act of the legislature allowed anyone to acquire an unclaimed lot for five dollars, roughly one cent per acre.[6]

Most of the settlers in South Georgia came from the eastern parts of the Carolinas and were of predominantly English stock. Religious affiliation among them by the 1830s and 1840s was about 35 percent. Of this number, about 48 percent were Primitive Baptists, 26 percent Methodists, and 24 percent Missionary Baptists after the division in the 1840s.[7] Travelers usually described the thin population in terms reminiscent of parson Woodmason. A railroad promoter wrote of the piney woods people of Irwin County, Georgia, in 1836: "As to the appearance of the people, and their cows and hogs, I can only say that they are the spontaneous growth of the country. For twenty-one years before we entered the country they had been living with the Indians and had imbibed most of their singular habits. They say little, despise to be encroached upon by settlement, live on their flocks, and, as you may suppose, exhibit many of the traits of the savage."[8]

The Georgia Methodists paid little attention to the Wiregrass country, but their circuit riders tended to keep journals more often than did Baptists competitors, so the earliest pictures of the religious scene in the region tend to be from their highly colorized and generally hostile viewpoint. The Methodists appointed Angus McDonald in 1806 to itinerate in the region, where he found no churches, no schools, and a population of which three-quarters had never heard a sermon. The people lived in log houses and supported themselves by stock raising. The houses were log cabins of the most ancient type, with a "pole weight" roof, lacking even pegs to hold the boards in place. McDonald found only horse paths through the open woods, marked by blazes on the trees. He encountered as the principal item of diet "hominy" and coarse grits made in hand mills. The people, though largely unchurched, inclined toward the predestinarian doctrine of the Baptists, and he had little success among them. The next annual conference dropped the infant circuit until the 1820s, when the Methodists appointed other preachers to the region, "perhaps the poorest and hardest in the State." And these preachers often broke down under the strain.[9]

In 1840, the Methodists appointed a young preacher from lordly South Carolina, Simon Peter Richardson, to the Irwinville Circuit, "one of the poorest appointments . . . in the Old Georgia Conference." He burst into tears and considered leaving the ministry rather than face single-pen log shacks with dirt floors, inhabited by stock drovers living sometimes ten miles apart in "a vast plain of long-leaf pine forest." He noted that the primitive accommodations did not always mark out new farms, as "some families had lived that way for years." The church buildings in the region consisted of log cabins with backless benches, but he conceded his hosts to be "hospitable." Richardson found his next circuit, in northeast Florida, almost identical.[10] The dominant predestinarian Baptists did little to ease his task. Early South Georgia Methodists and Baptists sometimes extended one another a grudging toleration. The 1822 Sunbury Association invited ministers "of all denominations" to assist in its session, and on a more personal level, John Hagan of Camden County, Georgia, had Baptist preacher Fleming Bates and Jeremiah Slade, the "Father of Methodism in Florida," both witness his 1822 will.[11] Mutual respect between the two competing denominations, however, soon dissolved in the *odium theologicum*. Union Church manifested more typical interdenominational attitudes when it excommunicated Mary Knight in 1832 "by the unanimous voice of the church" for having "joined the Methodist [sic] because she liked them best and disliked part of our faith."[12] Denominational jealousy as well as theological difference underlay much of this hostility. Circuit rider Richardson considered "Augustinianism" a heresy "that ought to have perished in the heathen brain that gave it birth." Richardson sneered at the predestinarian Baptists for preaching "a gospel that had no moral effect on the lives of the people," and did not hesitate to proselytize among their youth. They reacted angrily and argued the doctrinal differences between the churches. "Brother P.," described as "one of the leading preachers," challenged Richardson to a debate on the "five points." The local Baptists decided that "P.," probably Isham Peacock, did not have the ability to sustain a debate against Richardson. Incredibly, they asked him instead to state the position of both sides. "They ought not to have placed my purity under such a strain," Richardson ruefully recalled. The lecture became a fiasco when a Baptist preacher accused Richardson of unfairness, and attempted to reply to him. This nearly got the Baptist preacher in a fistfight with another Methodist preacher, effectively ending the curious meeting.[13] Except for a handful of Catholics, mostly around St. Augustine, and a few stray Presbyterians and Episcopalians in the better settled areas, Methodists and Baptists of one stripe or another had a virtual monopoly of the religious scene in most of antebellum South Georgia and Florida. Backwoods wiseacres pretended Presbyterians and Episcopalians were some rare "varmint" when asked about them.

Many travelers already cited noted the importance of cattle in the economy of the Wiregrass country. Prominent early settlers, such as the Gaskins, Averas, and Carters, removed to deep South Georgia primarily on account of the pasturage provided by the wiregrass that gave the region its name.[14] The good pasture of the longleaf pine–wiregrass biome, dominant in South

Georgia, also extended deep into Florida. The 1841 Circular Address of an association in South Georgia proudly noted that "nearly all the ancient worthies were engaged in that lawful and most honorable occupation of feeding of flocks."[15]

A large number of the settlers moving south into the Wiregrass country had long ago drifted beyond the reach of organized religion. When the Irish Catholic priest Father Thomas Hassett visited settlements of newly arrived pioneers in northeastern Florida in 1790, situated along the St. Johns, St. Mary's, and Nassau rivers, he found many who had never seen a minister of any faith in their lives. Their isolation from their own religious tradition was such that they greatly appreciated his instruction and the English catechisms he left with every family. Three Irish priests planned to establish parishes among the American settlers, but one of them went mad and the other two became broken in health before they ever reached their prospective flocks. The end of Spanish rule in Florida terminated the interesting possibility of Wiregrass Catholics.[16] Jesse Lee, a young Methodist circuit rider appointed to the region along the St. Mary's River in 1799, also found "many who had never heard a sermon."[17]

In the pine barrens west of Savannah, the fires of the Great Revival burned intensely after 1800. Isham Peacock, a profoundly influential minister in the region, commenced his long career during this period. "Old Father Peacock," as he came to be called, was an almost ubiquitous presence among the Baptists of South Georgia and northern Florida during the first half of the nineteenth century.[18] He was born in what would later become Dobbs County, North Carolina, on October 8, 1742.[19] His father, Samuel Peacock, reasonably well off for North Carolina, had joined Bear Creek Baptist Church by the commencement of the Revolution.[20] By 1776, Peacock and his family had settled in Anson County, North Carolina.[21]

Drafted at the beginning of the Revolution, he volunteered for further service, which consisted entirely of marching up and down the Carolinas for eight months, seeing no action at all. After he left the service, the Tories captured him and took his papers.[22] He drew a pension for his Revolutionary service from 1833 until his death. After the Revolution he joined the stream of emigration from the Carolinas into Georgia. Evidently a lover of frontier life, like many other early Baptist ministers, he settled in the pine barrens of Bulloch and Tattnall counties before 1800.[23]

Peacock's early religious impressions are unknown, but he burst upon the Georgia religious scene in 1802, during the Great Revival. A licensed preacher in the recently organized Lott's Creek Church, Bulloch County, he stormed a stronghold of wickedness at Black Creek, thirty miles southwest of Savannah. Henry Holcombe described the inhabitants of the region as "willing captives of Satan" and praised Peacock's work among them.

> Though young in the ministry, and without the advantages of a learned education, Mr. Peacock was eminently owned in converting sinners from the error of their ways. He commanded very general attention, and powerful impressions were made on the mind of many under his ministrations. Numbers who had never shown the least concern for their souls before, were emboldened, publicly, and with tears to request his prayers, and were under such engagements to find peace with God, that they spent whole nights, as well as days in religious exercises. In some instances, these arduous struggles of the mind were attended with convulsions similar to those which have so generally and strongly marked the present extensive and glorious revival of religion. It was feared in a few cases, that these bodily afflictions would terminate in death; but though from their strength, and continuance for several days and nights, with intermissions, they were truly alarming, they all issued in the unspeakable joys of assured salvation. Others who were exercised gently, gave, however, very satisfactory evidence that they had passed from death to life.[24]

Peacock's converts at Black Creek were organized into a church. Before a huge crowd, Peacock "rehearsed the leading articles of his faith," and received ordination in a grove near John Albritton's house from Henry Holcombe; John Goldwire, an aged Regular Baptist of South Carolina;[25] and Henry Cook, Peacock's pastor at Lott's Creek. He then baptized thirteen of the "first fruits of his labors" in a nearby stream. The presbytery that had ordained Peacock then constituted the neophytes into a church, which immediately elected Peacock pastor. That same evening, Peacock administered their first communion. "The behavior of the people through these various exercises would have done credit to a worshipping assembly in Philadelphia," Holcombe noted.[26] Black Creek joined the Savannah Association in January 1803, having grown from thirteen to seventy-seven members.[27]

The "leading articles" of Peacock's belief were illustrated in a set of articles of faith he signed for a newly constituted church several years later: "The existance of one triune God, the fall of man and his inability to recover himselfe, God's Sovereing choice of his people in Christ, their covenenat head, from before the foundation of the world, effectual calling, justification by the imputed righteousness of Christ alone, final perseverance of the saints in eternal salvation in glory, and baptism [by] immersion, and the Lords supper."[28]

Little evidence remains as to exactly where in the Calvinistic spectrum his preaching fell. His results at Black Creek seem to indicate that he, like John Leland, might have mixed "a little of what is called Arminianism" into his exhortations. On the other hand, Jeptha Vining's pure predestinarian doctrine seemed equally able to convert the wild frontiersmen. Whatever the exact details of Peacock's belief, the churches approved of his preaching. William A. Knight, clerk of Union Church, wrote: "His doctrin we believe to be the doctrin of Jesus Christ."[29] The Suwannee River Association declared him "a faithful old soldier in the cause of his master."[30] Old when he commenced his ministry, he became a more "high toned predestinarian" in his later years. In 1823, he warned churches against "filling the house of God with unprepared materials which cannot bear the fruit of God's elect nor bear the close discipline which God requires of us."[31]

Peacock excelled in "discipline" from the beginning of his ministry. He and other ministers silenced Rev. Wilson Conner in 1804 for "gross misconduct" at the behest of the Savannah Association.[32] In a vexing case at Beard's Creek Church, involving one Mark Adison and his "wife, or woman," Peacock cut through a Gordian knot of difficulties by discovering a flaw in the manner of their reception into the church, thus enabling the congregation to rule that the troublesome pair had never been members there to begin with.[33]

Perhaps Peacock's most lasting contributions to the character of the Primitive Baptists in his area was his influence on a rising generation of young ministers. Fleming Bates often traveled and worked with him. From his youth Matthew Albritton, at whose father's house Peacock had been ordained, knew him.[34] Henry Milton, who, with Matthew Albritton, frequently served as moderator of the principal association in South Georgia and Florida, also came into the ministry in Peacock's Black Creek Church.[35]

Peacock not only organized Black Creek Church but also assisted in organizing Beard's Creek and Salem churches in remote Tattnall County in 1804 and 1811, representing at that time the southern extreme of Baptist expansion in mainland North America.[36] In June 1819, he extended the Baptist frontier farther south with the organization of High Bluff Church in what is now Brantley County, Georgia.[37] In January 1821, he and Fleming Bates organized the first Baptist church in Florida, Pigeon Creek Baptist Church in what is now Nassau County.[38] Since Florida remained a Spanish province until July, this action by Peacock and Bates technically defied the law. Peacock made a preaching tour into Florida when eighty years old and baptized converts in the woods "south of the Altamaha" far from a church in his ninetieth year.[39] A certificate of baptism from him was as good as a church letter.[40] He last pastored the newly constituted Providence Church in Ware County, Georgia,

Shiloh Primitive Baptist Church, Pierce County, Ga. 1998. Courtesy of Elder Daniel Drawdy.

in 1844, when he was 101 years old.[41] Having become blind, he resigned his pastorate there in 1845, and moved with his second wife to Mayport Mills, near Jacksonville, where he spent his remaining years in retirement.[42] Indomitable to the last, he set out through the wilderness at age 107 on one last jaunt to visit his grandchildren in Pierce County, Georgia. The Old Warrior died there in February 1851, and the faithful buried him in an unmarked grave at Shiloh Primitive Baptist Church, the place of his last known membership.[43] The meetinghouse standing nearby is a most sufficient and proper monument.

Although not a constituent member, Peacock was the "father" of the Piedmont Association, the first Baptist association established in deep South Georgia and Florida.[44] In October 1815, delegates of Jones Creek and Sarepta churches of Tattnall County, Georgia, and Wesley Creek Church of Liberty County, Georgia, formed the Piedmont Association at Little Canoochee Meetinghouse in Tattnall County. Peacock assured the new body at the organizational meeting that Beard's Creek and Salem churches had an interest in joining the association. Upper Black Creek Church also expressed its "willingness to unite with us in an associate capacity if it should take place on proper principles." The circular address for the year admitted the small numbers and small ministerial gifts of the brethren but disclaimed any "sinister" intention in forming the new organization.[45]

Adiel Sherwood, a contemporary leading Missionary Baptist, believed the Piedmont Association had been organized simply to keep out missionary influence.[46] In this he erred, due to the long period that elapsed between the body's organization and its first formal correspondence with another association. "In consequence of a fall from a horse," Moses Westberry did not deliver an 1816 or 1817 corresponding letter announcing the formation of the Piedmont group to the Hephzibah Association. In 1818, Westberry again failed to deliver the associational letter, alleging "some occurences not neccesary to mention at present prevented his attendance at that appointment." When the Piedmont did succeed in opening a correspondence with the Hephzibah in 1819, Antimissionism was first stirring in Georgia.[47] Actually, the remote situation of the churches forming the association provided a sufficient reason for its organization. Jones Creek Church, for instance, had been organized in 1810 but had joined no association.[48] Beard's Creek Church, which sent delegates to the formation of the Piedmont Association and eventually joined it, had experienced some misgiving about whether to join the Hephzibah or the Savannah association, since it was equally remote from both.[49] The cession of Indian land in the treaty of Fort Jackson in 1814, and the inevitability of the American acquisition of Florida, no doubt also encouraged the formation of the Piedmont Association, providing a good prospect for southward expansion.

The name *Piedmont*, given both to this association and to an early southwest Georgia Baptist church, indicates the extent to which belief in a Baptist "apostolic succession" prevailed among nineteenth-century Baptists. By the 1800s, many Baptists asserted a continuous succession of adult baptisms by immersion and ministerial ordinations from Christ and the apostles. The Waldensian Church of the Italian Piedmont represented one of the oft cited links in this chain.

In 1816, the year after their constitution, the Piedmont Association adopted a decorum for their sessions, which was identical to that given as the Regular Baptist standard in Asplund's *Universal Register of the Baptist Denomination*.[50] They did not adopt articles of faith. However, by the 1820s, Beard's Creek Church had adopted a covenant declaring their belief "of all the doctrines of the Old and New Testaments preferring the explanation of them by the authors of the Baptist confession of faith, and such as agree with them to any that we have seen."[51] The "Baptist confession of faith, and such as agree with them" was certainly the 1689 London Confession or the "Abstract of Principles" derived from it.

This remote frontier association had few ministers, but its early preachers were quite interesting, mostly being examples of what William McElvey, another pioneer South Georgia preacher, referred to as "frontier men."[52] Moses Westberry, the first moderator, born at the High Hills of Santee, South Carolina, on March 2, 1772, moved in 1799 to Tattnall and then to Liberty County, placing himself on the extreme frontier of settlement in Georgia. Baptized by David Hennessy in August 1804, he became a charter member of Beard's Creek Church. Ordained a minister on July 19, 1809, by David Hennessy, John Goldwire, and John Stafford, he first served as a deacon. He organized Jones Creek Church in Liberty (now Long) County, Georgia, in 1810, which he pastored for many years, and he also served as a justice of the peace in Tattnall County from 1803 to 1808 and in Liberty County for several years subsequent to 1815. Soon after the region opened for settlement, he moved south of the Altamaha to Appling, later Wayne County. As he continued to serve Jones Creek Church, the congregation hired a man to "fetch and carry" him to and from the Altamaha River each month, showing a considerable affection for him on the part of the church. Not all he did pleased them, however, for in 1828, the church sent a committee to visit Westberry and "admonish him as he drinks too much." Like many Calvinistic ministers, Westberry suffered agonies of conscience. He asked the Jones Creek Church in March 1825 if "they thought he had ever been called and if he preached [the] gospel faithfully." They voted their approval of him and his preaching. Since he preached until his death at the advanced age of ninety-two, their vote of confidence doubtless overcame his scruples.[53]

Wilson Conner, an especially colorful early Piedmont minister, was born in Maryland in 1768 and went to South Carolina as a child, where he joined the Baptists in 1793. The Great Ogeechee Church in Effingham County, Georgia, had him ordained in 1803. After Peacock and others charged him with "gross misconduct," the fellowship defrocked and expelled him. Conner then took part in the abortive filibustering expedition that tried to detach eastern Florida from the Spanish Empire and went to Washington as a delegate from the short-lived East Florida Republic in 1811.[54] After the failure of this exploit in nation building, Conner returned to the United States, where he served as a justice of the peace in Tattnall County, Georgia, a position he had held since 1806. Restored to the Baptist Church and ministry by 1817, he served as a delegate to the Piedmont Association from Sarepta Church, Tattnall County, Georgia, and delivered the introductory sermon a day late.[55] Later he moved his membership to Jones Creek Church in the same association. Death claimed him in the pulpit after he had preached his last sermon at a church in Telfair County in 1844. This concluded a remarkable ministerial ordeal during which he had traveled over thirty-five thousand miles on horseback preaching in Montgomery, Screven, Emanuel, Liberty, Tattnall, and Telfair counties in South Georgia.[56]

From 1817 until 1825 the Piedmont Association expanded across southeastern Georgia and northeastern Florida, receiving ten new churches organized in those areas.[57] In 1817, a group of "sooners" had organized Little Satilla Church in the "Purchase," territory obtained from the Creeks in 1814 but not yet organized into counties or opened for settlement. The small church joined the Piedmont the same year.[58] In 1819, Isham Peacock and Fleming Bates organized High Bluff Church, in present Brantley County, Georgia, with members dismissed by Little Satilla. Settlers at Trader's Hill, on the St. Mary's River near the extreme southern frontier of Georgia and the United States, organized Sardis Church, also in 1819.[59] Beard's Creek and Salem churches obtained dismission also from the Hephzibah Association in 1819 and joined the Piedmont. This made Isham Peacock a member of the Piedmont Association, and it immediately chose him moderator. Due to its increased size, the association created two districts in 1819, one north of the Altamaha and one south of that river, and appointed one "yearly" meeting on fifth Sundays in both districts.[60]

Growth south of the Altamaha continued. In 1820, Spring Branch Church, Glynn County, Georgia, joined the association, followed in 1821 by Pigeon Creek Church, Nassau County, Florida, the first Baptist church in Florida. Symrna Church, in present Brantley County, Georgia, assumed the associational bond in 1823. Kettle Creek and Macedonia churches in Appling County joined in 1824, and the next year Union and Fellowship, in South Georgia's Irwin and Appling counties, respectively, brought the full number of churches to sixteen and the membership to nearly 400.[61] Many of these pioneer churches scattered through thinly settled country were quite ephemeral. Little Satilla, the first Baptist church south of the Altamaha, lasted only nine years.[62] Beard's Creek flickered in and out of existence several times before taking firm root in the early 1820s.[63] The early Piedmont Association's overall numerical size remained small despite its number of churches and geographical extension. In 1825, five ministers served its eleven churches and there were only 267 members.[64] Considering the sparse population of its territory, this number was not unusually small. By 1845, near the end of its identification with the Antimissionary movement, the Piedmont Association contained only seven churches with an aggregate membership of 216.[65]

The remoter reaches of South Georgia offered a daunting prospect for church growth. Isaac Hutto, a young South Carolinian immigrant and later a Primitive Baptist preacher, recalled his boyhood impression of Lowndes County in 1832: "This was then a new country, what few settlers were here were in almost a regular combat with the wild varmints: not much said about religion."[66] Union Church, near present Lakeland, Georgia, assisted in one way or another in the formation of most of the earliest Baptist churches of central South Georgia and north Florida. Ten Baptist settlers, under the leadership of William A. Knight, decided to organize a church, "a few of us having removed to this wilderness counterey and findeing each other oute." Organized, or "constituted," on October 1, 1825, by Matthew Albritton and Fleming Bates, with members dismissed from churches in the Piedmont and Hephzibah associations,[67] this church had organizing ministers who were among the most influential in the region. Fleming Bates was born in 1771.[68] William's Creek Church of the Georgia Association licensed him in 1810.[69] By 1814, he had moved within the bounds of the Hephzibah Association, and Big Briar Creek Church, Warren County, Georgia, ordained him in 1815.[70] In 1818 he appeared in South Georgia at the Piedmont Association as a visiting minister from the Hephzibah. He had united by 1821 with a church in the Piedmont, which elected him moderator in 1825 and 1827, years in which Isham Peacock did not attend.[71] Although Bates was not their pastor and was a member there only a short time, Union Church expressed collective admiration for "his fatherly admonitions and him as a brother and gospel preacher and his knowledge in discipline."[72] He assisted in the organization of Friendship Church near the present town of Hahira, Georgia, in 1827 and served as pastor there until some "eledged crimes" of an undisclosed nature caused him to resign and apparently lose the confidence of the Baptists in South Georgia.[73] Bates moved into northern Florida, where the early Baptist preacher John Tucker referred to him as "almost worn out," but he did help Tucker organize several churches in the area in 1835.[74] His "eledged crimes" followed him to his new home. Union Church hesitated to authorize Matthew Albritton to take part in constituting Providence Church in Florida, because some "expressions of the letter" led them to believe that Bates would also participate. Bates's trouble related to a "difference" between him and one Brother Tasset Douglass, which the Union Church believed serious enough to prohibit their pastor from assisting Bates in any ministerial work. Consequently, Union directed the brethren in Florida to call on others for help. That Bates still possessed considerable influence among some Baptists is indicated by the fact that the Union Church reserved a copy of their letter to the Floridians, "for fear some unpleasant thing might gro oute of our good intentions and friendly admonitions."[75] At their next conference, however, they authorized Albritton to go to Florida and take part in the constitution "if they be found in order."[76] Bates lived his last years at Newnansville, Florida. He died in February 1840.[77]

Of far greater influence than Fleming Bates was Matthew Albritton. He united with an unknown church in Bulloch or Bryan County, Georgia, prior to 1807, and began to preach in 1812. In 1820 he was a member of Upper Black Creek Church in Bulloch County, where he succeeded Isham Peacock as pastor, and he served there until about 1823, when he removed to Lowndes County, Georgia, settling north of what is now Quitman.[78] Albritton told the church "it had been presd on him to move and he wishd the church to inquire of the Lord by a day of fasting and prayer to know if it was the care of this world or the welfare of souls in a distant land."[79] His genuine and unaffected piety made him a beloved figure among the Baptists of South Georgia, as is expressed in an 1828 "pastorial call" from Union Church: "We the members of Union Church of Christ at Carter's meetinghouse do heare by say our harts have Rejoiced and we have been much Refresht and wonderfully delighted in the pastorial ceare of our beloved pastor father and brother Mathew Allbritton and do heare by Jointly unanimously and firvantly call Br. Allbritton to take the further Pastorial Ceare of us at les for one more yeare to go in and oute before us that we may still find pasture in his fatherly ceare heare ower cries our brother."[80]

By the mid-1820s, rapidly spreading settlement caused new churches to spring up beyond the bounds of any association. Hephzibah Church, located at the present Hopkins Cemetery in the extreme northern part of Gadsden County, Florida, grew out of a series of meetings at Matthew Fain's home under the leadership of William McElvey, a Baptist preacher licensed, though not yet ordained. At their initial meeting on June 12, 1824, one hundred people turned out to hear McElvey preach, "a numerous concourse for that newly settled country." Fourteen Baptists, members and former members of Beard's Creek and other churches in South Georgia, declared themselves interested in organizing a church. The organization did not take place at that time because the "means"—presumably an ordained minister—was not "available."[81] On January 23, 1825, McElvey, ordained minister Jeremiah Kimbrell, and William Whiddon, a deacon, formed a presbytery and constituted nine members as the Hephzibah Baptist Church, the second Baptist church organized in Florida.[82] Kimbrell came over from southeastern Alabama for the occasion.[83] The new church appointed McElvey as pastor, effective upon his ordination.[84] This apparently occurred soon thereafter, for on September 2, 1826, he assisted William Hawthorn in constituting Tired Creek Church, in what is now Grady County, Georgia.

McElvey and Hawthorn shared characteristics typical of pioneer Baptist preachers. Born about 1781, McElvey recalled, "I was raised as hard and at as bad a chance, if not worse than any free born in modern times, being born of European parents & they dying and leaving me an infant in the Revolution, without means, money, or guardian—according to the old proverb, a long shoot and a bad chance."[85] He and his wife became Baptists about 1808 in Burke County, Georgia. Like most Baptist converts, he experienced an initial reluctance. "I would not have been a Baptist, if I could have found any other way consistent with the word of God and my own conscience."[86] Ordained about 1814, at the ironically messianic age of thirty-three, he commenced a long, arduous career as a backwoods preacher.

> I lived always on the frontiers . . . two thirds of [the] time from home, travelling still on the outline of new settlements, planting churches and associations. . . . I never received ten dollars to aid me, I looked for none. . . . I lit on a settlement in Early county [Georgia], where I preached to men and women that had grown up on the frontiers without ever hearing preaching. . . . I tasked myself to the uttermost to supply their wants, having to go from sixty to seventy-five miles, through a wilderness where there were but five settlers, having to carry provision for myself and horse, camp in the woods, and when I would get to the place of preaching I assure you I cut a poor figure for a preacher. But nevertheless, I believed the promise; the Lord was with me, the heart's of God's children were made glad, and some were brought to witness salvation.[87]

William Hawthorn was a Revolutionary soldier, apparently converted during the war by a Baptist preacher named Benjamin Moseley, the father of William Moseley, a prominent Primitive Baptist minister in Middle Georgia. Many years later an article by the younger Moseley caused Hawthorn's "eyes to weep from a rememberance of my father, Benjamin Moseley, who preached to me in the time of the revolutionary war."[88] Moving from Sampson County, North Carolina, an area originally within the bounds of the strongly Calvinistic Kehukee Association, Hawthorn settled in Early (later Decatur) County, Georgia. His arrival between 1818 and 1820 made him one of the first in the region, officially opened to settlement in 1820.[89] Local tradition credits him with exploring the reputedly sickly region and discovering its great similarity to his home region in North Carolina. He encouraged many of his friends and neighbors to move south with him. The trail they followed into the section was known as the "Hawthorn Trail," and the community became known as the "North Carolina Settlement."[90] Both McElvey and Hawthorn were politically active. A local historian has observed that "nearly all the pioneers of Decatur were members of the Primitive Baptist Church."[91] Besides Union, Hephzibah, and Tired Creek, other churches soon sprang up in South Georgia and Florida. Matthew Albritton helped organize in 1826 Bethel Church in what is now Brooks County, Georgia, and Mt. Gilead Church in Jefferson County, Florida, among a people meeting as "the baptist convention near the macasookey ponds est floriday."[92]

With the increased number of new churches in the region, a move soon commenced for a new association in southwest Georgia and northwest Florida. A "council" met in Thomas County, Georgia, probably at the Olives Church, on August 24, 1827, to consider the feasibility of such a new organization. The Thomas County Council appointed another meeting at Mt. Gilead Church in September, requesting each interested church to send messengers with a statement of their faith and the date of their constitution together with names of the ministers taking part in it.[93] Such care seemed necessary, since many churches in remote areas tended to cut corners in their organizational procedure. (In 1833, the Ochlocknee Association refused to accept Shiloh Church of Ware County, Georgia, "on account of the illegality of her constitution"; the association instructed the church how to undergo a new constitution, which was done.)[94]

The Mt. Gilead council decided to go ahead with plans for a new association, for the Piedmont Association, at its October 1827 meeting, "received and read a petition from seven Baptist Churches situated between the Alapaha and Flint River praying ministerial aid to constitute them into an association." The Piedmont authorized Matthew Albritton and Fleming Bates, both members at Union Church, to oversee the organization. Union Church requested and received dismission from the Piedmont in order to join the new body.[95]

The organizational meeting took place at Bethel Church, Strickland's Meetinghouse, in Lowndes (now Brooks) County, Georgia, on November 17, 1827.[96] Six churches took part in the actual constitution of the new association.[97] Fleming Bates became the first moderator, serving until his controversy with Tassett Douglass in 1830. During the ensuing decade, Isham Peacock's disciples Matthew Albritton and Henry Milton continuously occupied the moderator's seat.[98] From an examination of scattered surviving records, the six churches were almost certainly Hephzibah, Gadsden County, Florida; Mt. Gilead, Jefferson County, Florida; Bethel, Lowndes (now Brooks) County, Georgia; Tired Creek, Decatur (now Grady) County, Georgia; Olives, Thomas County, Georgia; and Friendship, Lowndes County, Georgia. Located near the present town of Hahira, Friendship was an "arm" of Union Church and petitioned for a constitution in August 1827, in part for the "furtherance of a contemplated association."[99] A seventh church, almost certainly Union, joined at the first session of the new association, which took the name Ochlocknee, although several years passed before a standard spelling for that name developed. The new association had a total of 138 members and five ministers. Bates and Albritton reported to Union Church that "much harmony and love abounded" at the initial meeting.[100] Union probably did not join in the constitution because the ministers organizing the association belonged there. Early Baptists seem to have had the idea that for ministers to organize a church or association in which they themselves were included amounted to a sort of ecclesiastical incest. In 1855, when the Union Association organized at Union Church, Union followed the same procedure, because one of the organizing ministers, William A. Knight, held membership there.[101]

The Ochlocknee Association grew rapidly. Starting with seven churches and 138 members in 1827, it had thirty-five churches with a total membership of 1,010 in 1833. Migration did not account for all this increase. In 1833, the various churches of the association baptized 179 people. Friendship Church alone baptized twenty-four converts. Fourteen churches applied for membership in 1833. Neophytes apparently composed so many of the new churches that the association appointed William A. Knight to instruct them on the duties of churches toward the association. The new acquisitions prompted the association to "extend [its] boundary . . . so far as to reach the bounds of the Piedmont Association on the east[;] of St. John's River on the southeast." Within that large territory, it had churches in Baker, Decatur, Irwin, Lowndes, Telfair, and Thomas counties in Georgia, and Alachua, Columbia, Gadsden, Hamilton, Jefferson, and Leon counties in Florida. The geographical size of the association prompted a proposal to divide at the 1833 meeting.[102]

In 1834 the Ochlocknee Association dismissed eight churches: Friendship, Union, and Elizabeth churches in Georgia, and Providence, New Zion, Concord, Newington, and New River in Florida.[103] The Ochlocknee resolution reflected the intense territorialism of the associations, "designating a line beginning at the mouth of the Suwannee River and running up that stream to the mouth of the Withlacoochy thence up Little River to the boundary line." The new association took the name Suwannee River, and Concord Church hosted the constitutional meeting on the first weekend in December 1834.[104] Considerable difficulty attended the birth of the new association. The delegates met at Concord Church, but the ministers appointed to preside failed to attend, so another meeting was held at Providence Church in September

1835.[105] Only one of the designated ministers, Melus Thigpen, showed at Providence, so the exasperated delegates co-opted William A. Knight to act as the other member of the presbytery and proceeded formally to organize the association, "if done in order."[106] Matthew Albritton, of Union Church, served as moderator until his death in 1849.[107]

The Suwannee River Association grew rather slowly. Only three churches sent delegates to the 1836 Association, held in Lowndes County, Georgia, although two new churches had joined it. The 1837 Association convened at Union Church, and the first complete minutes, those of 1838, show twelve churches, with a total membership of 350.[108] Union Church, with seventy-six members, was the largest. All but three of the churches were located in Georgia, where every session had been held since 1836. None of the Florida churches was represented at the 1838 session.[109]

The Second Seminole War caused the Suwannee Association's slow growth and thin representation. The 1838 session "recommended to the churches, generally, to observe days of fasting and prayer amongst them, more frequently than heretofore, that the Lord might divert the judgements which seem to hang over us." They also "agreed that we attend to no business of a general nature, at this time, by reason of the unsettled affairs of our country."[110] In 1839, the association again met in the safer Georgia section of its territory. Not until 1842 did the association meet in Florida again. The 1839 delegates once more recommended fast days, "so that the war-whoop of a savage foe, might not be heard any longer in our land, to the great disturbance of our fellow citizens, while numbers of our women and infant children are falling victims to their relentless hands."[111] The Ochlocknee Association's 1836 session "lament[ed] the situation of the Suwannee River Association, on account of the Indian War in that vicinity."[112] John Tucker, who after the death of Fleming Bates was practically the only Baptist preacher in north-central Florida, bemoaned the effect of the Indian War on his work. Most of the churches, organized in the early 1830s, became scattered as a result of the war, and Tucker often preached at funerals in forts over the victims of the conflict. Ironically, one of the measures that helped subdue the Seminoles, the Armed Occupation Act, also served to scatter the settlers and to disrupt further the churches of the Suwannee River Association.[113]

While the Ochlocknee Association lamented the effects of the Seminole War, it also noted the early stages of a controversy destined to bring far greater destruction. The 1836 Association resolved "to join the Ebenezer Association in lifting our voice and using our best endeavors against the northern fanatics."[114] Local Primitive Baptists regarded Abolitionism as too far away and too visionary to be worth any further notice. The churches took slavery and the slaves' duty to masters for granted. In 1840, Richland Creek Church, Decatur County, Georgia, excommunicated "Bro Sam and Nancy his wife collerd persons the property of William Montgomery . . . on the charge of lying[,] harboring[,] and concealing runaway slaves."[115]

At the conclusion of the Seminole War, the Missionary Controversy at last reached the crisis point among the Baptists of South Georgia and Florida. It usually generated a fiercer rhetoric than that inspired by the depredations of Native Americans.

→ 3 ←

"Under the Dropings of the Sanctuary"

Worship and Discipline

William A. Knight, the first clerk at Union Church, described the congregation gathered there on Sunday, April 8, 1827, as "seting under the dropings of the sanctuary and the word delivered with power by Brs Bates and Allbritton."[1] Older local Primitive Baptist preachers still use the phrase "under the drippings of the sanctuary." Apparently not derived from any specific place in the Bible, it expresses their belief that true preaching and worship take place only when God condescends to impart a divine influence from above, a "dripping" from the heavenly "sanctuary."[2] The order of worship and the church discipline practiced in the antebellum settlement period has remained almost unaltered among some groups of Primitive Baptists in the area, and traces of it remain among virtually all of them. Therefore a detailed description of the church order of the 1830s reflects its principal features down to the present time.

Before the congregation could sit "under the drippings," it had to have a place to sit. In the case of some of the earliest churches, such as Hephzibah in Gadsden County, Florida, and Providence in Union County, Florida, meetings began in private homes with a meetinghouse built later.[3] In certain cases, like that of Union Church, the building of a meetinghouse in a new settlement preceded the organization of a church.[4]

Early Baptist meetinghouses usually consisted of small log structures in the earliest days. Jones Creek Church, in the Piedmont Association, erected a frame meetinghouse in 1832 but did not put glass windows in it until 1849.[5] With such small buildings, an unusual crowd sometimes necessitated outdoor services. At one 1832 Union Church service, the congregation "repaired to the association stand (the house not being roomy enough to accommodate the congregation with seats)."[6] Hartwell Watkins of Jefferson County, Florida, noted in the mid-1840s that although there was not "much increase,"

Top: Union Primitive Baptist Church, Lanier County, Ga. 1998. Courtesy of Nancy Ekstrom.

Above left: Interior of Union Church. Courtesy of Nancy Ekstrom.

Above right: Elder Marcus S. Peavey, pastor of Union Church 1935–78, in the pulpit. Courtesy of Mrs. L. H. Register.

The original bench, circa 1833, at Shiloh Church. Courtesy of Elder Daniel Drawdy.

Interior of Sardis Primitive Baptist Church, Charlton County, Ga., 1998, with original pulpit, circa 1830s. Courtesy of John G. Crowley.

Baptist meetings were often well attended. "At meeting times the houses are crowded with hearers."[7]

The present meetinghouse at Union Church, Lakeland, Georgia, is the oldest Baptist facility still standing in the area of this study. It is a post-and-beam frame building erected in 1854, measuring thirty by fifty feet.[8] Its interior layout is typical of Primitive Baptist meetinghouses in the area. The only pieces of ecclesiastical furnishing older than the benches and pulpit at Union are one seat at Shiloh Church, Ware County, Georgia, preserved from the original meetinghouse built about 1833, and the pulpit at Sardis Church, Charlton County, Georgia, which has bullet holes in it from the Indian Wars. Traditionally, men sit on the right hand of the stand and women on the left, with visitors in front of the pulpit. This is still the case in the majority of Primitive Baptist churches in the region.

Meetinghouses of the second generation, replacing the often cramped log chapels erected by the first settlers, were sometimes more elaborate. Some of the original log meetinghouses had significant appointments. John Dukes's meetinghouse, the original building of Bethlehem Church, Quitman, Georgia, had a slave gallery, the only one reported in a local Primitive Baptist church. The second Bethlehem meetinghouse, built sometime between 1861 and 1868, has a greater interior and better appointments than Union meetinghouse. However, the second Bethlehem meetinghouse did not have a ceiling in it until the 1940s. The basic form of these structures has continued unaltered among Primitive Baptists until the present.[9]

In some cases, the meetinghouses on the local frontier had better facilities than ones in the older regions. Commenting on criticism of "dilapidated" meetinghouses in North Carolina, P. T. Douglass of Bainbridge, Georgia, boasted that "in our parts, our meeting houses are ceiled, and in winter we have a stove which warms the house, so that in coldest weather, our families can go to meeting without danger to their health."[10] However, many if not most Baptist meetinghouses were distinctly rough. One observer noted in the late 1850s that Primitive Baptist "church buildings are generally erected in the woods, and most commonly are without windows and doors."[11] Many remained without ceilings or heat into the twentieth century.

The first churches constituted in South Georgia and Florida usually originated from a few Baptist settlers moving "to this wilderness counterey and findeing each other oute," as happened at Union Church. The number of members necessary for entering into a constitution sometimes barely exceeded the biblical "two or three." Union had ten charter members; Bethel Church, Brooks County, Georgia, had only six; Hephzibah Church started with nine members.[12] After locating potential members, the embryonic pioneer church had to obtain two ordained Baptist ministers. In earlier times, necessity forced churches to bend or compromise constitutional practices. In the period of rapid expansion during the Great Revival, the Savannah Association ruled that "in cases where proper helps could not be obtained without delays which might be injurious to the cause of God, we conceive that one ordained minister, with the assistance of a church, may perform [constitutions and ordinations], yet, we are of opinion, that ordinarily, they require—especially the ordination of ministers and the constitution of churches—at least two respectable ministers, and could *three* or more, be procured, it would be highly desirable, as adding to the dignity of such important transactions."[13]

Beard's Creek, Pigeon Creek, and Union all had two ordained ministers in their constitution.[14] Hephzibah, in a remoter situation, had one ordained

Bethlehem Primitive Baptist Church, Brooks County, Ga. 1998. Courtesy of Nancy Ekstrom.

Interior of Bethlehem Church. 1998. Courtesy of Nancy Ekstrom.

minister, a licensed preacher, and a deacon in its constituting presbytery.[15] In more settled times, associations became stricter in their review of the origins of applicant churches. In 1833, the Ochlocknee Association refused to receive Shiloh Church, Ware County, Georgia, "on account of the illegality of her constitution."[16]

The second generation of churches usually originated as "arms" of a previously established church. Union Church assisted in the formation of nineteen Baptist churches in South Georgia and Florida between 1826 and 1846.[17] Four of these commenced as arms. The first arm eventually became Friendship Church and left behind the most detailed records. On February 10, 1827, Union received a petition from Fleming Bates, Jonathan Knight, Elizabeth Knight, Mary Roberts, and Sam and Penny, slaves of Jonathan Knight, "for an arm of this church to be Extended to them on the withlacoochee with power to hold conferrences and commune and make there returns onste a yeare to this church as the body." The church granted the petition, expressed its confidence in the petitioners, appointed Jonathan Knight their clerk, and provided them with a copy of the church's decorum.[18] The members of the arm thanked the mother congregation for its "Liberality in granting the petition . . . [of] them distant Breathering for some of them cold not attend heare more then onste or twist a yeare." They appointed "Satterday before the third Sunday in June nex" for their first conference.[19] The first meeting convened at "Mr Saps and Johnstons," and after an "interesting discorse" by Fleming Bates, the congregation heard the decree of Union Church authorizing the meeting and the decorum provided. The arm chose Bates as its moderator. Four members joined by letter, including Bates's wife and daughter. Their hosts granted them permission to meet at the same place until construction of a meetinghouse. In May, Francis Akins, an ordained deacon, and his wife joined by letter, and the arm returned thanks to their hosts and planned to meet next at their new meetinghouse. At the June meeting, Matthew Albritton, the pastor at Union, presided. The arm drew up a petition to Union that Albritton and Bates be "clothed with authority" to constitute them a church "at the new meting house on the withlawcoochee River . . . for their conveniancy and furtherance of a Contemplated association." As if to place a divine seal of approval on their efforts, Samuel Henderson came forward at the end of the meeting and related an "expearence to the joy and gladness of our harts." Bates baptized him in the Withlacoochee River the following morning, and the arm afterward celebrated its first communion service. Union "cordially granted" their request at its July conference and constituted the arm as Friendship Church, near the present city of Hahira, Georgia, on July 15, 1827.[20]

In 1852, the Suwannee River Association officially discouraged the practice of "extending arms," probably because the long period of tutelage under a superior congregation reminded them too much of the religious hierarchies of the Methodists and Presbyterians. Also, the practice seems to have had no obvious biblical precedent, an important point to Baptists. In spite of this ruling, however, the practice of extending arms has continued sporadically until the present.[21]

The constitution of a church required the presiding ministers to examine the ecclesiastical standing of the charter members. At Hephzibah, for instance, only nine proposed charter members had letters of dismission. The embryonic church received five others who had not obtained letters as yet "under care" but did not permit them to be enlisted as charter members.[22] A letter of dismission surviving from Hephzibah in the 1830s has the typical form followed at the present:

> W. Florida, Gadsden County
>
> We the church of Christ at Hepzibah holding to the doctrine of election, particular redemption and the final perseverance of the saints in Grace. whereas our beloved sister Mariah a coloured having applied to us for a letter of dismission is hereby recommended to be in good order, in union and fellowship and is dismissed from us when joined to another church of the same faith and order. done for and in behalf of the whole church.[23]

Women and slaves sometimes lacked the opportunity to obtain letters when moving. Union Church took note of Amelia Corbitt's "destitute condition haveing . . . not appertunity to git a letter of dismission," and wrote to Hebron Church, Emanuel County, Georgia, for her letter.[24] Union received "br Poledo a black man upon relateing over his Experience formally [sic] a member of a church in Savannah baptised by marshell a black man fully autherised and allso receved Sister Tamer a black woman on Relateing over her Experience formally a member of the baptist church in bryant County baptised by Parson Sweat[.] both these Black peopple ware braught a way from there churches with oute haveing the appertunity of gitting letters of dismission."[25]

Richland Creek Church gave "Brother Shade a man of colour belonging to the estate of Robt. W. Sanders" a letter of dismission, hinting at the tragedy of a slave community scattered by the owner's death.[26] At least Brother Shade had the opportunity to get a letter, unlike Poledo and Tamer. Sometimes even a male white member moved to a new country without a letter, as when Reason Swilley requested Union to write for his and his wife's letters from Sarepta Church, Tattnall County, Georgia.[27] Sometimes a scapegrace, excommunicated by a distant church, rediscovered his faith on the Wiregrass frontier, as when a Brother Prescott requested Union to write on his behalf to Little Saltcatcher Church, Carter's Ford, South Carolina. Prescott admitted "he was turned oute of that church for neglecting to attend to disiplin wheare in the church was Rite and him self Rong." He wished "through us to confess his falt to them and craves there forgiveness . . . and . . . to be Restored to them again that he might be dismist in order . . . to be united with us." Prescott claimed he had "tried to deport him self as well as he cold," and the Church, knowing "nothing to the contrary," granted his request.[28]

During the frontier period, Baptist preachers occasionally baptized settlers in remote areas on their own authority and furnished them with certificates of baptism to use in place of a church letter. Union received Frances Gill by "surtificate" from Baptist preacher James Steely of Crawford County, Georgia, who had baptized her on a profession of faith and recommended her to any church "holding the Baptist faith in common."[29] Union Church specifically empowered William Knight, a newly ordained minister, to receive and baptize members while "travelling." The church required him to consult other members or other Baptists of the "same faith and order" before baptizing anyone. However, with no other Baptists at hand, he might "proceed himself and give the person or persons a certificate."[30]

A Baptist without a church letter found him or herself like a person abroad without a passport. On one occasion, Union Church member Roswell B. Darling resorted to the desperate expedient of forgery in order to join a Baptist Church in Tennessee. Apparently Darling aroused his new brethren's suspicion, causing them to send a copy of his "letter of dismission" to Union. Upon examination, the letter proved to be "a forgery" and "in his own handwriting." Outraged that Darling had dared to go "away from us without a letter of dismission" and then "impose" on distant Baptists, Union Church excommunicated him as a matter of course.[31]

The ephemeral nature of many early churches generated problems when the former members of extinct churches sought to join others. The Ochlocknee and Suwannee River associations ruled that in the case of "excommunicated members, or members removing and churches afterwards becoming extinct, to which no acknowledgement can be made, nor from which no letter can be obtained, that we recommend to the several churches composing our body that in all such cases that after due examination and sufficient evidence being had of their being Baptised and in faith and order, that they shall be received into full fellowship, and if satisfactory testimony cannot be obtained, then received in the usual manner by Baptism."[32]

Apparently in a matter as serious as valid baptism, a prospective member's mere word did not amount to "sufficient evidence." In the highly mobile frontier society, churches usually granted any member in good standing a letter upon demand. However, as a church did not have to accept a member, it also did not have to let one go. Bethlehem Church refused Simeon McLeod and his wife letters of dismission because "there was no church at present close to him."[33]

Once the members produced documentation verifying their standing as "orthodox" and "orderly" Baptists, they then formally joined in a covenant. The covenant recapitulated the founding motions of the church and the ministers and members taking part, and stated the faith of the church and the obligations the members assumed toward one another. That of Bethlehem Church, Brooks County, Georgia is fairly typical.

> We whose names are before written having bin duly Baptised upon a profession of our Faith [and] . . . hav[ing] obtained previledge and letters of dismission to become a Constituted Body to become a Church . . . Independent as to our internal wrights of any church or churches Presbytary . . . for which purpose we do call our beloved Brethren Matthew Allbritton and Ryon Frier to act as presbetery In our Constituion and the said brethren being present . . . first Cauld for our letters of Dismission from our Mother churches Examoned the same and Findeing no Impedement pronounced us a Church of Christ on the Principles of the gospel that is to say Beleving the Scriptures of the Old and New Testament to be the word of God and contains Every thing nessery for our faith and practice In perticular the Existance of one Tryune God the Father Son and Holy Gost the fall of man and his Inabillety to recover himself Gods Sovereign Choice of his people In Christ there covenant head from before the foundation of the world Effectual Calling Justification by the imputed Righteousness of Christ alone the Final Perseverence of the Saints In grace and Eternal Salvation in glory the Duty of Baptisom by Immersion and the Lord Supper washing the Saints feet &c.[34]

Some churches set forth a more detailed confession of faith. Beard's Creek explicitly stated its adherence to the 1689 London Confession.[35] Hephzibah Church adopted more detailed articles than the brief "principles of the gospel" adopted at Bethlehem. More explicit in their trinitarianism, they declared the members of the Trinity "equal in essence power and glory." They also clearly expressed belief in particular redemption.[36] Emigrants from strongly predestinarian North Carolina, Tired Creek's founders stated that "God foreordained whatsoever comes to pass."[37]

Union Church closed its covenant with an express mutual bond, vowing to "delibertly and Sollomly give our Selves to the Lord and to each other . . . Covinanting and promising each other to Live to geather as becomes Breathering in gospell bondes for the m[ain]taing of christian fellowship and gospell diciplin a greeable to the holy Scriptures and as true yoke fellows in the gospel a gree to stand or fall to geather in order."[38]

After being "pronounced a church in order," a new congregation adopted a decorum, or rules of order. These were standard rules usually copied whole cloth from those of older churches, but sometimes later amended by the adopting church. Many later churches adopted Union's decorum, which contains all the basic features of such documents.

The decorum required each conference to begin and end with "devine worship." Union Church met on the second Saturday and Sunday in each month, a practice which continues to the present. All but a very few Primitive Baptist churches in the area under consideration still meet monthly. Services consisted of singing, prayer, and preaching by whatever Baptist ministers, if any, were present.[39] Singing formed an important part of worship, and in the absence of a preacher, it furnished the bulk of the devotions.[40] Beard's Creek Church bought a single copy of Jesse Mercer's *Cluster of Spiritual Songs, Divine Hymns and Sacred Poems* from which to "line out" hymns.[41] This hymnal enjoyed "uncommon success and popularity," at least until its editor turned Missionary. Accordingly, his "success and popularity" among Primitives declined. The arrangement of the book was similar to that of Rippon's hymnal, one of its main sources. The *Cluster* contained hymn texts, without musical notation. It was in its third edition by 1810, and the 1835 edition contained 691 songs.[42] At Upper Black Creek Church, a "singing clerk" had custody of the book and lined out the hymns.[43] Hymn lining developed into an art form. Elder Ansel Parrish, of Berrien County, Georgia (1824–91), had a remarkably beautiful voice, and his hearers long remembered the antiphonal beauty of his lining.[44]

Extemporaneous prayer by the preachers present, and by laymen in their absence, constituted the second important part of the regular service. Since Union Church only met once a month, the church authorized prayer meetings on the fourth Sunday. They also held prayer meetings on the numerous occasions when the pastor or other ministers did not come.[45] The members and neighbors met to sing, pray, "exhort," and read the Bible aloud.

The sermon formed the centerpiece of the meeting. According to the Union Church minutes, a sermon differed from an exhortation, since it reflected doctrine, usually preached by an ordained minister from a text. Belief in inspired sermons remained strong among the local Baptists. William Knight recorded that on Sunday, August 9, 1829, Matthew Albritton preached from Mark 15:16 and "was in the fullness of the gospel and by inspiration deliverd to us a hart cheareing and affecting Surmond[.] A goodly number gave him there hand to be praid for."[46]

Fortunately, the early clerks at Union often gave the text and a brief synopsis of the sermons. Preachers often dwelt on the main points of Calvinist theology, as when Francis Akins held forth from I John 3:9 on "justifying righteousness," "effectual calling," and "perceverance of the saints in grace."[47] Sermons tended to be highly allegorical, dwelling much on "types and "shadows." For example, William Knight preached at Tiger Swamp, Hamilton County, Florida, from Revelation 16:22: "From these words he was enabled to show us the sea of God's grace that [none] could navigate but those taught by the Spirit[,] and it was navigated with the love of God[.] Showing us the beast his image his mark and the number of his name and how they stand on the sea and what was the harps of God the souls prepared and cleansed from all guilt filled with all fullness[.] we desire to thank and praise god for this wonderful display of his glorious gospel[.] the effect was almost genral[.] we hardly ever saw a softer time[.] a goodly number desired an interest in prayer[.] we hope the good spirit is at work in the hearts of some of the people."[48]

A critic mentioned that most Georgia Primitive preachers were of the "wang-doodle sort and played upon the harp of a thousand strings," references to two popular burlesque Old Baptist sermons of the 1850s.[49] Many Primitive preachers delivered their sermons in the chant mocked by the parson Woodmason in the 1770s. Harden E. Taliaferro described the "heavenly tone" in the Wiregrass "cow counties" along the lower Chattahoochee in the 1840s as having the "suck-in and the blow-out of the breath, the *uh!* and the *ah!*"[50] Some still employ that tone. A more recent and less charitable observer described one South Georgia preacher as "sounding like an old John Deere tractor hitting on two cylinders." Outsiders unfamiliar with Primitive Baptist theological terms and with sermons delivered in the "heavenly tone" experience difficulty in understanding them. Primitives believe, however, that if one has a "portion," a predestined message, it will be understood no matter what the delivery. Several years ago, a rather prim Methodist attended "Big Meeting" at Bethel Church, Echols County, Georgia. As the members waxed enthusiastic over one particular sermon, the Wesleyan sniffed that all she got from it was *"hoo!"* and *"ha!"* "Well," remarked a Primitive, "that was your portion." Many older Primitive Baptists still doubt the inspiration of a preacher who delivers a sermon in a normal tone of voice.[51] However, many highly respected Primitive Baptist ministers have not preached in this manner. Jordan Smith, a prominent minister of the Hephzibah Association during the 1820s, preached "slow and deliberate, though quite tender and pathetic."[52]

Preachers tended to be longwinded. When several minsters appeared, all might be called upon to preach. At Bethany Church, Brooks County, Georgia, in 1831, visitors heard three "discourses" on Saturday and two on Sunday. When several preachers followed one another, the church sometimes granted "a few minutes for refreshment" between sermons.[53] William A. Knight of Union frequently gave "verry lengthy" sermons and exhortations.[54] Other preachers shared his predilection for lengthy discourses. Bethel and Bethany churches, Brooks County, Georgia, had to omit the footwashing ceremony at their 1833 annual meetings because the preaching lasted so long.[55] Union also deferred the ritual at the 1833 annual meeting. Small wonder, since Melus Thigpen, William Knight, Ryan Frier, and Matthew Albritton all preached in succession.[56] Such marathon services sometimes frayed the patience of members and often reduced small children to extreme hunger. Elderly South Georgians still relate horror stories about all-day services crowned by a long wagon trip to a member's farm, where children, often served last, were told, "Take a cold tater and wait."[57]

People in such thinly settled country, with bad roads, found amusement scarce. Many came to "meeting" to "see and be seen," as Elder T. W. Stallings recalled of his unregenerate days.[58] In good weather large crowds often gathered. In 1832, Union Church moved one meeting outdoors to the "association stand, the house not being roomy enough to accomodate the congregation."[59]

The churches met on one Sunday of each month, and on the preceding Saturday, after preaching, they held their conference and took care of the church's business. The minutes consist chiefly of conference accounts. These records reflect a remarkable social history of their communities, mainly due to the strict discipline the churches kept. They reprimanded or excommunicated members for offenses that ranged from drunkenness, fighting, adultery, dancing, nonattendance, and horse racing to joining the Methodists. Drinking was a major problem for frontier Baptists, as well as for others throughout the United States during the 1830s and 1840s. Between 1800 and 1830, per capita consumption of spirits reached the highest point in American history.[60] As a pioneer Georgia Baptist minister recalled, "in those days, almost everybody was in the habit of drinking; young and old, rich and poor, saint and sinner, all would drink, and many of them get drunk into the bargain."[61] Some observers stigmatized Primitives as "Whiskey Baptists" or "Forty Gallon" Baptists.[62] About 1829, an itinerant preacher found a minister of the Piedmont Association keeping a grog shop.[63]

Habitual drunkenness brought one under the displeasure of the church. Between 1835 and 1840, eight Union Church brethren acknowledged "intoxication." All were forgiven and "admonished . . . to be more on . . . guard hereafter."[64] Drinking often accompanied—if it did not cause—rowdy behavior. In 1842, a Brother Lee reported to Union Church that his "feelings was hurt with Brother Wrice[.] he also stated that br Wrice had abused him considerable and that Br Wrice was intoxicated." The accused "made no defense[,] but said we had better turn him out[.] this proposition was made to him[:] would he forsake spirits [?] we would wait [i.e., bear] with him[.] he gave this answer[:] he allways had drunk spirits and expected to as long as he lived." "Seeing no hopes of reformation," the church expelled him unanimously.[65] His frank reply seems the main cause for his expulsion, perhaps coupled with abuse of a brother while drunk. Others repeatedly confessed mere drunkenness, but as long as they begged humbly for forgiveness, they received it as a matter of course. In time, these confessions became almost pro forma among the hard-drinking settlers. In one Primitive Baptist church in southeast Georgia, several members at one meeting confessed having "a *leetle* too much to drink." Finally, one brother arose and said, "Brethren, I haven't had a *leetle* too much to drink. I got *plumb drunk*." "Now that," observed the pastor of the church, "is the kind of acknowledgement I like to hear."[66]

Male drunkeness, then as now, injured women. Although the government of the churches "more peticular" belonged to male members, women could vote.[67] An old matriarch, "Grandma" Alderman, who at her death had 450 living descendants, held membership with Bethel Church, Brooks County, Georgia. There she once put the sister's latent power to work. A brother in the habit of intemperance regularly confessed his fault and just as regularly received the church's forgiveness. A report that he had been "tipsy" once again circulated and he appeared at church "with the same tale again." Sister Alderman told the sisters, "Girls, if you will follow me today, we will put a stop to it." When the usual move to forgive the brother's lapse came forward, all the male members stood to forgive him, but the women kept their seats. When the moderator put the negative of the question, all the women stood and, being the majority, turned the old soak out of the church.[68]

Even ministers occasionally had trouble with liquor. Isham Peacock was long remembered as "a whiskey drinking anti-missionary preacher," who "lived to a great age."[69] As the Missionary Controversy grew more heated, their advocacy of the temperance movement became grafted onto their other controversies with the Primitives. During this period Peacock carried a hollow cane full of whisky, from which he would drink before his congregation to demonstrate the bounds of Christian liberty with regard to ardent spirits. Missionary Baptist Adiel Sherwood shuddered to "see a minister nearly one hundred years old using such *strong* but *dangerous* arguments to carry his point." Peacock's opponents admitted that he did not drink to excess.[70] Moses Westberry, one of Peacock's fellow ministers in the Piedmont Association, and possibly the grog shop keeper of Jones Creek Church, developed problems as a consequence of sampling his own wares. In 1828, Jones Creek appointed a committee to "visit Rev. Westberry and admonish him as he drinks too much."[71] The cure often was worse than the disease where drinking was concerned on the frontier. With temperance societies among the many "benevolences" arousing frontier Baptists' suspicions, Westberry found himself on Isham Peacock's enemies list in 1833 for having joined a temperance society.[72] William Hawthorn, a prominent pioneer minister in southwest Georgia, suffered a number of slips in regard to liquor, as is recorded in church minutes. In 1828, Hawthorn acknowledged "intemperance" after returning from Milledgeville. Tired Creek Church concluded that "he should lay down his preaching gift until the church thought proper to restore him to his former office." Having decided this during a Saturday conference, it occurred to them overnight that they would have no preacher on Sunday, so they relieved Hawthorn of his interdiction the next day. In 1829 Hawthorn once again "came forward and made an acknowledgement to the church for intemperance in drinking on his way from North Carolina, for which the church [thought it] proper to silence him from preaching which he humbly submitted to with[out] a murmer." This time Tired Creek kept him on the bench for two months. Hawthorn's reputation for drinking evidently became so widespread that the church took steps to counter rumors relative to it. In 1832, the church instructed its members to employ their "utmost endeavors to contradict . . . a report . . . in circulation that . . . Brother William Hawthorn was drunk at the last association [which] is well known to this church to be false."[73] Although there was an obvious tendency to treat drunkeness as a venal sin, it did not always go unreproved. On one occasion, William A. Knight of Union Church "rose and adressed himself to the church verry fellingly [feelingly] on the subject of useing ardent spirits intemperately."[74]

Worldly amusements called forth much sterner rebukes than occasional lapses with the "creature." In 1838, John Guthrie confessed to Union Church that he had not only gotten drunk but had done so at a horse race, a compound offense for which the church "admonished him to be more on his guard hereafter."[75] He got off lightly. William Shepherd confessed the exact same combination of offenses to Richland Creek Church, Decatur County, Georgia, which excluded him for his "disorderly conduct."[76] Doubtless, the church's objection to horseracing stemmed in part from disapproval of gambling. Bethlehem Church excluded James McLeod for "falsehood and gambling." Ironically, two years previously McLeod received license to "exhort, pray, and admonish if his gift be found profitable." The church eventually restored him to membership, but his advancement toward the gospel ministry had apparently suffered a fatal setback.[77]

Dancing was anathema to the churches. David Fender of Union Church reported himself "imposed on in feeling by admitting frolicking in his house and if he had hurt his brethrens feelings thereby he was sorry for it and asked forgiveness." Since he had apparently succumbed to the solicitations of nonmembers to host a party, the church forgave him while "admonishing of him to be more upon his guard for the future and think more of himself and the profession he has made than the worlde."[78] Nancy Greene, a merry and independent-minded South Carolinian, along with a Brother Boyt, "suffered fiddling and dancing in their house." "After several remarks and remonisters [remonstrations?] against such conduct by professors," the church appointed a special meeting to deal with them.[79] Boyt, or Boyett, and his wife acknowledged their wrong, but Nancy Greene sent word that she "did not feel hurt for suffering the like in her house." Cited to appear before the church, she finally confessed and was forgiven.[80] A year later, Sister Greene again fell into "disorder" with the brethren's "feelings hurt" by her conduct. This time she scorned the church's citation, saying she "would not come and to turn her out or she would turn herself out." The church concluded that "her obstinance toward us is a sufficient cause for her expulsion." Departing from previous accounts of excommunication, the clerk specified that she was excluded by a rising vote and formally declared excommunicated by the pastor, "and that the church had no more charge over her."[81]

The horror that dancing inspired among the devout of the period is exemplified by the young slave woman Dinah Sermons, who lived near Union Church as a young woman. One of her most serious religious impressions came from the death of a "Missionary woman in the settlement" whom Dinah "saw dancing and sporting with worldly amusements[.] She was taken suddenly sick and died. And one day as I was walking along and thinking of her, I spoke and said—'She once professed to know the Lord, and now she is dead, what has become of her soul?' A moment after I felt a shock in my breast that seemed to jar my heart till it filled me so full I thought it would choke me to death."[82]

Later in the century, some Primitive Baptists slightly modified their stance on dancing. In Lowndes County, Georgia, younger members of pious families held "play parties" where they danced to chanted songs, reminiscent of the *peurt a beul*, or "mouth music," of Scotland and the "ballad dancing" of medieval Scandinavia. Rhythmic moving to chanted songs was only "playing," whereas the same movements to instrumental music constituted dancing and a grave offense. In the 1880s, W. N. Redding, a member of Cat Creek Church, Lowndes County, gave his musically talented son a fiddle for Christmas, showing a distinct slippage in two puritanical biases: opposition to secular music and to "Popish" festivals.[83]

Surprisingly, when a circus visited the backwoods of Jefferson County, Florida, in the late 1830s, some of the members of Mt. Moriah Church attended, paying a stiff fee for admission. However, they had not given their pastor, Henry Milton, anything for several years. At the May 1838 conference, they found lying on the communion table a satirical poem by fellow member Nancy Hagan, later a vigorous proponent of missions.

The worldlings they with minds so rash
To circus riders pay their cash
But we are young and strong as they
And yet our preacher gets no pay.[84]

The cracker on her whip was in the form of a ten-dollar bill pinned to the poem. Milton quickly received a generous contribution.[85]

Many early local Baptists held strict views of Sabbath observance. Tired Creek Church charged Rachel Gordon with "misconduct in selling bread on the associational ground on the sabbath day." She confessed her fault and was forgiven.[86] In Elder Ansel Parrish, of Berrien County, Georgia, strict sabbatarianism vied both with his sense of humor and with his well-known appetite. Leaving home to preach, he admonished one of his sons, "Boy, don't you go fishing Sunday, but if you do and catch any, be sure and save some until I get back." On another Sunday morning as he left for church, he called one of his sons to him, saying, "Son, I don't want you to be racing your horse today, and if you do, I'll thrash you." Reflecting a moment, he dismounted and said, "Son, I know you will race that horse, regardless of my warning, so I'll just go ahead and thrash you now."[87] Among the Primitive Baptists, respect for the Sabbath never outweighed fear of clerical meddling in national affairs. The Primitives staunchly opposed sabbath blue laws as an unconstitutional establishment of religion.[88]

Among the worldly entanglements Baptists were to avoid, "Secret Orders" and the Masons in particular ranked high. Opposition to Freemasonry was endemic in ninteenth-century America, but the Primitive Baptists reflected a particularly longstanding opposition. Beard's Creek Church "jerked up" that inveterate joiner, Rev. Moses Westberry, together with a Brother Lane for joining the fraternity in 1807. "They both confess they were sorry for what they had done and begged pardon of the church, which was granted."[89] In 1831, the Ochlocknee Association adopted a rather mild anti-Masonic resolution: "We recommend our brethren of that order to withdraw themselves from that body as much as they possibly can to save their obligations. And we further recommend to those who have not joined them to refrain from it entirely, and have christian forbearance toward their brethren."[90] The wording of this resolution indicates that membership in Masonic lodges was a fairly widespread phenomenon among early South Georgia and Florida Baptists, despite church opposition to it. The reprinting of an 1831 resolution in 1853 indicates that Masonic membership continued to be a problem despite efforts to eliminate it. In 1852, the Suwannee River Association also condemned Masonic affiliation, again rather mildly, stating that "we do not believe it to be according to gospel order, and recommend the members in our connection, to keep themselves from it as much as possible."[91] The Pulaski Association in South Georgia took a harder stance in 1852 and dropped correspondence with the Echeconnee Association in central Georgia because it held Masons in membership.[92] In 1857, the Alabaha River Association approved the excommunication of a Mason by one of its churches.[93]

Not merely the Masons but all secretive organizations came under the adverse scrutiny of the church. A scandalized brother complained about church members participating in the parades of "a new sect," the Odd Fellows. "There were two or three of my young brethren, tricked out with ribbons, and tin stars, and other gingleties. Oh, how my heart was grieved. . . . I was told that Odd Fellows was a charitable concern, and that was the reason that they joined. Well, is the Church of Christ not charitable enough? For shame, brethren, for shame! . . . These poor blind brethren say there is no scripture against them!!"[94]

One positive result of this attitude was that the churches discouraged their members from belonging to sinister secret organizations, which became more and more common in the antebellum South. The 1847 Ochlocknee Association forbade its members to join a local Regulator Company. "This Association does not pretend to determine as to the neccessity of the formation of said Company; but for brethren to continue to persist in a course fraught with so much danger to civil society, as well as to the affliction of their brethren, is not following the things that make for peace. . . . We, therefore, request all of our brethren who have been connected therewith to withdraw from said company; and further advise the churches to excercise all the Christian forbearance possible toward their brethren upon the subject."[95]

The fondness of antebellum southerners for fighting reflects a common problem in the social history of the region. Louis Leclerc Milfort reported that backcountry Georgians in the 1790s were called "Gougers" as well as Crackers, from their habit of gouging out eyes in fights.[96] George Washington Harris's Sut Lovingood described the antebellum southerner's *summum bonum* as, after sex, eating, and drinking, to play "short kerds, swap horses wif fools, and fite fur exercise."[97] Southerners frequently "exercised" by fighting, and South Georgians and Floridians were no exception.[98] Even church members did not avoid the vice entirely. As recorded in the Union Church minutes, Peter Wetherington admitted attempting "to make a fight with one of his neighbors," for which he was forgiven. The church forgave Brethren Lastinger and Brown for having "transgressed by laying violent hands on their fellow men." Four months earlier, the church had authorized Lastinger to "excersase his gift by prayer and exhortation within the pales of this church." No doubt someone did not care for his efforts at preaching. Lastinger again "transgressed by manifesting a desire to fight his fellow man" and received forgiveness. Jacob Giddens "arose and reported that he had been insulted inso much that he had a fight with a man and was sorry for it." The church forgave him. On a later occasion Giddens "got into an affray and drunk too much sperets," probably the cause of that "affray" and several others. The brethren at Union seem to have regarded fighting even more mildly than they did excessive drinking. In one case, they did not even deem it an offense. Jeremiah Shaw "reported he was purvoked in to a fite[.] [H]e was truly sorra for feare it had hurt his brothers felings but he could not avoid it and he hoped his brethren would forgive him." His brethren "manifested no hard feelings."[99] Fighting on the frontier was so general that it was hard to avoid. Tired Creek Church forgave Elias O. Hawthorn after he had "inadvertently falen into a riot."[100] At Richland Creek Church, in present Grady County, Thomas Wright, and Robert W. Sanders "charged themselves with a fighting scrape with persons out of the church." Richland Creek called for help from three nearby churches to advise them on the case. "After being fully discussed and meditated on by this church and thirteen visiting brethren[,] the brethren . . . were unanimously restored to the affections of the brethren and their former standing in the church."[101]

Fighting sometimes did not have to be reported to the church but actually took place there. Fellowship Church, a Madison County, Florida, congregation going back to the 1840s, was once known as "Wildcat" because local pugilists favored its yard as a place for settling affairs of honor. Fights did not stay confined to the yard there. A preacher once put forth a doctrine not to the liking of a brother, who jumped up into the pulpit and knocked the preacher out of the open window behind him. During the Missionary Controversy of the 1840s, tradition holds that several Baptist churches witnessed fistfights on the grounds between the adherents of the two opposed parties.[102] Fighting during services at Beard's Creek Church reached such a pitch that the church held a special meeting at which they authorized a member to report Cordy A. Sands to a justice of the peace for "disorderly conduct."[103] The church then sought an incorporation from the state and appointed trustees to "take special care of all property belonging to said church" and to prosecute anyone "injuring the house or well of water," or "any person attending our worshipping congregations" and behaving "incosistent with law, good order, and peace, to the interruption of the said worshipping congregation or any one of them."[104] Small wonder then that the clerk at Union Church gratefully wrote of one meeting, "such composur and order is worthey of aney peopple."[105] Associational minutes specifically thanked the local community for their "good order" during the session.[106] Good behavior at any large gathering was not a given.

Even the sisters sometimes engaged in brawls. In 1833, Jane Yawn apologized to Tired Creek Church for "for getting into an affray with one Jacob Miller." Sister Yawn possessed an unhappy temperament; Tired Creek finally excommunicated her for "profane swearing."[107] The pioneeer women of the region no doubt possessed a good bit of fortitude and also stubbornness. Union excluded three sisters for "obstinancy" in refusing to answer various charges against them. One of the accused sisters, Martha Sermons, did not exercise her "obstinancy" in silence. She "said things very unseemly of the church and did not say whether she would come or not but if she did come she should give the church no satisfaction."[108]

Even if the church decorums declared the government of the church to belong "more particularly" to the male members, the sisters did not always meekly submit. In 1829, Harty Sermons refused to take communion at Union Church. At the next meeting she explained that "Br. Robarts had not given hir full sattisfaction for a hard word spoken and not fully explaned[.] Brother Robarts rose and explaned and talked tenderly and beged pardon of the sister which was granted[,] giveing each other the rite hand of fellowship[.] Thank the Lord for peace."[109] Bethel Church, Brooks County, Georgia, in 1831 expelled Sarah Holloway, the new second wife of William Holloway, for her "long absence, having moved out of reach of the church and also for her disorderly walk." Her disorder was her disgust with her sixty-nine-year-old husband for leaving relatively well settled Bulloch County and removing to the wilds of deep South Georgia. Finally, she left him and returned on her own to the old neighborhood.[110] Even slave women asserted themselves, especially where their church privileges were concerned. Dinah Sermons, then a slave in her twenties, united with Union Church to its "great joy" in 1841.[111] "I offered myself to the church, and told them what great things the Lord had done for me. They said they were willing to take me before I told them all, but I told them I was not through."[112] She perhaps meant not to be deprived of the one time in her life when the white people had to listen to her.

Sexual offenses were relatively rare, perhaps because many early Baptists in the region were middle aged or old when they joined the church. In the 1840s, Simon Peter Richardson noted that the Primitive Baptists, especially the ministers, were old.[113] Nonetheless, the Old Adam occasionally revealed himself. In 1814, Upper Black Creek Church turned out one Brother Roberts after Elizabeth Davis accused him of begetting her child.[114] Beard's Creek Church dealt tersely and summarily with the case of the unfortunate Sister Nancy Moody, "it being made to appear to the church that [she] is a fornicatress."[115] At Beard's Creek, at least, church members had to be above reproach. That rather precise body expelled Amy Groover "on an accusation for adultery[,] [n]ot supported by church evidence but a want of fellowship on acount such report with the members of this church."[116] The early minutes usually called everything by its name, but as time went on, some Victorian sensibilites penetrated the backwoods. Tired Creek Church heard the case of G. L. Holton, who accused himself of "things contrary to gospel order." "It being a delicate matter," the church appointed an all-male committee to hear his confession. The committee decided the case "merits expulsion." However, the fellowship unanimously restored Holton five months later, which indicates an offense more embarrassing than serious.[117] As in many other developing areas, the post–Civil War generation in South Georgia and Florida adopted the mealymouthed conventions of the Victorian era at about the time that they were fading out elsewhere. As a result, they lived in constant dread of what their rough and outspoken "Old Settler" parents and grandparents would do or say next.[118]

Given the pugnacity of the Georgia-Florida border settlers, it is not surprising that when the controversy over missions finally arrived in the region, all parties leapt into it with gusto. The struggle against the Missionaries constitutes the burden of the next chapter.

4

"Always Primitive"

The Missionary Controversy

"The Ochlocknee has always been Primitive," Elder Prior Lewis wrote in 1843.[1] Most frontier Baptists of South Georgia and Florida opposed doctrinal and organizational innovations appearing in the early nineteenth century. Their opposition to the new institutions formed their subsequent character, distinguished by a conviction that far from the "Missionaries" was close to God. As late as the 1970s, the sneering remark, "That sounds like the Missionaries," quickly put to death any proposed novelty in a South Georgia Primitive church. Certain hymns in the standard Primitive hymnal, but also popular among Southern Baptists, elicited disdain. Several years ago, a recent convert from the Missionaries often requested the hymn "Oh, to be robed and ready." Eventually, he requested his favorite once too often, and a snide voice remarked, "He likes *Missionary* songs." "Robed and Ready" declined sharply in the repertoire thereafter. Even melodies popular among the Southern Baptists are disparagingly referred to as "borrowed tunes." At the "Old Side" faction of Valley Grove Church, Irwin County, Georgia, one venerable brother, now deceased, would throw down his hymnbook in disgust if anyone requested a song he regarded as Missionary.[2]

The missionary impulse in England grew out of the Great Awakening and in America out of the Great Revival. As seen in chapter 1, the English Baptists during the 1730s disputed the "Modern Question," concerning "whether saving faith in Christ is a duty . . . of all those who live under the gospel revelation." Baptist ministers led by Abraham Taylor argued in the affirmative, while John Gill and others dissented. Gill's position dominated many Particular Baptist churches, and in the opinion of Charles Haddon Spurgeon, the prominent nineteenth-century Baptist evangelist, "chilled many churches to their very soul." Ironically, one of these "chilled churches" converted Andrew Fuller, who introduced among the Particular Baptists both missionary zeal and its supporting theology. Young Fuller discovered Abraham Taylor's *The Modern Question,* which "set me fast." In 1785, with Gill safely interred in Bunhill Fields, Fuller published *The Gospel Worthy of All Acceptation,* in which he asserted the duty of all persons to believe savingly and exhorted the Baptists to assist in the evangelization of the world.[3]

The early Missionary Baptists faced an uphill battle. A strong tradition holds that William Carey, later the first Baptist missionary to India, asked the 1785 Northamptonshire Association whether the "Great Commission" was still in force. John Ryland, Sr., moderator of the meeting and friend of the late John Gill, dismissed the query and called Carey a "most miserable enthusiast." If Ryland did not actually say such words, many "Gillites" surely thought them. Less reliable accounts claim the chairman said, "Young man, sit down. When God pleases to convert the heathen, he will do it without your aid or mine," a sentiment American Primitives heartily endorsed.[4]

In spite of opposition, Fuller, Carey, and others pressed for a Baptist missionary effort. Andrew Fuller proposed the formation of a missionary society, which took place in 1792.[5] This first Baptist missionary society represented the initial swell of a wave that would introduce a generation of internecine conflict among Georgia and Florida Baptists.

In Georgia, where only one association existed in 1792, new measures got off to a slower start than in England. Blazing from the Great Revival, the 1800 session of the Georgia Association approved a meeting for encouragement of itinerant preaching. It refused, however, to send delegates to a proposed general conference of all Baptists in the United States.[6] Both the Georgia and Savannah associations endorsed the formation of a "General Committee of the Georgia Baptists . . . consisting of three members from each Association in the State, the leading object of which should be, to meet and confer with other Christian societies, in order to remove differences, and if possible, bring about a more general and close union among real Christians, on the principles of eternal truth."[7]

The General Committee recommended the formation of a missionary society for "sending the gospel amongst the Indians," and the Georgia Association "unanaimously and cordially approbated" the proposal, though they appear to have done nothing more. In November 1804, the Savannah Association "unanimously" approved both the "general committee of Georgia Baptists" and its attempts to establish a "Georgia Baptist College."[8] Little came of the attempt to establish a college, but Matthew Albritton and Isham Peacock, both later leading Antimissionaries, represented Upper Black Creek Church at this session. Embarrassment resulted years later, when a Missionary Baptist in Thomas County, Georgia, appealed to the early example of the Savannah Association in answer to the Primitive charge that the Missionary plans represented a complete novelty and that the Primitive brethren had never supported them.[9]

The General Committee of Georgia Baptists accomplished little besides the formation of an ephemeral academy, which soon perished along with its parent organization.[10] The 1812 conversion to Baptist principles of Luther Rice and Adoniram Judson, Congregationalist missionaries to India, stimulated missionary organization in the Baptist denomination and eventually generated the Primitive secession.

Judson and Rice, with their wives, set out to India as Congregationalist missionaries. They embraced believer's baptism in principle, as a result of their biblical studies during the voyage. Their Congregationalist sponsors' desire to convert "the heathen" did not extend to paying Baptists to do it, so Reverend and Mrs. Judson proceeded to Burma, while Rice returned to America to enlist Baptist support for their mission. Many American Baptists, delighted to have a foreign mission of their own, embraced the new cause with enthusiasm.[11] In 1814, representatives from local mission societies in eleven Atlantic states, including Georgia, met in Philadelphia. They organized the Triennial Convention to coordinate missionary activities, and they set up a subsidiary standing body, the Baptist Board of Foreign Missions for the United States, a well-meant organization soon to be a veritable modern Dagon in the eyes of dissenting Baptists.[12]

In South Georgia some interest appeared in organized missionary exertions. The 1811 Savannah River Association "agreed to encourage itinerant preaching, and urge . . . establishing a missionary fund in this body."[13] In 1812 this association, with "a majority . . . warmly in favor," took up an initial collection of $160.25 for a missionary fund. In 1813, Luther Rice, "a missionary to the East, and now on his tour through the Southern States, for the purpose of promoting missionary exertions . . . was affectionately invited to a seat in this body." The same session organized an associational missionary society and expressed their "cordial approbation of the great design now forming in America, for sending the Gospel to the Heathen."[14] In 1817, the association recommended the establishment of missionary societies within the individual churches.[15]

Farther inland, in the "wiregrass and lightwood knot country," beginning in 1804, the Hephzibah Association appointed pairs of itinerants to preach in "destitute" areas.[16] Local farmer-preachers, the itinerants toured in late summer when the laying by of the crop gave them and their hearers leisure to attend to such preaching. Itinerants received no money from the association until 1815. In that year, Caliborne Bateman received eighty-one dollars "to itinerate in the counties of Montgomery, Tattnall, Liberty and Emanuel."[17] Paying a minister to preach in a certain predetermined area represented a definite novelty among Baptists originating in the Separate tradition. Still, societies distinct from the churches and cooperation with a national organization constituted far more of a departure—more so than the Hephzibah Association and many others wished to make.

The 1815 session that appointed itinerant preacher Bateman also received "a number of copies of the First Annual Report of the Baptist Board of Foreign Missions, at Philadelphia." In 1816, supporters of missions organized a Hephzibah Baptist Society for Itinerant and Missionary Exertions.[18]

Opposition to missions soon appeared in the Hephzibah Association. "When the mission spirit waxed hot, the anti-mission began to wax warm also," recalled Antimissionary Elder Robert Donaldson.[19] In 1816, the association thanked the Board of Foreign Missions for its report but raised no money for it. In 1817, the association again acknowledged a communication from the board but refused to contribute. Those in favor of missions resolved to form a private missionary society with no connections to the association. In 1819, opposition came to a head when the association "negatived" a proposal "to know whether this body will take any part in the missionary." The association "agreed not to correspond with the Foreign Missionary Society."[20]

In 1822, mission advocates organized the "General Baptist Association of the State of Georgia," the second Baptist state convention in the United States.[21] The new state convention got off to a slow start, but it nowhere else met with quite the reception the Hephzibah Association gave it. By 1822, the association violently opposed mission efforts, rather than simply declining to take part in them. At that year's session, William T. Brantley obtained leave to read an invitation to join the state convention. According to the minutes, "On motion, the above plan was rejected."[22] J. H. T. Kilpatrick, a missions advocate present on that occasion, provided some details of the rejection not mentioned in the minutes. "A motion was made to lay the papers on the table, this was amended to a motion to throw them under the table, this by another to kick the bearer out of the house; the motion carried by a rising vote, some of the voters leaping up two or three times to give emphasis to the vote. The last amendment, in its execution, was so modified that the bearer of the unfortunate documents was escorted to the door, and with very demonstrative gesticulations threatened with dire consequences if ever again he pronounced the word 'missions' in the presence of that body."[23]

In 1825, a few petitions from mission advocates to allow members at least privately to cooperate with mission programs elicited a new amendment to the associational decorum: "This Association shall have no right to correspond by letter or messengers with any General Association or Committee, Missionary Society or Board. Any brother moving either of the above subjects in this body shall be considered in disorder and therefore reproved by the Moderator."[24] The Antimissionary party reached its high water mark with this resolution. In 1826, Jordan Smith, a strong opponent of missions, lost the moderator's seat, and the association repealed the "gag rule" enacted the previous year.[25] In 1827, in the midst of this conflict, the Kehukee Association of North Carolina sent the Hephzibah Antimissionaries copies of their minutes containing the "Declaration of the Reformed Baptist Churches in the State of North Carolina," written by Joshua Lawrence (1778–1843), and adopted by the Kehukee.[26] The Declaration anticipates virtually all Primitive Baptist arguments against Missionary Baptist practice: lack of a definite biblical mandate, overemphasis on money, overvaluation of secular learning, large and potentially subversive organizations, and friendship with "the world."

The strongly predestinarian Kehukee Association led the southern Antimissionaries in declaring nonfellowship—virtual corporate excommunication, as opposed to mere noncooperation—with missions and those who supported them.[27] The association flirted with various modern institutions for twenty years, but in 1827 took a decided stand against them, as being a "fruitful source of argument, strife, and contention." "The missionary proceedings and beggars who have come among us have been the principle cause of our distresses." Lawrence condemned "Missionary Societies, Bible Societies, Tract Societies, Theological Schools, &c., and hiring agents to beg for the support of such institutions. . . . Our early ministers, who bore the burden and heat of persecution and sufferings and . . . brought the Baptist society to that amount of numbers and influence which they have since obtained . . . would indeed . . . have blushed at such conduct and proceedings as have lately been resorted to." The churches subscribing to the Declaration therefore asserted "NON-FELLOWSHIP with all such societies and proceedings and with all churches who hold members of such societies in them."[28]

The "Reformed Baptists" itemized their objections to the several modern innovations. They condemned missionary societies as being "only the inventions of men" and "without any warrant from the New Testament, or any example in the purest ages of the church." No person belonging to a missionary society could belong to a "Reformed Baptist" church, and "no missionary preacher or beggar . . . shall be invited into our pulpits . . . to beg and cheat the people." Lawrence feared large organizations for their potential subversion of liberty, a common concern of the Jacksonian era. He arraigned tract societies for publishing "fictitious accounts and narratives to mislead the mind and promote the interest of their own sect . . . one great design of these societies is to bring the youth of our country . . . to be of some sectarian opinion, and thus pave the way in time for an established religion and priestly dominion . . . such an event ought to be guarded against by every friend to true religion and the rights of conscience."[29]

Lawrence, in common with many of his contemporaries in the Baptist ministry, had a limited formal education. "Joshua whilst a lad was discovered to be shrewd, witty, and gave early presages of great powers of intellect and diversified talents. . . . His father sent him to school only a very short time, so that he learned to read and write but imperfectly." When, about 1801, he started preaching, he was "unusually awkward, and . . . could scarcely read without spelling his words as he went," although he made rapid improvement thereafter.[30] To such men, theological schools ascribed insufficiency to God, and implied an insufficiency not only in their own ministry but in that of the Apostles and the early Baptists as well. "Theological seminaries are the inventions of men and have no warrant or sanction from the New Testament, nor in the example of Christ and the apostles . . . none of the apostles . . . ever went to such a place to be taught rhetoric, oratory, or any other human accomplishments. . . . The Baptist denomination . . . long existed and flourished without any such institutions. . . . This new invention . . . will be the greatest curse to our own as well as other denominations . . . substituting forms for realities, introducing a proud, pompous, and fashionable ministry, instead of a humble, pious, and self denying one. We . . . declare a nonfellowship with all such human institutions . . . and . . . all societies and travelling beggars for their support, believing them to be the emmisaries and agents of antichrist, and opposed to the true kingdom of Jesus Christ."[31]

Other Antimissionaries opposed seminaries on a more fundamental level. Theological studies implied that "the revelation which God has made of himself is a human science, on a footing with mathematics, philosophy, law, &c. which is contrary to the general tenor of revelation, and indeed to the very idea itself of a revelation." Although the Declaration did not mention Sunday schools, mission opponents disliked them for the same reasons. Sunday schools were unscriptural, usurped the rights of parents to oversee the religious instruction of their children, and, most important, implied that saving faith could be taught by human means. Sunday schools were "grounded upon the notion that conversion or regeneration is produced by impressions made upon the natural mind by means of religious sentiments instilled in it; and if the Holy Ghost is allowed to be at all concerned in the thing, it is in a way which imples his being somehow blended with the instruction, or neccesarily attendant upon it; all of which we know to be wrong." Extensive religious instruction by "giddy, unregenerated, young persons" of children devoid of saving grace "only made hypocrites of the [Pharisees] and . . . we cannot believe it will have any better effect on the children in our day."[32]

Bible societies seem beyond reproach. Lawrence's scale, however, weighed them and found them wanting on several points. Reports of foreign missionaries translating the entire Bible into native languages in a short time aroused his suspicions as to their accuracy. He did not "think any two or three men of a particular sect, very likely to give the heathen, or others, a correct and impartial version of the Bible, by reason of those particular views and prepossessions which influence, more or less, the members of every religious persuasion. We fear, indeed, that there will be as many incorrect and spurious Bibles as there were in the time of King James, when he was induced to select fifty-four persons, eminent for learning and knowledge in the ancient tongues, to give his subjects our present translation of the Bible."[33] Lawrence pointed out the Bible had been translated into Native American languages since the 1600s, with the result that, "for want of a true call to this work, bad management, or through a neglect to set a proper example, or all these put together, the Indians in almost every instance have been made more dissipated, and have been brought to a more speedy and certain destruction."[34]

Another failing of the Bible societies lay in their practice of selling memberships to wealthy contributors. "Who can believe these societies will advance the cause of Christ's kingdom, when the great men of this world, the mighty, the rich, the fashionable, and ungodly, are received into half-brothership with the church, and are made life members, managers, and directors[?] . . . It would be well for some . . . to recollect . . . that *charity begins at home,* and first learn their own negroes to read the Bible, who have sweated and toiled for the very money perhaps they are giving to others." Lawrence charged contributors to such societies with neglecting poor ministers and individuals in their own communities in order to donate to foreign causes and obtain "the praise and honor of great and wicked men. . . . We therefore declare our . . . non-fellowship with all such societies, and such connection between the church and this world, knowing that *Christ's kingdom is not of this world.* . . . We are fully assured that as a worldly minded Judas betrayed

Christ, so will these worldlings in Bible societies betray the cause and church of God."[35]

Inspired by the Kehukee Association's uncompromising stand and stung by Missionary accusations of "ignorance and . . . covetousness," six Hephzibah Antimissionary churches met on Fox Bay in Tattnall County, but they concluded themselves too weak to attempt a new association. This meeting appointed another in Emanuel County, where nine churches attended, and at a final meeting at Limestone, Washington County, thirteen Antimissionary churches met, containing eleven minsters. Though feeling themselves "sheep-like in the midst of wolves," they determined to confront "them unholy warriors, the missionaries." The Antimissionaries petitioned the Hephzibah for letters of dismission to form a new association south of the Ogeechee River. The Hephzibah refused their request, so they seceded and organized an association on their own authority.[36] As one eyewitness to the bitter 1828 meeting later recalled, "I tell you, sir, we fout them missionaries that day—I tell you, sir, we fout them—and at last we just tore ourselves loose from them, sir, and have had nothing to do with them since."[37] The seceding Antimissionaries organized the Canoochee Association, which in 1833 contained sixteen churches with 365 members.[38] This schism represented the first actual division over missions among Georgia Baptists.

The Sunbury Association, organized in 1817 by the Georgia churches of the Savannah River Association, supported missions as zealously as did any association in the state. However, Isham Peacock's old foundation at Upper Black Creek became increasingly uneasy toward the association's stance. In 1820, with Antimissionism rising in the nearby Hephzibah and Piedmont associations, Upper Black Creek "took into consideration the plan advised by the association for the purpose of supporting home missions and after investigating the subject the sense of the church was taken which terminated in disolution of the same among themselves."[39] Matthew Albritton, Isham Peacock's successor as pastor at Upper Black Creek, preached the introductory sermon at the 1822 Sunbury Association. However, at the same session he "begged leave to withdraw" from the association's standing committee for missionary concerns.[40] In 1823, Henry Milton and Matthew Albritton, delegated to the year's association, reported that "the association had cooperated with the General Association." The church unanimously disapproved.[41] The next year, Upper Black Creek "received a letter from the Powers Church . . . which was read and after much debate was received with the exception of the education for the ministry for the gospel," which the Powers Church letter apparently favored and Upper Black Creek did not. The rising tension over missions prompted Upper Black Creek to "set apart . . . the first sabath in April" for a day of fasting and prayer that God "would remove the difficulty among us as touching the Missionary [and] education for the ministry."[42] God did not "remove the difficulty," and the church petitioned the Sunbury Association "for a letter of dismission as we cannot fellowship the general committee and the education for ministers."[43] The association, "after a long and very affectionate discussion of the subject," agreed to grant the church a letter of dismission "expressing the reasons of their withdrawal, and our fellowship for them as a Church of Christ." Notwithstanding, the association inserted a sugarcoated Parthian shot in its minutes: "It causes us sincere grief to be obliged to state, that there are still some among us opposed to the cause of Missions. Dear Brethren, let us not exercise unkindly feelings toward them, but rather pray for them. Let us wrestle with God, that the veil which darkens their understandings may be removed! and that, by the enlightening influence of the Holy Spirit, they may have a spiritual discernment of our dear redeemer's farewell injunction—`Go ye into all the world, and preach the gospel unto every creature.'"[44]

Adiel Sherwood wrote of the Piedmont Association, "It is to be presumed that this little body was organized to keep away from the light of missions and other benevolent associations!"[45] If this is true, this association formally opposed missions virtually before any Baptist body in the United States. At any rate, it manifested opposition as early as any Baptist association in America. Whatever its founders' exact motivation, the Piedmont opposed missions from its intial contact with them. In 1818, Thomas Sumner Winn, a minister of the Sunbury Association, "presented two printed circulars from the Kentucky Missionary Society and after being read they gave rise to considerable debate, which being put to vote was laid over till next association." The Piedmont Association did agree to "receive as tokens of love and respect by the hand of Bro. Thos. S. Winn five copies of the fourth annual report of the board of foreign missions."[46] In 1819, with Isham Peacock in the moderator's seat, the association took up the previous year's reference and a "circular from the secretary of foreign missions." In response to both, the association "voted unanimously that they have nothing to do with missionaries and the clerk is directed to forward one copy of these minutes to the corresponding secretary."[47]

In 1822, however, a strange mixture of sentiments became evident. With Isham Peacock moderating the association, "a letter was presented from the board of managers of the general convention of the Baptist denomination in the United States for foreign missions and other important objects relating to the redeemer's kingdom which gave rise to some debate." Despite the favorable language adopted by the clerk, Moses Westberry, the delegates did not deem the "important objects" important enough to receive even a reading. "Brother [Wilson] Conner moved that the letter be read not being seconded the motion was lost." Remarkably, Fleming Bates wrote the circular address for that year, and he rejoiced in the "encouraging thought that the time is not far distant when knowledge will cover the earth as the waters do the great face of the deep and to effect his purpose the Lord is sending his word through his servants to distant and destitute parts of the world for the purpose of establishing his kingdom which shall never be destrouyed. Amongst benighted heathen we have the encouraging hope that Christ is soon to have the heathen for his inheritance and the uttermost parts of the earth for his possession. This should animate our spirits and raise our affections above the perishable objects of time and sense and cry unto God and say thy kingdom come."[48] The association received the circular "without alteration with love and respect for the author Brother Fleming Bates," hinting that the author may have been more acceptable than the writing itself. Bates concluded his address hoping God would cause the churches to "grow and thrive abundantly and may many more be raised up and unite themselves to the church."[49] "Old Father" Peacock wrote the 1823 circular, sobering the association with a strongly restrictive predestinarian doctrine: "Brethren, if it is true that every church . . . is a branch of the living vine in him before the foundation of the world planted by his own hand, has he not a just right to expect the same fruit the vine produced? . . . . Do we find the spirit that governed the Lord Jesus abiding in us richly? If so, we are . . . faithful in receiving members. We shall not be willing to fill the house of God with unprepared materials which cannot bear the fruit of God's elect nor bear the rein of close disciplin which God requires of us. . . . . Every unfruitful branch shall be taken away, and have no more a name of place among the [saints]."[50]

His admonition bore fruit at next year's session, when "Brother Ripley rose and stated that he had been appointed by the general association of this state as a corresponding messenger, that he had minutes of that association if this association would receive them; this association votes no correspondence with the general association." In fact, the Piedmont Association also "voted that we discontinue correspondence with the Sunbury Association," by then a decidedly Missionary body. On the next day of that 1824 session, however, the association reconsidered, and dispatched delegates to the Sunbury and Savannah River associations, after "much friendly debate."[51] But by the following year, the Piedmont had had enough of modernism and "resolved that we discontinue our correspondence with the Sunbury and Savannah River Associations because they are so much engaged in the Missionary concerns." This did not represent too harsh a repudiation of those bodies since John Brooker, the messenger from the Sunbury, preached the next day. The 1825 circular address warns the churches to "stand unshakeable in the doctrine of the gospel and that you hold fast to your church liberties."[52] In 1828, Beard's Creek Church, a member of the Piedmont Association since 1819, sent Isham Peacock, then moderator of the association, to the Antimissionary Limestone Convention.[53] In 1829, the association, with Isham Peacock presiding for the last time, warned the churches "concerning the faith," admonishing them "earnestly [to] contend for the faith which was once delivered to the saints." Paul, they noted "does not only recommend but commands that an heretic shall be rejected after the first and second admonitions."[54]

In the next couple of years, however, a revolution took place in the Piedmont. In July 1830, Beard's Creek adopted a motion by Isham Peacock "that we suffer not any person to address this church or any people in this house on the subject of foreign missions or the Temperate Society. Knowing the times to be very pregnant with doctrinal error. The move was seconded and the nature of the subject closely examined, and finding no authority for no such society or traditions in the word of God we accordingly adopted the . . . resolutions and appointed the brethren J. Peacock, R. Brewer, S. Knight, and J. Taylor whose duty it shall be to object or silence any person treading on such errors."[55]

All the association's churches did not agree with this resolution. Salem Church favored the Missionary party and joined the Sunbury Association late in 1831.[56] In May of 1831, four members from Salem applied for membership at Beard's Creek as "they were not satisfied to remain in Salem Church and that they could not obtain letters of dismission." Beard's Creek, "being personally acquainted with their good conduct as pious and orderly Christians," accepted them as members without letters, virtually declaring war on Salem. As a result, in July, after a month's consideration, Beard's Creek withdrew from the Piedmont Association without leave of that body and joined the newly formed Antimissionary Canoochee Association.[57] With Beard's Creek and the redoubtable Isham Peacock out of the way, ministers of the Sunbury Association reappeared at the 1831 Piedmont session, which thanked "the brethren from the Sunbury Association for their zealous labors of love at this meeting."[58] In 1832, the Piedmont passed a frosty judgment on the Beard's Creek defection by "withdraw[ing] from a place called Beard's Creek Church formerly a member of this body as a disorderly church."[59] Beard's Creek wrote to the 1833 Canoochee Association protesting that "we do not believe it to be our duty to make any acknowledgements to the Piedmont association for ending off and joining the Canoochee association."

Relations thawed slightly after a while. In March 1834, Moses Westberry of the Piedmont preached at Beard's Creek "according to previous appointment." In April, the church reconsidered its ban on temperance members and "unanimously agreed to leave everyone to his own free will as regard communion and to invite any that they had fellowship for to commune with them." Perhaps coincidentally, one year later Isham Peacock resigned the pastorate at Beard's Creek and called for a letter of dismission.[60]

The Piedmont alienated its extreme Antimissionaries, and began a slow movement toward their opponents. James MacDonald, later a Missionary Baptist leader in east Florida, took a prominent part in the 1833 association.[61] McDonald and other Missionaries remained active in the Piedmont area. In 1836, he held a meeting at Spring Branch Church, Wayne County, baptizing several and presiding over a "revival . . . which has brought within its compass many precious souls, saved by the grace of God."[62] From 1828 until 1835, the Piedmont corresponded with no other associations. In 1836, 1837, and 1838, the association made abortive attempts to correspond with the Antimissionary Suwannee Association, which lay to the west and south.[63] However, in 1837, Wilson Conner, one of its ministers, attended a Missionary minster's meeting at Eatonton, Georgia. Conner sat on a committee appointed to answer the query: "To what should the divisions now existing in our denomination be attributed?" The committee blamed the Baptist division on "covetousness" and "an unrighteous opposition on the part of many, to the benevolent plans of the day."[64] Conner also published a preaching itinerary for the spring of 1837 in the *Christian Index,* the organ of the Georgia Missionaries. He projected a preaching stop at the Georgia Baptist Convention.[65]

Despite such Missionary leanings in a principal minister, the 1839 association petitioned the radically Antimissionary Canoochee Association for correspondence. Isham Peacock visited the 1839 association and preached several times during the services.[66] Nothing appears to have come of this initiative. Beard's Creek Church may have scuttled the attempted rapprochement. It "clothed with authority" its delegates to the 1840 Canoochee Association "to demand an acknowledgement from the Piedmont Association for their advertising them a disorderly church, that is if they call for a correspondence with us."[67]

While the Piedmont vacillated in isolation, member churches dropped away, the defection being most noticeable in the southern part of the association. Sardis Church, Camden County, Georgia, did not send delegates after 1825. Smyrna Church, Wayne County, Georgia, dropped out of the association after 1827. Pigeon Creek, Nassau County, Florida, attended no further sessions after 1829. After 1830, High Bluff (temporarily renamed Big Creek) attended no further sessions. The association frequently dispatched letters and messengers to the unrepresented churches but to little avail. Only one church, Fellowship, Ware County, Georgia (renamed Mt. Pleasant), responded to the association's repeated summons—but only to request a letter of dismission. The association "advise[d] the church . . . to stay some longer." At the next session, 1836, the association granted this church a letter of dismission. In 1839, Spring Branch, Pigeon Creek, and Smyrna churches all applied for and received letters of dismission. This left only six churches with a total of 180 members in the once extensive Piedmont Association. The 1839 circular address lamented that "our Association appears to be in a cold and declining situation."[68]

As the isolated Piedmont declined, the decidedly Antimissionary Suwannee Association grew at its expense. In 1833, dissidents organized Shiloh Church in Ware County, Georgia, well within the bounds of the Piedmont. The church attempted to join the distant Ochlocknee Association, which rejected it because of a constitutional defect.[69] Reorganized on a sounder basis, Shiloh joined the Suwannee River Association by 1837. In 1838, Mt. Pleasant took its letter of dismission from the Piedmont to the Suwannee River. Elizabeth Church in Telfair County, Georgia, logically within the bounds of the Piedmont, also joined the Suwannee River instead.[70] In 1839, High Bluff and one other former Piedmont church joined the Suwannee River, meeting that year at Shiloh in Ware County. In 1842, the Suwannee River Association dismissed most of these churches to form a new association.[71] This new association, the Alabaha River, organized at Mt. Pleasant Church, Appling County, Georgia, on October 8, 1842. Wesley Creek Church of McIntosh County, Georgia, deserted the Piedmont to assist in organizing the new association. At its first session the Alabaha River body firmly "declare[d] nonfellowship with all unscriptural institutions of the day."[72] Its decided stand won it most of the rest of the Antimissionary churches of the Piedmont. In 1843, Smyrna and Big Creek churches in Appling County, Georgia, both switched their allegiance. Finally, in 1847, Pigeon Creek Church joined the Suwannee River Association and, in 1860, transferred to the Alabaha River.[73] While the Piedmont did not suffer a violent schism over missions as did other associations, its neutral stance caused it slowly to bleed away churches and territory to its more decidedly Antimissionary competitors. In the Alabaha River Association, the Piedmont essentially found itself confronted with its Antimissionary successor. Within three years of its organization, the Alabaha River Association, organized with four churches, grew to sixteen, with a total membership of 391.[74]

The Piedmont began to move toward the Missionaries during the 1840s. In 1845, the association appointed an associational itinerant and adopted a tedious circular address on "religiously training up our children," a topic hardly indicating Antimissionary sentiments. The 1845 session dispatched a messenger to Big Creek Church to "endeavor to reclaim her in the spirit of meekness."[75] Big Creek already belonged to the new Alabaha River Association, and the attempted reclamation failed.[76] On the other hand, two churches, Ten Mile Creek and Elizabeth, defected to the Piedmont in 1846 and 1847.[77] In 1847, the association recommended "protracted meetings," the forerunners of present Southern Baptist revival services.[78] Antimissionary Baptists frostily dismissed these meetings as "got up either for the purpose of inducing the Holy Spirit to regenerate multitudes who would otherwise not be converted, or to convert them themselves by the machinery of these meetings, or rather bring them into their churches by means of exiting their animal feelings, without any regard for their being born again."[79] Far down the slippery slope to Missionism, the Piedmont no longer claimed to be Antimissionary. The 1847 Association adopted an explanation of their position: "Whereas, believing that various opinions exist among Churches and Associations of our denomination as regards the true position occupied by this body in regard to the missionary doctrine; Resolved, therefore, that we, as heretofore still endeavor to avoid either extreme of missionary or antimissionary, but hold forth the hand of fellowship to all who are in good standing with their churches, and make them welcome to all the privileges of the Piedmont Association."[80] This trimming policy satisfied no one. The Piedmont voted in 1848 to abandon its neutral stance and join the Georgia Baptist Convention.[81]

In Florida and remoter regions of South Georgia, the Missionary tide arrived weak and late. In the "always Primitive" Ochlocknee Association, Wiley Pearce reported in 1838 that "we have had no difficulties with the missionaries."[82] O. T. Hammond, an educated northerner appointed by the American Baptist Home Mission Board, arrived in Tallahassee in June 1837. His wife taught school, enabling him to return his salary to the mission board. He soon returned himself as well.[83] Remoteness and the proximity of the Seminoles may have kept other Missionaries away. The Baptist settlers of the area having originated from heavily Antimissionary areas in eastern Georgia and North Carolina, they arrived already prejudiced against missions. Pioneer preacher William McElvey attributed to the controversy some of his love of frontier life: "I lived in Burke County [Georgia] when that system entered the State, the society was I thought unequally made up, it was church and world mixed together. . . . I insisted that the plan did not agree with the word of God. . . . Unwilling to war with my brethren, [I] let it alone and I have kept ahead of it ever since till now it seems to be overtaking me."[84]

A local eruption of heresy helped explain the uphill battle of Missionism in the Wiregrass country. Although Missionaries were few, Wiley Pearce bemoaned the presence of "a few Whiteites, or . . . Free Wills, or soft shells, who appear to be walking in their silver slippers, as it is a pleasant time with them."[85] In November 1830 after a two-year struggle, Tired Creek Church expelled Lewis St. Johns, a licensed preacher, for heresy.[86] In 1835, Richland Creek Church excluded nine members for "holding faith hetridose to the constituted articles."[87] A reference in the Richland Creek minutes identifies the heretic group as "Free Will Baptists." Elias Hawthorn of Tired Creek commented that "even in the Ochlocknee Association, which has never bent the knee to nothing but what is found in the Scriptures as touching faith, our churches exclude men for heresy, and our distant Free Will friends come and gather them up that nothing be lost. And this is not all, no matter what the crime is that we orthodox Baptists exclude a man or woman for, they will have them and call them brother or sister; any thing and every body that will turn against the Primitive Baptist will do them. I for one, say that it is right: the carrion crow has as much right to his food as the dove; therfore, I do believe that the true church is better off, for designing men and women love to go with the crowd, and the little flock will not suit them."[88]

The "Free Wills," or "Whiteites," originated with Cyrus White, a Baptist minister in Middle Georgia. In 1829, White published a pamphlet contending for the Arminian doctrine of universal atonement.[89] The Columbus Association expelled White and his followers for having "published a faith differing from the orthodox Baptists." The expelled Arminians formed the United Association in September 1832. By 1839, they had added enough churches in the Chattahoochee River Valley to form a second association, the United Chattahoochee. Although remaining aloof from other Baptist groups, they supported the missionary work of the Georgia Baptist Convention.[90] Exposure to this heretical group convinced many predestinarian Baptists that Missionism and heresy went hand in hand. Conservatives suspected Jesse Mercer, the leader of the Georgia Missionaries, "of drinking out of Fuller's spring along with White." Mercer sprang to his own defense with *Ten Letters Addressed to the Rev. Cyrus White in reference to His Scriptural View of the Atonement*. Mercer attempted to square the circle by claiming that White's doctrine differed heretically from Fuller's, and that it in turn differed from the Calvinism of John Gill by "a mere shade—a difference only in the modus operandi of the great plan."[91] The Antimissionaries did not believe him, and the presence of Free Wills in southwest Georgia prior to orthodox

Missionary Baptists doubtless inoculated the churches against any sympathy for their doctrines and practices.

The Ochlocknee Association opposed Missionaries before significant numbers appeared among them. Jonathan Gaulden, a preacher from Liberty County, Georgia, moved to South Georgia and joined Bethel Church, Lowndes County, in 1831. At the November 1832 conference, the church called into question "the doctrine which he has been advancing Publicly." Gaulden persuaded the church to "dismiss the case . . . of preaching unsound doctrine as there is no evidence he did at Suwannee Springs or Tiger Creek [Florida]." Gaulden then called for a letter and became a "trunk Baptist," one who obtained dismission and then placed the letter in his trunk. He remained unchurched for eight years until he organized the first Missionary Baptist church in Lowndes County.[92]

The 1833 Association expressed concern over Missionism in other places, basing their objections on an uncompromising adherence to *sola fide* and *sola gratia:*

> Can man forward the purposes of God, inconsistent with the word of God? No other plan can be laid than that already laid; we hear of their setting up societies, calling themselves by different names, the Saviour never called or spoke of, it is man's plan; by this, they say we are preaching the gospel, and what do they preach by their plan, temperance and morality and call it righteouness, by this they are going to reform the heathen nations and teach them practical righteousness, as they call it; try this by the word of God. Has God planted this by the example of his son and word? the answer must be no, for Christ has become the end of the law for righteousness to everyone that believe[.] . . . The assistance of man without inspiration, and revelation, to hasten God's promises . . . would be something like old Sarah when the Lord seemed to delay . . . causing old Abraham to know her handmaid Hagar, and . . . it produced an Ishmael, a son to the bond woman, destroyed Abraham's peace and was her vexation.
>
> . . . To carry this wonderful plan into effect, . . . they will send youths to seminaries . . . and they come forth and bear the likeness . . . like counterfiet does to the true coin, not being called of God, but only by man. . . . Let us choose Christ and his gospel, and God's appointed way through his own means, strength and time.[93]

A number of factors at last brought the Missionary Controversy to the Ochlocknee and Suwanee River associations. Several mission-oriented ministers arrived in northern Florida and began quietly, and sometimes abrasively, to advertise their views. William Blount Cooper, a South Carolinian and a graduate of Columbia College, Washington, D.C., emigrated to Florida in 1838 to help his rheumatism. Raised in another persuasion, he had become a Baptist minister in South Carolina. He joined the Hickstown Baptist Church, Madison County, and preached throughout Madison, Jefferson, and Leon counties as well as in Lowndes and Thomas counties in Georgia. At his death the Florida Association attributed "the present status of the Missionary Baptists of Florida and Lower Georgia . . . in great measure to the efficient labors performed by brother Cooper." Cooper later served sixteen times as moderator of the Florida Missionary Baptist Association and three times as president of the Florida Baptist Convention.[94] A stranger to the mores of backwoods Baptists, "one of these effort preachers from South Carolina," almost certainly Cooper, irritated Elias Hawthorn by saying "he would fellowship a horse thief as quick as he would a brother who would give his brother or friend a dram to drink." Hawthorn indignantly replied that "there are as honest Christians and men that drink drams when they want them as any men upon earth; but I cannot think that he was, if he would fellowship a horse thief so easy."[95]

John Tucker commenced his ministerial career in 1806 as a Methodist, but joined the Baptists in 1828 and moved to Florida in 1832.[96] The nearby branch of Friendship Church in Lowndes County, Georgia, a branch soon to become Columbia Church, ordained him in March 1833.[97] Always an active evangelist in northeastern and central Florida, he reportedly carried an Indian bullet in him until his death. Although not an early advocate of missions, he accepted support from the American Baptist Home Missionary Society in 1843 and in the ensuing year traveled two thousand miles under their auspices. "I am a missionary, and I must travel," he wrote.[98]

John B. Lacy, born in Virginia in 1793, joined the Baptist Church in Middle Georgia in 1824, being baptized by the sometime heresiarch Cyrus White. He moved to Thomas County, Georgia, in 1830. Intensely evangelistic, he walked as much as twelve miles to appointments, "warning and exhorting as he went." He left South Georgia in 1840, on the eve of the Missionary schism, but returned five years later and preached for the Missionary Baptists in South Georgia and Florida until his death in 1878. "Full of pathos, he appealed to sinners with tears to give their hearts to Jesus."[99]

William J. Blewett moved to Decatur County, Georgia, in 1833 at the age of twenty-one and joined Richland Creek Church. He accepted the pastorate of a church in Randolph County in time to escape a general massacre of Blewetts at Richland Creek.[100] Three Blewetts figured among the members excluded in 1835 for "hetridose" sentiments.[101] William J. Blewett identified with the budding Missionary movement in north Florida and preached along the state line until his emigration to Texas about 1870.[102]

Richard J. Mays, a wealthy South Carolinian who settled the Clifton Community of Madison County, Florida, also espoused the Missionary faith. A prominent planter, educator, and political leader, he organized the Concord Missionary Baptist Church in Madison County in 1841 and entered the Baptist ministry the same year.[103]

One of the more colorful Missionary exponents, James MacDonald, moved to northeast Florida in 1837, where he remained until 1851. Born in 1798 of Scottish ancestry in Limerick, Ireland, and raised a Catholic, McDonald emigrated to America at seventeen. A wild youth and a virtual atheist, he began to have some stirrings of conscience and a desire to read the Bible. As a result of his Catholic upbringing, he regarded this as a satanic temptation. Fleeing from his troubled conscience, he set out to become a mercenary in Central America, but a scrape in Havana landed him in prison. In jail, he resolved to study the Bible if he obtained his freedom. On his release, he went to Georgia and in 1830 joined a Baptist church near Macon. After preaching for a several years in Georgia, he moved to war-torn Florida, where, in his opinion, "If . . . there has ever been a real revival of religion I do not know it; and if there is on the peninsula one intelligent Baptist minister, I do not know it."[104] Not surprisingly, some described him as "not popular with the masses . . . reserved and even stern."[105]

This influx did not go unnoticed by the Antimissionaries. In 1839, William McElvey sarcastically grumbled that "ranging missionary and temperance men begin to invade our coasts, . . . endeavoring to get our people to sign petitions to the Legislature of Georgia to prohibit the use of all drinks but water."[106] Elias Hawthorn declared that the Ochlocknee Association had fifteen "faithful ministers of the Primitive order. . . . We have three or four more which I am not able to state what they are; therfore, I leave that with them and their God."[107] Hawthorn also rejoiced that "the institutionists have given us such an appropriate name as that of hardshells," which suited him to "a gnat's eye. . . . We have a goodly number of hard shells and some are getting harder and harder while others are getting softer and softer." He noted that lowland Georgians possessed an intimate familiarity with turtles and knew that the hardshelled ones were much more difficult to kill than the softshelled ones. Antimissionary intransigence was "almost enough to start a civil war, that we unlearned, wire-grass raised boys should attempt to dispute with a Goliah of Gath," or seminary-trained Missionary preacher. Prior Lewis also expressed concern over "some [that] have crept in unawares to spy out our liberties."[108] He rejoiced that the "Arminians" failed to get the

"Temperance Bill" passed. "I think that the missionaries are somewhat down in the dumps, seeing their entering wedge has jumped out." Lewis and his coreligionists feared that such legislated morality portended religious establishment. "The Old School Baptists . . . do not want our religion established by law." Comparing the Missionaries to Reformation era Catholics, Lewis wished "these . . . fellows had Luther to deal with."[109]

Antimissionaries attributed an ingratiating underhandedness to the Missionaries. William McElvey complained that Missionaries subverted a church he founded on the pretense of holding services on those Sundays he could not attend and filling in for him while his wife was dying. By the time McElvey could give his attention to the church again, the interlopers had gained such ascendancy that when he confronted the Missionaries, "they hissed me out of the pastoral authority of the church, and it is manifest from the gestures and manners of some, that they would have hissed me out of the world." McElvey salvaged those members "who had received the engrafted word of truth" and organized them into another church.[110]

Other Antimissionaries accused the opposition of outright fraud. Hardy Brooks of Nassau County, Florida, lamented that "we in these Southern piney woods are not entirely exempt from those pious beggars, who call themselves missionaries." He alleged that a traveling Missionary, "peddling out the gospel," had his horse fall ill and reported it dead. The local people pledged money for "two such horses." The Missionary's horse recovered, but "the pious scoundrel" collected the money anyway, and then "had the impudence to mount his dead horse, and ride him around to preach to the very same people who had "contributed . . .. And what is more strange, some of the people were silly enough to go and hear him preach—did I say preach? He called it preaching, but no one else did."[111]

Missionaries' emphasis on money generated hostility among frontier Baptists, primarily because they had so little of it. Money on the frontier always presented a problem, and in the depressed economy of the late 1830s, a particularly vexing one. The 1833 Ochlocknee Association committee on contributions reported that a total membership of 1,010 had contributed ninety-eight dollars and twenty-seven and one fourth cents.[112] In such a situation, the associations occasionally had to exhort their members to assist, if not support, their own ministers. The 1841 Ochlocknee Association exhorted deacons to "look into the situation of their pastors . . . and if the faithful servant stands in need of support in any way to enable him to go and discharge his duty giving to him is a special duty of the church."[113] William McElvey, old enough to need no further support himself, offered "a few lines of admonition" on ministerial neglect. "The Primitive Churches are too slack in doing their duty, and their preachers too often oppressed. . . . They that preach the gospel should live of the gospel; and when the church neglect their preacher they sin against God." If a church lacked the means to do a great deal for their preacher, they should still do as much as they could. McElvey admitted that members hospitably entertained preachers while they were with the members but cared nothing for their neglected families left at home. As a result, he feared that Missionaries and other opponents would criticize the Primitive ministry for neglecting their families.[114] The 1842 Ochlocknee Association denounced "Gospel speculators" for taking up so much money that as a result "there is great neglect of duty towards God's true ministers."[115] The 1844 Association echoed McElvey, asking how "any reflecting Christian, in easy circumstances, could receive the repeated services of their preacher without compensating his destitute family! and whether destitute or not, it is a compensation of reward, as the ministers of the gospel cannot be considered as subjects of charity, but should be esteemed for their work's sake. . . . But if self is not denied, it may discover many obstacles in the way, expecting to attend to those Christian duties at some distant period of life, until our aged ministers are worn down in the services of the churches, and their families may be happily removed to the enjoyments of a better inheritance."[116] The 1841 Suwannee River Association and the 1842 Alabaha River Association both adopted a circular address similar in sentiment, though to little effect.[117]

The churches acknowledged such obligations in theory but seldom in fact. Although Hephzibah Church, Gadsden County, Florida, covenanted to "honour, obey, and maintain them who the Lord may . . . set over us . . . according to our several abilities . . . for the Lord hath ordained that they who preach the gospel should live of the gospel," other church records indicate only a token compliance with this duty, although many private contributions doubtless went unrecorded.[118] Neglect of their pastor by the Mt. Moriah Church was noted in the previous chapter.

Isham Peacock, one of the longest serving and most respected Baptist preachers in the region, received little material reward for his services. In 1817, Beard's Creek Church proudly recorded that John Tilmon gave Peacock three dollars and "one buisel seed pees."[119] In 1839, the Suwannee River Association voted him twenty dollars as "a free donation of the churches, as we believe him to be a faithful old soldier in the cause of his master," and gave him ten dollars in each of the next two years.[120] These donations represent the most generous, and indeed, almost the only examples of such support to a minister.

Unfortunately for the "oppressed" preachers, many Antimissionaries heeded Elias Hawthorn's advice to "get clear" of the "money hunting preachers" by not giving preachers "one cent of money for ten years." He promised that "when the money grows scarce they . . . will go down, as my old mill does when the water is falling." Orthodox ministers, thus deprived, would continue to preach and would not be afraid to "trust God for ten years," in order to get rid of the Missionaries.[121] After the Missionary Controversy, Primitive preachers found themselves trusting God not for ten years but for a century and a half.

Ministerial education was no more popular among Antimissionaries in the Ochlocknee Association than among others. This association observed that "it is not uncommon for professional men of learning to expect a living from the sweat of the laboring men, and it would be less exceptional in any other class than that of the clergy." They further asserted that a professional clergy tended toward an established church, with legally enforced tithing.[122]

Although the Ochlocknee Antimissionaries boasted of their "illiteracy," some of them not only read but wrote as well. In 1838, the *Primitive Baptist*, published since 1835 in eastern North Carolina, began to circulate in South Georgia and Florida. The Kehukee Antimissionaries founded the *Primitive* as an organ for the southern Antimissionaries, and their adoption of the name "Primitive Baptist" as a denominational title bears witness to its influence. Elias Hawthorn used the title for the Ochlocknee Baptists as early as 1838. As might be expected, some of the Primitives suspected that the paper itself was only another religious "speculation." In spite of this, Hawthorn believed that "it appears to go down better than I could have expected; for some of our brethren say they like it better and better," though "some find fault." To Hawthorn's delight, the "Free Willites say it should not stay in their house."[123] Soon, Hawthorn reported the paper "gain[ing] applause in this section of Georgia."[124] James Alderman of Hephzibah Church, Gadsden County, Florida, reported that "the paper is greatly beliked in this part of the country."[125] Scarcely an issue of the paper appeared without a letter from William McElvey, Elias Hawthorn, or Prior Lewis, all ministers of the Ochlocknee Association.

The *Primitive* served multiple purposes. It consisted almost entirely of letters from Antimissionaries all over the South, and so served to encourage each otherwise isolated group of them to stand firm against the Missionaries. Daniel O'Neel, of Decatur County, Georgia, wrote, "I there see brethren a few, yes, a goodly number scattered over our wide extended country, contending for the faith once delivered to the saints[,] . . . that have not bowed the knee to Baal." Chloe Hurste, of Jefferson County, Florida, a "simple female," rejoiced to see "the old brethren from so many quarters travelling on and chopping down the noxious weeds." James Alderman and his neighbors believed it "to be the means of uniting the Primitive order."[126]

The paper also served to keep isolated believers in contact with the Antimissionary movement. Jane Stokes moved to Milton, Santa Rosa County, Florida, a "very wicked place" with no preacher. Missionaries and Methodists sometimes preached there, but she considered their sermons "all stuff," preferring to "stay at home reading the Bible and my sweet little winged messenger."[127]

The *Primitive* further served as a sounding board for concerns over doctrine and practice. Scruples over details of observance troubled Hephzibah Church, Gadsden County, Florida. In 1839, concern over "unscriptural" practice made the brethren stop handing the communion cup about on a plate, no doubt because the Bible mentioned a cup but not a plate. In the same year, the church resolved to write to the *Primitive Baptist* soliciting views on the propriety of holding funeral services.[128]

The greatest influence excercised by the *Primitive*, however, lay in the biblical quotation emblazoned on its masthead: "Come Out of Her, My People," a war cry echoed by its correspondents in South Georgia and Florida.[129] This uncompromising demand for total separation from the Missionaries spread the separatist position of the Kehukee Association to many other Antimissionaries.

Another important Antimissionary paper, Gilbert Beebe's *Signs of the Times*, published in New Vernon, New York, circulated in the Ochlocknee Association but not to the extent of the *Primitive Baptist*.[130] Books as well as magazines figured in Primitive reading matter. The 1845 Ochlocknee Association exhorted its members to hold evening devotionals in their families, with "good books on the stand." Besides the Bible, one such "good book" might have been the Georgia Antimissionary leader William Moseley's one-volume reprint of the Englishman William Huntington's *Universal Charity* and *The Naked Bow of God*, together with some minor pieces also by Huntington.[131] The Hassells wrote that Huntington "is regarded by many genuine Baptists in England and America as one of the most spiritual writers of the present century; but Mr. [Andrew] F[uller] says he never saw any marks of genuine religion in his writings."[132] William C. Thomas of Decatur County, Georgia, announced his intention to subscribe for *Universal Charity*, and recommended it to other Primitives.[133] Prior Lewis noted Moseley's advertisement and hoped "he will use some method to circulate them through the lower part of Georgia and Florida, as I think his work would meet with a general patronage among the Baptists here." Lewis's references to Huntington indicate a prior acquaintance with the radical Anti-Arminian's works.[134]

Increasing numbers of Missionary exponents, the Antimissionary background of most of the settlers in the region, and the circulation of Antimissionary literature moved the Ochlocknee Association ever closer to an openly declared rupture with Missionism. Another compelling force in that direction came from corresponding associations. The Ochlocknee exchanged letters and messengers with all neighboring associations except the Piedmont pariahs. One of these, the Ebenezer Association in central Georgia, divided bitterly over Missionism in 1836, with two factions both claiming to be the orginal association.[135] The Ochlocknee responded by dropping correspondence with Ebenezer Association.[136] Such a course, had it continued, would have left the association nearly as isolated as the Piedmont. Sentiment for a more decided stance grew during the late 1830s. Elias Hawthorn complained that the 1838 Ochlocknee Association received correspondence from "an Association that had declared non-fellowship . . . with the institutions of the day; and also from one . . . of the go-between faith . . . that [believed] those things should not break fellowship. Now, brethren, the fact is, that there is no middle ground between . . . true Christianity & hypocritical pretensions; therefore, I predict a distress in the Ochlocknee, . . . for I think the seed is sowing fast, which will breed discord. The Ochlocknee sheep have not been sheared very closely and I think that there are some of the wool-gatherers that begin to think it high time that they were fleeced." Hawthorn feared that the Missionaries, if not publicly disfellowshipped, would work quietly and subvert the younger members of the association, who, like young birds, were "as apt to swallow a pebble as a berry."[137] With such attitudes among leading members, and increasing pressure to choose sides building up without, what little neutral inclination existed in the Ochlocknee soon vanished.

Antimissionary Baptists considered doctrinal deviation the principal Missionary error and the foundation of their organizational innovations. The Ochlocknee and Suwannee River associations especially emphasized doctrinal differences between them and the new order of Baptists. The Missionary Baptists claimed to believe in predestination, but Primitives saw their reticence on the subject as equivocation. A Missionary critic, claiming to be an orthodox predestinarian, scandalized Prior Lewis, claiming that his strongly Calvinistic doctrine "was not profitable, though it was the truth."[138] In a similar vein, a Madison County, Florida, Missionary Baptist wrote that election was "dangerous for those unskilled in the word of God to tamper with."[139] Such a policy of believing Augustine but preaching Pelagius made William McElvey proclaim the Missionaries "inconsistent men" who "subscribed to the . . . calvanistic faith" and then "condemn[ed] the principles of the gospel."[140] Another Antimissionary labeled the "Society Crew" "Arminian Baptists" and "Enthusiasts."[141]

The 1843 Suwannee River Association adopted a lengthy circular address by their clerk, Owen Smith, on the principal theological problem of the controversy: the extent and nature of the atonement, "this point of Doctrine so essential to salvation." Smith immediately declared the Missionary doctrine a mere equivocation since "a universal Atonement without a universal application makes the eternal state of sinners no better, however plausible to men." Employing the logic foundational to High Calvinism, he pointed out inconsistencies in the universal theory. If Christ died conditionally for all men, but the Holy Ghost only applied the benefits of the atonement to the elect, then the persons of the trinity worked at cross purposes. Also, if the Holy Spirit applied the benefits of a conditional atonement to a sinner in response to an act on the sinner's part, then salvation depended upon works, not grace. Texts cited to prove a universal atonement, Smith continued, if taken at face value, actually proved universal salvation, which the Missionaries themselves did not believe. Since both Missionary and Antimissionary believed the "application wholly dependent on the sovereignty of the Holy Ghost," Smith saw "no use nor advantage for an atonement without an application or that it betters the state of sinners to whom the Holy Ghost refuses to apply it." In a lengthy passage, Smith argued that the very doctrine of election implied a limited atonement, as did the lack of response to the gospel in many of its hearers, all of which manifested "this golden chain of God's purpose from his foreknowledge to the special sinner's glorification." Smith acknowledged that "all this does not supercede the neccesity of God's means to accomplish his ends."[142]

On the practical level, Smith condemned agitation over the atonement as the Devil's plot to use a "hair-splitting mysterious doctrine to destroy the peace and fellowship of the Church of God." In a final conciliatory note, he exhorted the brethren to lay aside such useless contentions and "enforce as the Scripture says, "Repentance towards God and Faith in our Lord Jesus Christ," and that "Jesus came into the world to save sinners," and that "ye must be born again or not see the Kingdom of Heaven, and leave the issue to God who paradventure may give repentance to the acknowledgement of the truth . . .. Let not your prejudices rise so high against the many institutions of the day, that you should forget your bounden duty to the true ministers of Christ."[143]

The local Missionaries themselves sometimes wondered about the tendency of their doctrines and the consequences of the divisiveness they engendered.

> It is unfortunate for the people of God that when they disagree on certain points of doctrine . . . they become perfect antipodes to each other. . . . Those that are opposed to the work of benevolence, that is to missions, . . . thinking that Missionary Baptists are Arminians, or Freewill Baptists, have betaken themselves almost entirely to preaching about the great fundamental truths of the Bible—neglecting practical religion. They seem to think we are unconverted, or that we are great backsliders from the Gospel. . . . Missionary Baptists, ever anxious for the conversion of sinners to God, have become almost entirely practical in their preaching, and frequently neglect the inculcation of primary truth on the hearts of their brethren. . . . Our preachers may mean to affirm certain truths which are not always satisfactorily explained. . . . Our ministers, intending to induce the unconverted to come to Christ, do extend their invitations in words that sometimes need great qualification.[144]

With doctrinal, economic, social, and denominational pressure building, the churches of the Ochlocknee and Suwannee River associations moved toward open schism. The individual churches led the way in adopting nonfellowship resolutions. In 1839, Hephzibah Church declared against the "institutions of the day benevolent faulcely so called" and disfellowshipped anyone "that holes to the mishionarys and temperince societies[,] Sunday school union which we conceive to be unscriptural and the inventions of men." They forwarded their nonfellowship resolution to the Ochlocknee Association and the *Primitive Baptist*.[145] Tired Creek followed suit in declaring to the association "that we stand opposed to all the new invented societies of the day."[146] At Union Church, in the Suwannee River Association, Joshua Lee queried whether it was right "for Primitive Baptist Churches to invite missionary preachers believing them to be such and holding them institutions of the day etc. to preach among them?" The church ruled the practice disorderly and appointed a committee to question traveling preachers "whether they are under missionary influence," and if so, to refuse them the pulpit.[147]

Antimissionary action on the associational level proceeded in stages. In 1839, the Ochlocknee Association officially changed its name to Primitive Baptist and dropped correspondence with all associations "in favor of the institutions of the day."[148] Jesse Mercer's *Christian Index*, perhaps believing the Wiregrass Baptists would never hear of it, made a major contribution to the Antimissionary spirit in the association. The *Index* swooped down upon the Ochlocknee Association, declaring them to "have been fighting against the light for years, and what have they accomplished—have they been instrumental in the conversion of souls? No. Have they succeeded in promoting their own personal holiness? There is no evidence that they have. Satisfied that they can maintain a bare existence, they are disposed to encourage each other in the opposition to everything good, and still sleep on, perhaps we had better say, pout on. May God grant them repentance for their sin, in attempting to throw impediments in the way of his glorious cause."[149]

Elias Hawthorn replied to Mercer's "unfeeling remarks." Hawthorn found it "rather distressing" that "a man who I have heard my own father and many others of the Baptist denomination . . . speak of as the champion of the Baptists" could thus "publish to the people in general, known . . . untruths." The Ochlocknee fought against "false doctrine," not against light. "We who try to preach in this part of the country are as much in favor of the spread of the . . . gospel . . . as any people that you ever was acquainted with in your life." However, they opposed "the spread of erroneous doctrines, and the kind of statements . . . you have made." Hawthorn pointed out that as early as 1834, the Ochlocknee Association had 891 members, indicating their success in making converts. Mercer wrote his editorial in response to an anonymous communication from Early County, Georgia. Hawthorn declared "any man who comes out in public print against any individual or individuals, and does not assign his proper name to his writing . . . unworthy of notice." He called upon the Primitives to consider how disgruntled Missionaries "come to see us, . . . express a desire to keep up a correspondence with us, and shed tears at the idea of our withdrawing, &c."—and the Missionaries then abused them in print as "opposed to everything that is good." Hawthorn called upon those "on a stand whether to non fellowship those men that can write and talk this way about you" to doubt no longer "the propriety of coming out from among them."[150]

The association soon followed Hawthorn's advice. The 1839 dropping of Missionary correspondence had not smoked out any significant number of Missionary churches or preachers. Therefore, in 1842, "after some discussion," the association adopted a new article for the associational decorum: "It is the duty of this Association to provide for the general union of the churches, and will not fellowship any church, or churches, nor hold them in union, that support any modern Missionary, Bible, Tract, or Sunday School Union Societies, or Theological School either in themselves or in any other persons or any other society that now is or may hereafter be constituted, under a pretence of circulating the Gospel of Christ, nor will she correspond with any Association that support or fellowship any of the above named societies."[151] As a result, five churches in the Florida Piedmont belt withdrew from the association: Hickstown, Madison County; Ebenezer, Jefferson County; Indian Springs and Shiloh, Leon County; and Hebron, Gadsden County. Elizabeth Church, Jefferson County, withdrew before the next associational meeting. Twenty-seven churches containing 874 members remained in the association.[152] Prior Lewis rejoiced that such schisms would "eventually result in the glory of God and the burning up of much dross among Christians."[153]

The burned up dross did not respond kindly. The *Christian Index* called the 1842 Circular "such a specimen as you never saw in print" and, as regards the nonfellowship resolution itself, considered that "the best apology we can make for the man who wrote it is, he must have been drunk when he did it—Certainly no man in his senses could have produced such an article."[154] After a preliminary meeting elsewhere, the withdrawn churches met the next October at Ebenezer Church, Jefferson County, Florida, and organized the Florida Baptist Association. Eleven churches joined the six seceders, bringing the new body to a total of seventeen churches with 670 members. One new church, Little River of Lowndes County, Georgia, was the only one in South Georgia.[155] Jonathan Gaulden, in exile from Bethel Church for eight years, had joined with seven others in organizing the church. Until the organization of the Florida Association, the small group, like Gaulden himself, existed in isolation, hoping for better days. It is today the First Baptist Church of Valdosta, worshipping in an edifice that Jonathan Gaulden would mistake for a gothic cathedral rather than a Baptist meetinghouse.[156]

The new association, freed from the restraints imposed by their former Antimissionary connection, adopted the liberally Calvinistic New Hampshire Confession, which emphasized "the freeness of salvation," and down -played, without denying, election and predestination. "The awful and portending cloud of *'false doctrine,'* which, like an incubus, has so long hung over the churches of our denomination in Florida, and settled its members down into a death-like lethargy and lukewarmness, is now rapidly passing away before the pure light of the gospel of truth." The circular address asserted that the seceding churches had taken this step in order to preserve the freedom of action to which they were entitled as American citizens, and compared the "dogmas" of the Antimissionaries to the decrees of the "Roman Pontiff." Had they remained in the Ochlocknee Association, they would "ere long . . . be brought to groan beneath the absurdities of bigotry and prejudice, and our devotions burdened and perplexed with a long train of traditionary ceremonies."[15]

The Wiregrass Missionaries had more problems with identity than did the Old Baptists. In a move inconsistent enough to merit them Elias Hawthorn's scornful name "Softheaded Baptists," the 1844 Florida Association sent a corresponding letter to the Ochlocknee, as though to an association of its own faith.[158] The Ocklochnee committee on correspondence did not even deign to report the letter, but the circular address noted with dour amusement the inconsistency of desiring correspondence with a body they had recently denounced as "enemies of the American Constitution, and just ready to unite with a Roman Pontiff." The circular derided Missionary interest in money and governmental incorporation and aid as more ominous signs of incipient Popery than their own nonfellowship resolution.[159]

Some Primitive churches at first took a relatively mild stance toward the few adherents of the new party, perhaps expecting them soon to come creeping back to their old allegiance. Bethlehem Church in Lowndes County, Georgia, resolved that "this church shall not receive . . . any member who is a Missionary or advocates the Missionary cause," and that any member who should "here after turn over from the primitive order to the Missionary shall forthwith call fore a letter of dismission" or be excommunicated for disorder.[160] This indulgence was soon withdrawn. The 1845 Suwannee River Association reproved Forest Grove Church, also of Lowndes County, for "dismissing two members from her body to become members of a different society, which we believe to be contrary to strict discipline." The association forgave Forest Grove on account of its "repentant manner" but hoped its action would not set a precedent.[161] As attitudes hardened, Nancy Hagan, a vociferous supporter of Missions, found herself trapped in Mt. Moriah Church, Jefferson County, Florida. The pastor, Henry Milton, was a decided Antimissionary, bred at Isham Peacock's old foundation at Upper Black Creek.[162] Despite her having raised the first collection for the pastor in five years, the church voted to exclude her for her Missionary stance and expelled her for "joining of a church of the Missionary faith and order and saying she was harty in the faith of the Florida Association which we believe is not the faith of the Oaklocknee Association." At her request, Mt. Moriah gave her a copy of the excommunication decree to use as a recommendatory letter at her new church.[163] Active among the Missionaries, she died two years later at Grooverville, Thomas County, Georgia, soon after happily "exhorting" among "convicted" girls during a "protracted meeting" there.[164] Curiously, her son John F. Hagan, of Jefferson County, Florida, avidly read the *Primitive Baptist,* declaring it "the work of the Lord," and detested the "soft side or . . . money beggars."[165]

The Suwannee River Association declared against missions in 1840, adopting a resolution similar to that later adopted by the Ochlocknee in 1842.[166] With Isham Peacock a member of the association and Matthew Albritton, from Peacock's Upper Black Creek, as moderator, Missionism stood little chance.[167] Nevertheless, the new system had its adherents. John Tucker and William B. Cooper both belonged to the Suwannee River Association in the early 1840s. Ryan Frier's defection caused the most grief, however. Possessed of impeccable Antimissionary credentials, Frier had belonged to Peacock's Upper Black Creek Church and had married Peacock's granddaughter Sarah.[168] He joined Union Church by letter in 1832, and the church called on him to preach and "liberated" him to the pulpit the same day.[169] Union ordained this immediately popular minister in 1833 at the request of Friendship Church.[170] In 1842, however, Friendship reported to the Suwannee Association that, "painful as it was," it had dropped Frier for "departing from the faith under which he was received and ordained." The association sustained Friendship's action. Frier had refused to surrender his ministerial credentials, so the association warned "our brethren generally not to encourage him in error by inviting him to any public excercise." John Tucker, soon to turn "Softheaded Baptist" himself, served on the committee that proclaimed Frier an excommunicated and disorderly preacher.[171]

Frier had in fact adopted the Fullerite doctrine of general atonement. Before a committee assembled at Friendship Church, he had asked, "How could unbelief be a transgression, if Christ did not by the grace of God, taste death for every man?" The church replied by silencing him over the objections of some of the members, withdrawing fellowship from him, and demanding his credentials "for holding forth doctrines at variance with her faith." Frier then approached the Little River Missionary Baptist Church, which, not surprisingly, found "no error of doctrine or practice" in Frier and unanimously received him as a member and minister. A member of Friendship Church summed up Frier's offense as consisting wholly in preaching "a full atonement and that upon the impenitent sinner rested the fault of his condemnation."[172]

Other than Frier's defection, Missionism made little inroad on the remote Suwannee River Association. In 1845, the association finally noticed that Concord Church of Hamilton County, Florida, no longer attended its sessions, having joined the "Missionary Association (so called)." The 1845 Association also added their 1840 nonfellowship resolution to their decorum.[173] Two years later, the association sustained a minority faction at New River Church, Columbia County, Florida, "having been defrauded out of their rights and priveleges as a church, by those favorable to the popular institutions of the day." The same session dropped Providence Church, and its pastor John Tucker, as "unsound in faith and immoral in practice."[174]

Several ceremonial adjustments finalized the schism. The Primitives perceived a vast difference between their faith and the general atonement doctrine of the Missionaries. Reflecting this, the 1844 Ochlocknee Association adopted an amendment to its decorum that "recommend[ed] to the Churches comprising this body to receive members who went off with the Missionary Baptists at the time of their separation from us, who may return with a suitable confession; and not to receive any who have been baptised by them since said separation, only by experience and baptism." In the next year, the Suwannee River Association adopted the same resolution, as did the Alabaha River.[175] This action, together with the adoption of the Primitive Baptist name, clearly established the emergence of two separate denominations, which henceforth largely ignored each other.

The practice of footwashing after communion was one of the "long train of traditionary ceremonies" to which the Missionaries objected. The 1793 Georgia Association ruled it "an ordinance of the gospel" and "binding on the churches."[176] Union Church, organized in 1825, added footwashing to its list of sacred ordinances.[177] The Missionary-minded Savannah Association, on the other hand, did not "consider this humble duty . . . in the class of sacred ordinances" and considered its practice a thing indifferent.[178] The Primitives, with their strict adherence to narrow biblical interpretation, valued the practice more highly as the Missionaries depreciated it. In 1842, the Suwannee River Association added the "washing of the saint's feet" to baptism and communion as "ordinances of Jesus Christ." The circular for that year declared it a distinguishing mark of the elect to prize all the ordinances of Christ equally, including the "blessed, meek, and humble ordinance of washing the saint's feet." To adopt practices not in Scripture, or to declare biblical practices "non-essential" were equally wrong.[179] In 1845, the Alabaha River Association also added footwashing to its articles of faith.[180]

One final ceremonial change took place in the 1840s, which remains firmly in place among most South Georgia and Florida Primitive churches. Jesse Mercer's hymnbook, the *Cluster,* became unacceptable to the Primitives as later editions added more and more hymns of a Missionary complexion. In 1842, Benjamin Lloyd, a Primitive Baptist preacher in Chambers County, Alabama, published the *Primitive Hymns,* a collection of standard hymns, similar in content and format to Rippon and Mercer's early hymnals.[181] Considering that for the most part only individuals purchased hymnals at that time, the success of Lloyd's hymnal was remarkable. By 1847, its fourth edition was out, and Lloyd expressed delight in its extensive use.[182] It remains the most widely used hymnal among the Primitive Baptists of South Georgia and Florida, and the esteem in which it is held is difficult to exaggerate. One elder once remarked in a South Georgia church that, unlike the Bible, the *Primitive Hymns* was not inspired, only to be heatedly informed by the members that indeed it was.[183]

→ 5 ←

"Wars and Rumors of Wars"

The Civil War Era

Except in times of extreme crisis, the outside world might as well not have existed as far as Primitive Baptist church records were concerned. For example, the Mexican War received no mention in the minutes of the Ochlocknee and Suwannee River associations. In 1849, a revealing exception took place when the Ochlocknee, Alabaha River, and Suwannee River associations, in concurrence with the North Carolina Primitive Baptists, sent resolutions to Congress and the Georgia and Florida legislatures opposing the establishment of a chaplaincy for Congress and the army and navy and the incorporation of religious societies.[1] In North Carolina, the Kehukee Association opposed such laws because of the "rapid encroachments of ecclesiastical power and clerical corruption" and because "the Kingdom of Christ is not of this world."[2] They opposed tax exempt status for churches and religious institutions, holding mere toleration quite enough in the way of government assistance. They favored the North Carolina law that excluded clergymen from political office and feared that incorporation would be the forerunner of religious establishment.[3] "Christianity in its infancy needed not the puny arm of man or human laws to sustain it . . . whatever therefore seeks to unite itself with the state and trusts in the power of human enactments for existence . . . is not and cannot be the religion of Jesus of Nazareth"[4] They called on Congress to abolish chaplaincies and any state support to religious schools. Ministers could pray for Congress and the armed forces on their own time.[5] "If ministers cannot preach and pray for the Army, the Navy, for Congress, and the Indian Tribes, for the love of Christ, without conferring with flesh and blood and a salary in filthy lucre, . . . then they cannot acceptably to God do so with this salary, for such constitutes them hirelings . . . in whose counsels there is no safety."[6] Given such attitudes toward the world, it is unsurprising that the events of the 1850s and 1860s brought little comment in Primitive Baptist records.

During the mounting national crisis of the 1850s, business continued as usual in the local churches. Prospect Church, in the barren sand plains of Hamilton County, Florida, "jerked up" and turned out Joseph Holder in 1847 for "cohabiting with and keeping a black Negro slave instead of his white wife and abandoning his wife from his bed and board."[7] John C. Johns fell victim to the majesty of the church in the same year for "disorder," which consisted of fiddling and dancing. Two years later, the church cast out James and Nancy Parrish, he for adultery and she for being five years absent from meeting and for "living with a man not her husband."[8]

Up the Alapaha River in Georgia, religion grew cold at Union Church during the 1850s. The pastor, William A. Knight, in his seventies, often missed meeting.[9] Many members were "cited to the conference" for long absence, including seven at one time. Brethren fought over geese lost in the woods, drank to excess, and joined the Masons.[10]

The Primitive Baptists enjoyed considerable growth during the prewar period. By 1854, the Ochlocknee Association had thirty-five churches spread from Wakulla County, Florida, to Irwin County, Georgia, with 778 members in all.[11] Within four years of its organization, the Alabaha River Association grew from four churches with 107 members to fifteen with 377.[12] Between 1838 and 1855, the Suwannee River Association increased from twelve churches and 350 members to twenty-four with 627 members. In 1855, this association dismissed its churches in Georgia to form the Union Association with thirteen churches and 334 members.[13]

As the crisis of the 1850s deepened, national concerns finally found their way even into the associational minutes in South Georgia and Florida, apparently by way of the *Signs of the Times.* Gilbert Beebe editorialized in the *Signs* against the anti-Nebraska petition submitted to Congress by three thousand New England clergy. The petitioners protested against the admission of slavery to the territories as "a great moral wrong and as a breach of faith . . . subversive of all confidence in national engagements" and calculated to bring down the wrath of God upon the nation.[14]

Beebe attacked the petition as an example of priestly arrogance emanating from "the Babylon of New England theology," and declared that the New England clergy and the Roman Catholics differed only in that the former believed that they were God's "viceregents to act for him on earth" and the latter believed only the Pope to be such. Taking the prevailing anti-Catholicism a step further, Beebe inquired "why it should be thought less extravagant or wicked for the clergy to assume the name and attributes of the almighty God and hurl the thunder of their anathemas against the senate of the United States, or to dictate to them what laws they may enact, and what they may repeal, than for the Pope of Rome to exercise the same authority over the Kings of the earth, is hard for us to perceive."[15]

Beebe usually avoided all political topics in the *Signs,* having "higher and more sacred matters to dwell upon; matters which concern the Kingdom of our Lord and Savior Jesus Christ. His kingdom is not of this world, and he has commanded the subjects of his kingdom to mark the distinction he has made between church and state." He excused reference to this matter because, as a protest by clergymen acting as such in the name of the deity, he believed that the "Mammoth Petition" represented a dangerous breach in the wall of separation between church and state. As an egalitarian Baptist, Beebe found the distinction between clergy and laity repugnant. "In the church of the living God, there are no such distinctions as that of *clergy* and *laity*. There is no aristocracy in the spiritual kingdom of our Lord Jesus Christ. . . . The ministers of the gospel of our redeemer, are not allowed to lord it over the church, much less are they to exercise authority over the state."[16] Beebe rejoiced in the castigation given the petition in the Senate by Stephen A. Douglas and Andrew Butler of South Carolina and hoped that such a display of clerical arrogance and intermeddling would lead to the abolition of the chaplaincy and thus "sever these unnatural ligaments which now unite the church and state."[17]

Influenced no doubt by Beebe's editorial, the Warwick Association of New York, to which he belonged, hastened to proclaim themselves as one northern religious body not in support of the protest. While acknowledging the right of citizens to petition the government on any topic, they denied that Christians as such should meddle in political affairs and strongly condemned the New England ministers as presumptuous for speaking thus in the name of God. The Warwick Association denounced such actions on the part of ministers as "calculated to destroy every vestige of civil and religious freedom, and prostrate all the institutions of our land at the foot of an irresponsible and arrogant priesthood."[18] The association forwarded copies of their resolution to the President of the Senate, the Speaker of the House, the *Signs of the Times, Southern Baptist Messenger,* and the *Banner of Liberty.* The Delaware and Baltimore associations also denounced the protest, denying that the three thousand New England clergy represented "the gospel ministers of all the religious sects and denominations of our country."[19] They forwarded their resolutions to the same congressional officers and periodicals as those addressed by the Warwick association.

The 1854 Suwannee River Association "resolved that we concur with our sister Associations North, to wit: the Baltimore and Delaware Old School Baptist Associations in their Resolutions set forth in their minutes against the act of the three thousand clergymen of New England who have threatened our Congress with the vengeance of Almighty God upon the passage of the Nebraska Bill."[20] The phrasing of their resolution and the mention of associations far beyond their normal range of correspondence indicates that they probably acted in response to the accounts carried in the *Signs* or the *Southern Baptist Messenger,* which appears to have enjoyed some circulation in South Georgia. This resolution is the only overt antebellum political statement made by the Primitive Baptists of the region.

The Wiregrass Primitive Baptists did not commit to writing what they thought of the slavery controversy. However, their principal organ, the *Primitive Baptist,* departed from its usual neutrality on political issues to print a "discourse" by Elder John Clark of Virginia on "The Relation of Master and Servant," which probably spoke for most southern Primitive Baptists and very likely most of the northern ones as well. Elder Clark delivered his discourse before a racially mixed congregation at Stafford Courthouse, Virginia, on April 29, 1860.[21]

Clark first declared himself "a *strict constructionist*" in his reading of the Bible. "What it teaches as doctrine we must receive as truth, and what it enjoins upon us in precept we are under obligation to observe; and all that is not expressly commanded therein is forbidden." Clark traced the institution of bondage from the curse upon Canaan, the grandson of Noah, recorded in Genesis 9:25–27. Clark derived, "as I understand it," the Jews from Shem, the whites from Japheth, and the blacks from the accursed Canaan. He pointed out that in both the Patriarchal and Mosaic dispensations, servants were purchased, and further that the Scriptures made a distinction between bought and hired servants.

Clark next answered the objection that the Christian dispensation had abrogated the former order of things. "When Christ came . . . he found the institution of Slavery in existence; and although he never failed to reprove the people for their sins—all manner of sins—and in the severest terms, yet there is no case on record where he ever protested against slaveholding as a sin, or that he ever commanded that it should be abolished."[22] He quoted several passages from the Apostles exhorting servants to obedience and masters to kindness. In commenting on the force of these passages, Clark left the relatively safe ground of scriptural exegesis and ventured to prophesy: "I have presented the testimony of the Apostle Paul . . . and of the Apostle Peter . . . in which this relation is recognized, and explicit instructions given to the parties respectively; and of course, it is consistent with the Christian economy. In the same connection instructions are given to husbands and wives, parents and children, and as long as these relations shall endure, which shall be as long as the world stands, or until `time shall be no longer,' so long will there be masters and servants, otherwise that portion of the Bible would be obsolete; but that shall never be with anything belonging to the new covenant, and the gospel dispensation; and therefore I would as soon think of laboring to abolish the conjugal and parental relations which God has established as to abolish slavery."[23]

Clark found the "Abolition Party of the 19th century . . . in spirit and in letter" in Paul's admonition in I Timothy 6:3–5: "If any man teach otherwise, and consent not to wholesome words, even to the words of our Lord Jesus Christ, and to the doctrine which is according to godliness: He is proud, knowing nothing, but doting about questions and strifes of words, whereof cometh envy, strife, railings, evil surmisings, perverse disputings of men of corrupt minds, and destitute of the truth, supposing that gain is godliness; from such withdraw thyself."

Clark closed his sermon by pointing out that he had traveled in sixteen states, six free and ten slave, and proudly stated that he never knew a Primitive Baptist "who had any standing in the Church, or any character for orthodoxy, who was an abolitionist." He denounced abolitionism as a species of theft and related that the "notorious Anthony Burns"—the famous escaped slave whose recapture and deportation from Boston under the Fugitive Slave Act had nearly touched off an insurrection there—had been baptized by him and later excommunicated by the Primitive Baptist Church for running away from his master. Clark denounced the English and American Baptists who called for abolition as Missionary and Fullerite heretics, not to be confused with genuine Old School Baptists. He singled out Charles Haddon Spurgeon, the celebrated English Baptist preacher, as a particularly prominent example. Spurgeon wrote a letter on slavery stating that he would as soon fellowship a murderer as a slaveowner, causing the southern Missionary Baptists who had previously idolized him to burn his books. Clark smugly declared himself to be "under no such necessity" since he seldom read one whom "we never owned as being of our faith and order; never considered him sound either in doctrine or church polity; nor do our brethren in England recognize him. . . . His egotism in this production is disgusting in the extreme."[24]

Politics, as usual, made for strange bedfellows. In conclusion, Clark quoted with approval a passage from the Missionary *South Western Baptist*: "We defend slavery because of our honest conviction that it is socially and morally right. This is the true Southern platform, and it is as scriptural as it is Southern."[25]

Even with the actual commencement of the war, there was no direct reference to political or military matters in either the church or the associational minutes in the region of this study. The 1861 minutes of the Alabaha River and Suwannee River associations described their ongoing doctrinal debate over the role of the gospel in salvation. The *Primitive Baptist* served as the principal organ of the South Georgia and Florida Primitives and several letters from the region appeared in the paper during the secession crisis. Typically, not one of them referred in any way to matters in the political sphere. Asa McCrary wrote from Thomas County, Georgia, in September 1860 on church discipline. After the fateful 1860 election, the same correspondent held forth on the doctrine of salvation by grace alone. McCrary's letter of January 1861, in the midst of Georgia's secession, made no reference to politics at all.[26] David Hickox of Pierce County, Georgia, penned his first letter to the *Primitive* in May 1861, with the war actually begun. His letter commented extensively on John 4:24 but said nothing whatever about secession or war.[27]

Though the South Georgia and Florida correspondents of the *Primitive* did not comment on the secession crisis, the editor, Elder Burwell Temple, did devote one editorial to the looming crisis. In the first number for 1861, Temple made a colossal understatement: "The present year, dear brethren, from its introduction, does not flatter us with the tranquillity of the past." Nonetheless, he rejoiced that all "true" Primitive Baptists, North and South, remained united. He claimed to have long believed that "priest-craft" would be the ruin of America and declared the secession crisis the result of "abolitionist priestcraft." He compared the Union to a Primitive Baptist association, wherein erring or heretical churches were dropped from the union and left in isolation by their orderly brethren.

Temple's theory of federalism was typically southern, plainly asserting the states to be superior to the federal Union in power and the Union itself a compact of states. The constitution does not provide for putting down a rebellion of states; therefore to act against secession was unconstitutional. The North had profited from slavery, yet northern states had passed personal liberty laws, depriving southerners of their property. Such states ought to be dropped from the Union, like disorderly churches from a Baptist association. Abolition, according to Temple, was heresy since slavery was in the Bible. It was also theft and, as practiced by John Brown, murder as well. "The very first step toward the abolition of slavery in this country, was of the spirit of the devil himself, under the garb of preachers, with an eye single to the upsetting of this republican form of government, in order to set up one more congenial to their love of filthy lucre and aggrandizement; to fatten faster on the labors of the unsuspecting part of the community."

Temple concluded with a sentiment probably widely shared among Primitive Baptists and the white South generally. "I am in favor of the Union on the strict principle of our Constitution; and if the Southern States, in their sovereign capacity, shall be debarred of their just and equal rights, I am for secession as the last resort—though I much prefer the Union, if it be indeed a Union of rights, interest, and honor." He ended by remarking that if his "decided stand" on this issue cost him subscribers, he was prepared to endure the loss.[28]

Some Primitive Baptists participated in the secession debate. Elder Henry Crawford Tucker of Colquitt County, Georgia, won election to the Georgia secession convention on the cooperationist ticket.[29] Fifty-eight years old, he had never sought public office before. T. W. Stallings described him as "the most awkward and ignorant man in all God's creation. . . . I thought he preached the most foolishness of anybody I ever heard."[30] His main claim to fame lay in fathering thirty-three children by three wives.[31] He finally submitted and voted with the secessionist majority at the convention.[32]

Other Primitive Baptists seemed lukewarm toward secession. Benjamin Sirmans of Union Church, a former Whig, served as one of Clinch County's delegates to the convention. According to tradition, like his coreligionist H. C. Tucker, he voted against secession until the last ballot, when he caved in and went with the majority. Seventy-nine years old, he died two years later.[33] Loyalty to the Union may possibly have been stronger among older people. Two younger Primitive Baptist preachers, Ansel Parrish and E. J. Williams, preached for the Fiftieth Georgia Regiment while it was encamped at Savannah. T. W. Stallings found the sights of the city more alluring than their preaching.[34] South Georgians speaking of the war in later years often referred to it as the "Confederate War," leaving the impression that it was a war between the Confederates and the Yankees, with themselves perhaps only bystanders.[35]

In a remarkable instance of how far some Primitive Baptists went to avoid the ministry, William Hollingworth volunteered for Confederate service at the outbreak of war because his church called for his ordination. Then twenty-six, he had joined Mizpah Church in the Ochlocknee Association in 1854. With great misgivings he had begun to preach occasionally and the church had licensed him. He had no taste for the "cruel war." "I was not a fighting man. I did not want to leave my wife and five little children." But when, to his horror, the church discussed plans for his ordination, he fled to Macon and enlisted. He thought his three years of service in the Confederate army "the longest years of my life." His thoughts were often on his brethren in Georgia. On one occasion when he felt he would certainly die in a "storm of lead," he felt a divine assurance that the church had prayed for him and that he would live to preach again. However, he admitted that "I met with circumstances after that many times that made me fear I was mistaken." He served until the surrender at Appomattox and returned home in May 1865. As might be expected, he interpreted his war experience in religious terms, concluding that like Christ, he "there learned obedience by the things I suffered. Though surrounded with the horrors of war and the vices of men, I would sometimes enjoy the sweet presence of Jesus." With typical Primitive Baptist single-mindedness, the church proceeded with his rather delayed ordination as soon as he returned home.[36]

During the war church business proceeded much as usual. While secession loomed, Bethlehem Church, Brooks County, Georgia, discussed moving the church to the new railroad.[37] When federal forces pressed into Georgia, the same church excluded a sister for fornication.[38] With the end in sight in early 1865, Bethlehem "jerked up" William Smith for joining the Masons.[39]

Cedar Creek Church, Baker County, Florida, with raid and counterraid blundering through the local woods, found time to conduct an ecclesiastical vendetta with nearby North Prong Church over some unspecified "disorder."[40] When the surrender came, Cedar Creek spent April through July deciding to expel Sister E. M. Yelvington for "disorder."[41]

Several of these church discipline cases reveal an interesting pattern. Prior to the war, cases of church discipline involving sexual transgressions were rather rare. During the war years and after, such matters seem more common. In February 1865, Salem Church, Berrien County, Georgia, heard Brother W. W. Williams accuse himself of "unseemly acts" with Sister Nancy Edmondson. In March, Sister Edmondson "being present [and] acknowledging her self equally concerned in the Transgression," the church withdrew from both of them. In September 1866, Williams returned and "reported himself dissatisfied and manifested a desire to enjoy church priveleges Confessed his faults and asked forgiveness."[42] Sister Edmondson does not appear to have returned to the church. The sisters at Salem became rather rowdy toward the end of the war. In May 1866, "the fact was established beyond a doubt that one of the members of this boddy Sister Patience Crausby was guilty of fornication and having treated a committy who waited on her in regard to the matter verry insultingly," the church voted her "no more a member of this boddy until reclaimed."[43]

The financial pinch of the war showed in several ways. In 1864, Cedar Creek took up $24.16 to help print the associational minutes, about ten times the amount usual before the war.[44] The 1864 minutes of the Suwannee River and Ochlocknee associations are much shorter than usual and are poorly printed in small type on what appears to be one half of a single sheet of writing paper. In September 1862, Union Church had to omit its yearly communion because the deacons could obtain no flour or wine. In practically all the minute books for the war period, the ink is obviously homemade and often almost illegible.

At least two Primitive Baptists may have descended from the famous probity of the denomination to some of the shady profiteering common in wartime. H. P. Mathis of Union Church confessed his "unthoted acts in trading the same stock to two persons to the wounding of the feelings of the church."[45] Elder Andrew G. Connell of Emmaus Church, Berrien County, Georgia, confessed to operating a "still house" in June 1863 and promised to discontinue it.[46] The church's objection may have been more to the use of scarce grain than to the manufacture of spirits as such.

One Lowndes County community reached the point of boiling over in the spring of 1864. At the May conference of Union Church, Brother John Lee arose and informed the church that "three of the members of this body to viz. Sister Hetta Peters & Sister Rachel Chitty & Bro. W. S. Peters has bin sensured of pertisipating with a mob that had assembled at Naylor for the purpos of taking of spun yarn cloth and bacon for which cause they have come under the displeasure of the church."[47] W. S. Peters cleared himself; Hetta Peters confessed and was forgiven "with joy." Rachel Chitty refused to answer the church's summons and was excommunicated.[48] Local tradition held that the Confederate Commissary thoroughly worked over the area, leaving little in the way of livestock or provisions behind.[49] In Primitive eyes, that evidently did not justify stealing the stuff back.

That two of the accused in the Naylor mob incident were women indicated the survival in South Georgia, as in other parts of the Confederacy, of the ancient European tradition of bread riots led by women. The incident also hints at the tremendous struggle endured by South Georgia women during the Civil War, although the region was not a theater of military operations. C. W. Stallings, Elder T. W. Stallings's son, recalled with simple eloquence the hardships of his mother, Susan Newton Stallings, during the war: "Father was called off to the war and left her to battle through the best she could."[50] Warren Ward recalled, "About the close of the Confederate war the woods in South Georgia was filled with . . . deserters, details, runaway negroes, tramps and rogues of all sorts. The country was inhabited mostly by women and children and they were always in some fear that . . . harm would come to them."[51]

A rash of conversions accompanied the war. In 1861, the Union Church minutes show six baptized after several years in which no one joined. In all,

Elder Timothy William Stallings and his wife, Susan Newton Stallings, members of Pleasant Church, Berrien County, Ga. Circa 1885. Courtesy of Roscoe A. Stallings.

thirteen baptisms took place during the war years, a higher rate than usual. Cedar Creek records show six baptized in 1861. Sardis Church in Colquitt County gained eighteen members during 1863–64. Salem Church also had a considerable revival during the war years, with the pastor frequently baptizing people on his own authority at a distance from the church, a practice frowned upon in more settled times.[52]

T. W. Stallings of Brooks County, Georgia, left an account of his wartime conversion. He joined the "Brooks Volunteers" on March 19, 1862, and served in the Army of Northern Virginia.[53] In January 1863, he began to feel uneasy over his sins, having engaged in fiddling, horse racing, gambling "and many other vile practices." He began to feel that he would soon die and that his prayers were useless. The chaplain exhorted him to believe and pray, but he felt he could have "as easily made the sun rise at the hour of midnight." After the next engagement, however, he found himself one of only four unhurt out of the twenty-seven in his outfit. Feeling that God had heard his prayers, he found his spiritual distress eased somewhat, and the chaplain baptized him. He then dreamed that he could read the Bible, although he claimed never to have advanced beyond two-syllable words in a spelling book. He borrowed a friend's Testament and was astonished to find that he could read with perfect ease. The first passage he read was a fundamental predestinarian proof text: Romans 9. He suffered a severe, nearly fatal, wound in the arm in October 1864 and went to his mother-in-law's home to recuperate. Unable to attend church, he asked his mother-in-law to make a preaching appointment for Henry Crawford Tucker at her house. Although he had previously detested Tucker, Stallings now felt that "his every word was to my soul as apples of gold in pictures of silver. He did not preach Jesus as a co-worker with man, but . . . as having power over all flesh to give eternal life to as many as his father had given him." He eagerly repudiated his former connection with his chaplain's unnamed denomination and received Primitive Baptist baptism from Elder Tucker after he and his wife united with Bethel Church, Brooks County, Georgia, in February 1865.[54] By May 1865, he was preaching in local churches and Bethel licensed him in October of the same year.[55]

In 1864, Florida saw enough Federal action to rattle even the most solid predestinarian. Cedar Creek Church lay about two miles from the main road to Olustee. The minute book is blank for February 1864. The church met on the second weekend of each month, and in early February Union and Confederate forces jockeyed for positions around Sanderson and Olustee, the Federals "piloted by traitors familiar with every portion of the country."[56] Primitive abandonment to providence did not extend to meeting on the actual field of war. In March, however, everything at Cedar Creek proceeded as usual.

The 1864 the Suwannee River Association noted several churches unrepresented "on account of distress in the land."[57] The country around Black Creek Church, Clay County, Florida, and Etoniah Church, Putnam County, Florida, saw considerable raiding during the time of the association's annual session.[58] Elim Church, in Lafayette County, Florida, sent no delegates that year, its area being largely controlled by Unionist guerrillas.[59] The 1864 Alabaha River Association had intended to meet with Buffalo Church, Wayne County, Georgia, but met instead with Big Creek Church, Pierce County, "on account of the enemy being so near."[60] In the case of Wayne County, this was likely Federal troops operating on the coast, near Darien. This association's decision to drop fellowship with the Union Association for continuing to correspond with the Suwannee River Association took up more space in their minutes than any concern over invading Federals. The 1864 Pulaski Association made no direct reference to the war but lamented unspecified calamities coming upon the country.[61]

Primitive Baptists certainly shared in the war's human cost. To give just two examples, Sarah Milton Redding, of Brooks County, Georgia, widowed sister of Elder Henry Milton, lost three of her eight sons in the war. William Alderman, a member of Bethel Church, Brooks County, Georgia, lost three of his five sons.[62]

Those not already living in inaccessible areas often moved into them during the war. James Jackson Lee, a member of Bethel Church in Echols County, Georgia, moved onto Billy's Island in the heart of the Okefenokee Swamp soon after the war began and cleared the first farm there. His astuteness cost him his church affiliation, however, as Bethel expelled him for long

James Turner of Emmaus Church, Berrien County, Ga. Circa 1885. Courtesy of John G. Crowley.

absence on October 10, 1863.[63] In Florida, many neutralist families moved downstate into the remote Peace River country as a result of the war.[64]

James Turner, a forty-year-old farmer and wheelwright of Berrien County, Georgia, typified a common response to military service. According to formal records, he volunteered in 1863 in the Berrien Minutemen. Wounded in the eye while serving in the Army of Tennessee, he was hospitalized and furloughed home until the end of the war.[65] His aged granddaughters related a slightly different story. He thought the war foolishness and "volunteered" only when conscription stared him in the face. A jack of all trades, and something of a favorite with his commanding officer, he became the regimental cobbler. As he was mending boots in his tent, divine providence smiled on him and dropped a piece of spent shrapnel through the roof and hit him in the nose, leaving a slight permanent scar and a ticket home.[66] Soon after his return, he joined Emmaus Church, Berrien County, Georgia.[67] His oft expressed contempt for the war did not hinder him from applying for a Confederate soldier's pension, however.

Others did not wait for divine interposition. Joel Wooten Swain, a member of Empire Church, Berrien County, Georgia, deserted on October 30, 1863, and the church licensed him to preach the same year. They set his ordination for June 24, 1865, but then voted to postpone it indefinitely. He soon moved to South Florida.[68] The attitude of his returning comrades may have thrown cold water on his candidacy for ordination. On the other hand, Hebron Church, Hamilton County, Florida, excommunicated Matthew

McCullars on September 10, 1864, for deserting the Confederate Army. The church later reinstated him.[69]

The war did not seem to breed any lasting animosities among Primitive Baptists. One South Georgia deserter who joined the Union Army in Florida united with Empire Church in 1883 and later married the widow of a Confederate casualty.[70] Another deserter who joined the Union forces in Florida later joined Prospect Primitive Baptist Church, Clinch County, Georgia.[71] The Alabaha River Association expressed apprehension in 1865 of potential suffering at the hands of "our invading foe."[72] Such apprehension proved groundless. The Federals but lightly occupied South Georgia. Apparently the only Federal troops seen in Colquitt County, Georgia, during the war or Reconstruction were a pair of wretched Andersonville escapees taken in and helped on their way by J. B. Norman and his wife toward the end of 1864.[73] Mrs. Norman was a parishoner of Elder Henry Crawford Tucker at Sardis Church, in the southeastern part of the county.[74]

One last grim incident relating to the war and the Primitive Baptists took place in Irwin County, Georgia. One Bone, a reputed Unionist, took in two Andersonville escapees. One of them was later killed attempting to steal horses. Bone also took in a runaway slave named Toney. Toney's master, Jack Walker, disappeared in the woods on April 20, 1865. Bone behaved suspiciously and his teenage son, under threats from local vigilantes, told that Walker had apprehended Toney in the woods and that his father had killed Walker. Upon being led to Walker's shallow grave, they found one hand out of the earth; he had apparently been buried alive. With no functioning legal apparatus available, the vigilantes formed an impromptu court and elected Jacob Young, a member of Brushy Creek Primitive Baptist Church and a former justice of the peace, as chairman. The court found Bone guilty of the murder of Walker and hanged him with a homemade cotton rope supplied by Mrs. Young. Neither Toney nor the Andersonville escapee was recaptured.[75] Brushy Creek Church licensed Young to preach three months later.[76]

By then it was all over. The minute books continue, dry as the Anglo-Saxon Chronicle. Perhaps Elder Tucker preached from that favorite Primitive Baptist text, Daniel 4:35: "And all the inhabitants of the earth are reputed as nothing; and he doeth his will in the army of heaven, and among the inhabitants of the earth; and none can stay his hand, or say unto him, What doest thou?"

6

"How Are the Mighty Fallen"

The Post–Civil War Era

Most of South Georgia and the interior of Florida escaped direct harm during the Civil War because the area did not lie en route to any significant military objective. Casualties of faraway battles, depredations by the Confederate Commissary, and, outside the Florida Piedmont, the eventual freedom of the relatively few slaves represented the extent of the war's impingement on life in the vast pine barrens that constituted most of the territory.

Primitive Baptist Church records mainly indicate the war's outcome by giving former slaves surnames rather than distinguishing them as "the property of" someone. During the flux of nomenclature after the war, Bethlehem Church, Brooks County, Georgia, used the transitional phrase "formerly the property of."[1] Most churches in this region had few black members. Union Church, the oldest in central South Georgia, never had more than eight black members before 1860, out of a total membership for the same period of 120.[2] Also, excommunication fell on black members more often for moral rather than purely theological offences, such as in the case of one Henry, excommunicated by Friendship Church, Lowndes County, Georgia, for "lying, stealing and non-attendance."[3]

One slave member at Union, Dinah or Diannah Surmons, wrote an account of her conversion at the end of a long life. Her written experience was remarkable in being that of a woman, an African American, and indeed one of the most detailed of known written "experiences" from the area. She had joined Union Church as a young woman in 1841.[4] Fifty-five years later, in her "weak way," she described her experience. As a "poor negro," she had desired to "always . . . stay in my place . . . and I want all my race to do the same; and they will be better respected by both white and black people." Having thus nodded to the powers of her day, she proceeded in her account with the serene assurance of a strict predestinarian.[5]

As a small child she saw a vision of a "most beautiful white child . . . dressed in a strange snow-white covering." Terrified by the apparition, she ran screaming to her mother, who took her to their mistress, "a good Primitive Baptist." Her mistress questioned her closely about the vision for several days, and assured her mother that the vision was not a token of death, as she feared. Satisfied that it was a genuine revelation, she patted Dinah's head and told her, "You will see that again." Several years later, Surmons heard a voice say to her, "Dinah, you are born to die." These early impressions, however, proved superficial. At fifteen, she dreamed of Christ raising a building with the waving of his hand. In her dream she followed after Him, praying "Lord, will you remember me?" Some years afterward, as mentioned in a previous chapter, a Missionary Baptist woman of her acquaintance died suddenly after Surmons saw her "dancing and sporting with worldly amusements." While meditating upon such awful marks of apostasy, the young woman experienced such a wave of horror that "I thought it would choke me to death." For two years she wrestled constantly with the same sense of horrible oppression. Convinced that damnation awaited her, she began to lose her sense of sight and hearing and could not endure the company of her children or anyone else. While gathering wood, more to be alone than of necessity, she suddenly saw "a great light all about me, and in an instant . . . all my burden was gone; and I was so light I could not hardly stay on the ground." Then it seemed as if someone took her by the shoulders and said, "There is the way." "From within" she saw "a beautiful straight road . . . about three feet wide . . . and it went gradually up till lost." Although she soon doubted the reality of her deliverance, the horror under which she had previously labored never returned.[6]

Surmons asked her mistress's permission to "go to preaching" a month later and applied for membership at Union Church. Her newfound spiritual peace gave her assurance in dealing with the mostly white congregation. "They said they were willing to take me before I had told them all, but I told them I was not through."[7] The Church received her "with great joy," and William A. Knight, "Old Master Billie" to Dinah, baptized her the next day.[8]

Surmons remained at Union until September 1895, when she called for a letter of dismission, having grown "so feeble and old I could not well get there."[9] She placed her letter with Pilgrim's Rest, "a good orderly church of all colored people," near her home in western Brooks County, where she had moved at some unspecified time.[10] Pilgrim's Rest, started in Thomas County, Georgia, before 1889, had relocated to western Brooks County about 1900.[11] Constituted by Elders Wilson Johnson, John C. Rogers, and Allen Vincent Simms, it apparently was the only black church formally organized by white

Primitive Baptists within the bounds of the Ochlocknee Association.[12] Even so, the minutes of Bethlehem Church, where Wilson Johnson belonged, make no reference to his participation in the constitution, an unusual omission. The Ochlocknee Association toyed with the idea of admitting the black church. The 1889 minutes list Pilgrim's Rest, near Boston, Georgia, as "unrepresented." However, the "unrepresented" church made a donation of fifty cents to the association. Previous and subsequent minutes make no reference to this church, so the white brethren doubtless had second thoughts about admitting a "colored" church.[13] In 1906, Pilgrim's Rest had fourteen members.[14] Some black Primitives in the Wiregrass country remained in their old churches. Jacob Minton signed a church covenant at Big Creek Church, Wayne County, Georgia, in 1859. In 1900, the church granted him the privilege of attending "when he was able and his disabilites would permit."[15] As late as 1874, a black convert joined Union Church, and a black member joined Hebron Church, Hamilton County, Florida, by letter in 1890.[16] The tombstone of Sophia McLoud, buried in 1881 at Bethel Church, Brooks County, Georgia, proudly proclaims that "she was a member of the Primitive Church" and "as a colored citizen she had no equal." Indeed, within living memory, blacks attended and held membership in white Primitive Baptist churches in South Georgia. After the Civil War, however, in at least one case, racial solidarity may have outweighed theological conviction. Bethlehem Church excommunicated Milly Wright, a black member, for joining a "colored Missionary Church." However, Primitive Baptists excommunicated white members for the same offence.[17]

Friendship Church, near Hahira, Georgia, received more black members after the war than before. Twelve blacks joined the church by baptism in 1868–69.[18] Monday Strober, "a colored brother . . . not a member of this body," prayed at the baptism of black converts and interceded on their behalf in church conferences. The church noted his intercessions but ignored them.[19] The black members did not remain long at Friendship. The fellowship expelled one sister for adultery, although in a coincidental show of impartiality, the church charged a white sister with the same offense at the same conference and also expelled her. The following year a black brother came under church discipline for "hard sayings and for parting man and wife." In November 1872 the "colored brethren" were cited to the church for long absence. Soon after, the spiritual sword descended on another black brother for adultery. In 1873 four black members obtained letters of dismission, and in 1879 the church dropped from membership eight black members "not heard from for two years or more."[20] The Friendship roll from 1854 to 1879 shows a nearly equal number of black and white members, which is unique for a

Primitive Baptist church in that area. The excommunication rate of blacks was obviously higher than that of whites. Subsequent church affiliations of those black Friendship members dismissed by letter have not been traced. Their surnames are common in the Hahira black community, but no residents bearing these surnames are Primitive Baptists today. Black members who brought accusations against white members received short shrift, if the one surviving example is typical. An "old colored woman" belonging to a church pastored by Elder Robert Barwick charged one J. N. Gibson with "behav[ing] himself criminally" toward her. The church concluded that "the woman is a rogue and a liar" and denounced her report as being "black and false as the one who started it." The church had its proceedings in the case published in the *Pilgrim's Banner.*[21]

One South Georgia Primitive Baptist preacher played a role in establishing a major black Primitive Baptist association. In 1870, Hopewell Church in Mitchell County, Georgia, requested the advice of the Ochlocknee Association relative to a criticism concerning Elder J. D. Tennison, one its members.[22] Tennison had formerly belonged to a church in the neighboring Harmony Association. During Reconstruction, his church disbanded and he ran afoul of his brethren for several unauthorized actions in organizing churches and ordaining ministers among the freedmen. Two black churches petitioned the 1868 Harmony Association for admission. Harmony refused to receive them "owing to their informal and unscriptural Constitution . . . by one minister alone, without church authority or advice."[23] The association then rendered its opinion on Elder Tennison's part in such proceedings, together with his lamentable tendency toward *communio in sacris* with the hated Missionaries:

> Whereas, Eld. Jas. Tenison, an ordained minster among us, has for some years past been manifesting coolness, distance and indifference toward the course and interest of the Primitive Baptist, and also, has been giving encouragement to Missionary Baptist by preaching with them, and as we learn, taking part, and affiliating in their unscriptural course; and also, has been constituting Churches and ordaining Ministers among the colored people without the aid or advice of any other minister, or Church. And as the said Eld. Jas. Tenison is holding a letter of dismission from a church that has now ceased to exist and cannot be called to order thereby. Resolved, therefore, that we as an Association, declare our disapprobation to his unscriptural course; and we further say that we are not responsible for his course.[24]

Considering the *odium theologicum* between Missionary and Primitive Baptists, his brethren probably regarded Tennison's chumminess with "Soft-shell" Baptists as a far worse departure than his playing the bishop's role among the freedmen. However, the Harmony Association probably did not greatly regret finding a fatal flaw in the constitutions of the black churches. A black church, composed mainly of slaves, helped organize the Savannah Association in 1802.[25] During the postwar period, however, black churches seem to have been unwelcome in white Baptist associations, either Missionary or Primitive. In 1885, the Kehukee Association in North Carolina decided to "postpone indefinitely" the request for admission by the "Colored Primitive Baptist Church at Peter Swamp," "it being thought better, as in the cases of all the Primitive Baptist Associations in the United States, so far as known, for white and colored churches to be in separate Associations."[26] Of course, questions over the validity of a church's constitution have always elicited serious concern for Primitive Baptists. As noted in a previous chapter, the 1833 Ochlocknee Association refused Shiloh Church, in Ware County, Georgia, "on account of the illegality of her constitution."[27] The Suwannee Association declined to admit Sharon Church, Nassau County, Florida, in 1841 because of an unorthodox constitution.[28]

Tennison had held a preliminary conference with black preachers Solomon Jordan, Charles Smart, and Columbus McCombs at Gatewood Stand, Baker County, Georgia. There, they agreed to form a black Primitive Baptist association, Antioch, which when formally constituted at Guilfield Church, Macon, Georgia, in October 1870, consisted of twelve southwest Georgia churches.[29] This association adopted the decorum and articles of faith in common use among the other Georgia Primitive Baptists, except that the decorum made special provision for silencing disorderly ministers by means of a special conference under the supervision of the associational moderator. Antioch specifically forbade churches to use ministers thus defrocked. Displaying some of the closefistedness of their white counterparts, the black Primitives of the Antioch Association warned delegates from the churches to "provide themselves with money to return home, and not look for a distribution of the funds of the Association, for it will not be granted." Rapid associational growth occurred throughout the "Black Belt" of southwest Georgia, and there were forty-three churches with 1,510 members in 1879.[30] The Antioch Association, in turn, organized the black Union Association about 1880.[31] In 1891, the Union contained twenty-three churches with 947 members in southwest Georgia. Ritually and ideologically similar to their white counterparts, the members used Benjamin Lloyd's *Primitive Hymns* and "agreed to withdraw fellowship from Elder Jerry Holiday, for endorsing Sabbath Schools in his churches.[32] At some point between 1891 and 1905, Dinah Surmons's Pilgrim's Rest Church, rebuffed by the white Ochlocknee

Association, joined the black Union Association. Proud of their "orderly" constitution by three powerful white preachers, Pilgrim's Rest apparently did not find the black Union Association to its liking and called for a letter of dismission in 1906.[33] At some later time the church faded from existence. The black Union continued to grow across South Georgia. By 1925, it had churches in Decatur, Worth, Colquitt, Lowndes, Clinch, Mitchell, Grady, and Glynn counties, along with four churches among the black diaspora in Ohio and Pennsylvania. The 1925 minutes contain a "charity report," indicating a more organized approach to poor relief than among white Primitive Baptists.[34] Meanwhile, Elder Tennison satisfied his white brethren of his return to orthodoxy, and they forgave, though they never forgot, his Reconstruction rambles. On his death in 1883, the Ochlocknee Association damned him with the faint praise of having been "in his latter days . . . an orderly and consistent minister."[35] Hopewell, the white church of Elder Tennison's later membership, became extinct in 1990.[36] Ironically, Tennison's despised and irregular labors among the "colored people" constitute the most enduring fruits of his ministry.

The Harmony Association had the decency to offer what was from their point of view a reasonable excuse for not receiving the two black churches that had applied for membership in 1868. The Beulah Primitive Baptist Association of Florida in 1881 rejected a petition from "a colored church called Antioch" without any excuse or explanation whatever, despite their reputation at that time of being the most liberal body of Primitive Baptists in the region. A strong local tradition among both blacks and whites maintains that the Beulah Association helped organize the first black Primitive Baptist churches in the area.[37] However, no documented evidence supports this assertion.

The Tallahassee area developed a strong liberal black Primitive Baptist tradition during Reconstruction. The Florida Primitive Orthodox Zion Baptist Association, organized about 1870, grew to thirty-nine churches with 2,659 members in 1880. Its articles of faith were essentially the same as those of the white associations, but the presence of a "chief evangelist" and emphasis on the spread of the gospel and Sunday schools indicated a considerably different interpretation of them. The association encouraged "education, industry, self-reliance, general improvement, and especially spiritual elevation" among its members and emphasized that "color shall never form a bar to membership in this association, and that the fatherhood of God and the brotherhood of man are the two great truths in the Gospel of the Son of God that take precedence of all other truths in the Bible."[38]

Mystery shrouds the origins of this association. Supposedly, a white preacher, W. A. McDonald, and Henry MacDonald, a black preacher who had formerly belonged to McDonald's father, began preaching to the freedmen under a brush arbor near Tallahassee at the end of the war and later organized St. Mary's Primitive Baptist Church.[39] No preacher named McDonald appears in the minutes of the Ochlocknee Association, the only Primitive body in the region at that time. The phenomenal growth of this black association, together with its Missionary-style practices, suggest that it represented a secession of freedmen from the planter-dominated Southern Baptist churches of the Tallahassee area. Perhaps espousing the Antimissionary wing of the Baptist faith indicated a declaration of spiritual independence from the planter class, rather than real animosity to the Missionary ideology. The small, scattered antebellum Primitive Baptist churches of the Tallahassee area did not produce such a multitude from among their own ranks. On the other hand, Primitive determinism spoke to the insecurities of poor whites and may have exerted a similar pull among the freed slaves. Despite many Missionary trappings, the Primitive Baptists of this tradition remained officially committed to the doctrines of predestination and unconditional election. Recapitulating the history of the white Primitives, the Florida Orthodox Zion Association later suffered a schism over missions, Sunday schools, and conventions.[40]

Mt. Enon Association in South Florida suffered some unrest on the question of receiving black members into their churches. Isaac Berry, a black man, indicated interest in joining the church, whereupon Elders Andrew Kicklighter and J. M. Keen asserted that this would require eating at table and sharing beds with the black brother and would lay the groundwork for "social equality" and "amalgamation." The segregationists carried away three of the Mt. Enon Association's seven churches, but after the death of Kicklighter and Keen, all but a few members returned and confessed their error.[41] J. H. Purifoy, a visiting minister from Virginia, noted the long sequestration of the Jews as an encourgaging example of how one race lived alongside another without matrimonial entanglement. He further commented with a fine mixture of New South and predestinarian ideology: "There is no danger of social equality and amalgamation with the negro, and we can continue in the future to receive every regenerated one into *church* fellowship and *Christian* fellowship, without receiving them into *social* fellowship, or *matrimonial* fellowship. . . . God says, 'Ethiopia *shall* stretch forth her hand.' When God says a thing shall be done, the puny arm of man is too weak to prevent it."[42]

Reconstruction politics indirectly caused some upheavals in Primitive

Baptist churches. Piedmont Primitive Baptist Church, Decatur County, Georgia, found itself presented with a rare opportunity to express its opinion of Reconstruction politics. John Higdon, a member of the church, served in the 1868 Georgia Convention that drafted a constitution nullifying the Confederate debt, as required for the state's readmission to the Union. Piedmont Church construed his action a violation of his oath to uphold "that sacred instrument," the United States Constitution, since, in their view, it violated the provision against states enacting laws "impairing obligation of contract." As a result, "thousands of widows and orphans made by this late devastating war . . . are now left peneless and helpless being stripted of their just rights" and "left to the cold charities of the world." Higdon and his fellow conventioneers compounded their guilt in the eyes of the church by voting themselves compensation "at the exorbitant rates of $9 per day and 40 cts per mile." The church then cited a long catena of Scriptures denouncing injustice and oppression, adding that "many others might be referred to." Not surprisingly, the church voted unanimously to excommunicate Higdon.[43]

This uncompromising attitude toward financial obligation helps explain the church's violent reaction to another piece of Reconstruction legislation: the Georgia Homestead Law of 1868, permitting debtors to withhold a certain amount of property from their creditors. This enactment flew directly in the face of Primitive ideas of probity. Elder C. W. Stallings of Cat Creek Church, Lowndes County, Georgia, an invalid, once gave all he possessed to his creditors, depending entirely on providence for support for himself, his wife, and six young children.[44] The faith of some others gave out before that point, and as Primitive Baptists began to "ride the pony," or take advantage of the "bankrupt law," controversy erupted at one Primitive meeting after another.[45]

Bethlehem Church, near Quitman, Georgia, led the anti-homestead movement in the Ochlocknee Association. In January 1869, Bethlehem fired the opening shot by refusing to aid in the ordination of John Delk of Harmony Church "on account of his takeing the benefit of the homestead act for we believe it to be a transgression and unortherised by the scripture."[46] In response to a query from Harmony, Bethlehem further defined its position: "We as Primitive Baptist Church unanimously agree that we oppose the principle of the Homestead Act and we unfellowship a brother or sister who takes the benefit of the act until reclaimed."[47] In July 1869, the church adopted an anti-homestead resolution almost incoherent in its ferocity: "We agree to set up our standard concerning the Homestead that we invite no Minister of the Gospel to the priveledge of our pulpit that is a homesteader or that are living under the administration of a homesteader or that are living in the church with a homesteader or any member that is living with a homesteader in peace to seat with us or any that communes with a homesteader in peace knowingly until they are reclaimed."[48]

In October 1870, Bethlehem sent a query on the Homestead Act to the association, which sustained that church's strict view.[49] Bitterness and confusion reigned throughout the association to such an extent that Bethlehem held no communion meeting for two years.[50] The Union Association sustained the Ochlocknee's disapprobation of the Homestead Act, though in somewhat ambiguous terms.[51] Nonetheless, one of its churches, Wayfare in Echols County, Georgia, expelled a member for "taking the homestead" the same year.[52]

The Alabaha River Association suffered the most from the homestead controversy. In 1870, this association adopted the Western Georgia Upatoie Association's lengthy declaration against the Homestead Act. The Upatoie declaration recognized that the war had brought many members almost to destitution, but this did not authorize one to take advantage of the homestead law in order eventually to repay debts or to use one's creditors' money as if it were not theirs: "The law of God declares that the borrower is servant to the lender, but the Homestead law makes the lender servant to the borrower." If resorting to the homestead law with the intent of eventually repaying one's creditors was wrong, then of course to resort to it to escape obligations completely was very wrong. In either case, to Primitives, "riding the pony" was only legalized breach of contract. Homesteading betrayed a lack of confidence in divine providence and an unwillingness to shoulder the cross of suffering that fell to the lot of every Christian. The resolution concluded by exhorting churches to deal tenderly but firmly with homesteaders and to help brethren in debt as much as possible.[53]

Associational delegates reconsidered the act at their next meeting in 1871. The motion to repeal the anti-homestead resolution passed narrowly, with ten delegates voting for repeal and eight against. Seeing grave trouble ahead, the association suspended correspondence with other associations "for the present."[54] A special session of the association met in June 1872 and appointed a meeting with five churches dissenting from the homestead repeal. Representatives of the two parties met in August. The anti-homestead party behaved coldly toward the associational delegates, presenting letters of protest from their churches but refusing to elaborate on them or make any proposal for reconciliation. Consequently, the associational committee reported at the October 1872 Association that "they effected nothing satisfactory, but left matters rather worse than they found them." The Alabaha River then withdrew fellowship from the five dissident churches but appointed one more peace conference for January 1873, inviting both churches and concerned individuals to attend.[55] The five withdrawn churches offered a petition of reconciliation to the 1873 Association, but "inasmuch as the petition failed to give the cause of withdrawal but rather held forth impeachments for the Association's action," it did not achieve its end. Instead, the association dropped two more churches for "going off" with the five seceders. The same session commissioned two ministers to write an account of the division and a defense of the association's stance for publication in the *Primitive Baptist*.[56] Regrettably, all surviving files of that periodical lack most numbers from the 1870s, so it is impossible to know if the association's apologia ever saw print or what it contained. In any case, it neither healed the breach in the association nor attracted any support from former corresponding associations.

The homestead controversy generated considerable unrest among all the South Georgia Primitive Baptists, but the intensity of the conflict in the Alabaha River Association gained heat from the personal conflict between two prominent preachers, Reuben Crawford and Richard Bennett. Bennett championed the anti-homestead party and Crawford the opposing faction, and today, more than a century later, if one speaks of Primitive Baptists in southeastern Georgia, one must specify whether one refers to "Crawfordites" or "Bennettites."[57]

Born in Effingham County, Georgia, in 1801, Reuben Crawford later resided in McIntosh County, Georgia, where he served as second lieutenant in the militia in 1823.[58] He attended the 1835 session of the Piedmont Association as a delegate from Wesley Creek Church, McIntosh County. He began preaching by 1836, and in an unusual action, the association, rather than his home church, took charge of his ordination, appointing Moses Westberry, Sr., and his son, Moses Westberry, Jr., to perform the ceremony in November 1837.[59] Crawford's home church, Wesley Creek, joined in forming the Alabaha River Association in 1842, and Crawford attended every session after 1843. About 1845, he relocated in Pierce County, Georgia, joining Shiloh Church, where he remained a member and pastor until his death.[60] Elected moderator in 1846, he served in that capacity until the division of 1871 and continued to moderate the faction named after him until his death in 1887.[61] Although Crawford did not exhibit the longevity of Isham Peacock, he did retain a formidable vigor to the end of his life. He led Shiloh Church with a firm hand and single-handedly farmed his land at age eighty-eight.[62]

Less is known about Richard Bennett, Crawford's opponent. Born in 1825 in Appling County, Georgia, he served in the Confederate Army from 1862 to 1865 and was a company captain for about six months.[63] He is first mentioned

Elder Reuben Crawford, pastor, Shiloh Church, Pierce County, Ga. Circa 1888. Courtesy of Susie Crawford Thomas.

as an elder in the Alabaha River Association in 1869.[64] During the height of the controversy, he reportedly said that he had more fellowship for a horse than for Reuben Crawford. Tradition holds that Crawford foretold that Bennett would "die with his shoes on"—that is, commit suicide—which he did in 1898.[65] Bennett adopted a strict anti-homestead stance against Reuben Crawford. Crawford's son felt forced to take advantage of the Homestead Act, which led his father to oppose any harsh steps in connection with it.[66] Already isolated from much of its former correspondence by a doctrinal dispute to be considered later, the Crawford faction now found itself completely cut off from other Primitive Baptists. Several new churches soon joined the Alabaha River Association in northeast Florida, and in 1878, it dismissed four churches to form a new association, the St. Mary's River. Ironically, in 1911, the Crawfordites withdrew fellowship from their daughter association for some unspecified disorder. Although the Crawfordite Alabaha River Association still dutifully calls for correspondence each year, it has neither offered nor received any from any other group of Primitive Baptists for eighty-five years. Very conservative, these churches carried on most practices as in the time of "Uncle Reuben."[67]

The Bennett faction obtained recognition from other Primitive Baptists as the true Alabaha River Association. They declared the Crawfordites in disorder, and, while inviting them to return to unity, also called upon other Primitives not to receive any baptisms performed by them after the division. The Bennettites accused the Crawfordites of withdrawing from all other Primitive Baptists, "without reserve or explanation," an accusation not strictly true.[68] The Crawfordites responded to the Bennettite declaration in

1881, altering the official name of their association to "Original Constitution Alabaha."[69] The Original Constitution Alabaha River Association's 1884 circular address attacked their opponents as "using the Jew's language and carrying a form of Godliness, but denying the power thereof," comparing them to the Assyrians who besieged Jerusalem and calling into question the genuineness of their profession of religion. "They will claim that at a certain time they prayed to God; that at a certain time he showed them some glorious thing; that at a certain time they were most shamefully persecuted for Christ's sake, and some say I have been a Christian for ever so many years. One that is enabled to see with an eye of faith, and hears them make these declarations, are more fully convinced that they know nothing about the matter, than if they had heard them use the bitterest oaths."[70]

During the 1860s and 1870s, a number of new mutual aid societies became targets for church discipline. Apparently the longstanding Primitive opposition to secret societies underlay their suspicion of several new groups appearing during the post–Civil War era. In 1878, Cat Creek Church excommunicated a Brother Davis for joining the Grangers and ordered an account of their action published in the *Primitive Pathway,* a widely circulated Primitive Baptist periodical.[71] Wayfare Church, Echols County, Georgia, ruled in 1889 that "the Farmer's Alliance is not to be tolerated," and the Bennett Faction of the Alabaha River Association adopted a resolution against the alliance in the same year.[72]

Despite the divisiveness that attended the stresses of the Reconstruction era, some positive organizational advances took place. The Ochlocknee Association organized its western churches into a new association, the Flint River, with nine churches and 237 members.[73] The Ochlocknee also dismissed churches in the area of Taylor and Lafayette counties in Florida and organized them as the San Pedro Association.[74] This made the Ochlocknee the parent body of three other associations, five if one counts its "illegitimate" offspring, the Florida and Beulah. The Union and Alabaha River associations, organized from the Suwannee River, the Ochlocknee's first filiate body, made it a grandparent.

While conflict and reorganization occurred in the older settled regions, the Primitive faith spread with the frontier into southern Florida. Several Primitive Baptist families from South Georgia and northeastern Florida moved to the excellent cattle range west of Tampa after the Seminole War. In the wilderness they found abundant rough provisions, shared with the occasional bear or panther, but remained isolated from others of their faith for many years. The more methodical Methodists and Missionary Baptists evangelized the region, while these isolated Primitives, in the words of their historian E. I. Wiggins, "dwelt in the wilderness for twenty years tempted of the Devil through Missionarism." William Wiggins, one of the scattered Primitives and father of their chronicler, nourished his faith with the Bible and the *Signs of the Times*. Missionaries ill-advised enough to try and recruit him did "get their dose," as his son recorded, with Wiggins following them to the road and preaching at their backs as far as he supposed they could hear him.[75]

An elderly bachelor preacher from Alabama, James Mosley, felt impelled to travel south in 1865. Having no family and trusting to providence, he set out in an ancient spring carriage covered with raw deerskins. As he passed through South Georgia and northern Florida, the Primitives hospitably entertained him and invited him to settle. However, his impressions continued to lead him farther south, where he always found fewer of his coreligionists.[76] At length, he discovered the isolated group west of Tampa, who regarded his appearance as little less than a miracle. He preached his first sermon in a log chapel originally intended as a Missionary Baptist church. The Primitives and curious neighbors gathered for the services. The Old Baptists experienced such delight that "they could not behave themselves" but would exclaim aloud during the sermon. They presented Elder Mosley with a fresh horse and built a log meetinghouse for his use. He preached over a radius of some fifty miles from the Wiggins settlement, where he made his headquarters. Although no church could be constituted without a second ordained minister, the growing band of Primitives formed a "body" in 1865 to hear experiences and receive members, whom Mosley then baptized. Andrew Kicklighter, a Primitive minister from Bulloch County, Georgia, and later an opponent of black church membership, moved to the area in 1867, and he and Mosley organized Mt. Enon Primitive Baptist Church.[77] Three new churches soon developed in the area and in 1871 formed the Mt. Enon Association, assisted by a presbytery composed of Kicklighter, Joel Swain, and Isaac Coon, the latter from the Suwannee Association.[78]

→ 7 ←

"Contentions Among You"

The Crawfordites, Jackites, Battleites, and Coonites

All the mundane controversies of the Reconstruction era paled into insignificance before a ferocious series of doctrinal controversies that racked the Primitive Baptists during the 1860s and 1870s like ideological tornadoes, leaving slots of destruction behind them. Three of these controversies revolved around the role of the gospel in conversion and the style in which it should be preached. A fourth centered on the introduction of a form of the neo-Manichean "Two Seed" doctrine.

As already noted, the Primitive Baptists adhered strongly to a predestinarian theology. Nonetheless, they originally considered the gospel as the means by which God regenerated the elect, and they thought that preachers ought to address both saint and sinner. The 1689 London Confession, source of the Abstract of Principles used in South Georgia and Florida, taught that the "word and Spirit of God" raised sinners from spiritual death, though only at God's "appointed and accepted time." This confession of faith declared "elect infants dying in infancy" and "other elect persons, who are incapable of being outwardly called by the ministry of the word" to be regenerated by the Spirit alone.[1] At the 1833 Ochlocknee Association, the ministers appointed for the Sunday services preached "to the consolation of mourners, the establishment of saints, and the alarming of sinners."[2] As seen previously, Isham Peacock alarmed sinners into convulsions. The minutes of Union Church often speak of sermons as "alarming to poor careless sinners" and once as alarming to "poor dead sinners."[3] Several years after the Missionary division, the Suwannee River Association exhorted its ministers to "preach the word wherever you go, and whenever you can go; it is . . . for the consolation of his children, for the comforting of mourners and the alarming of sinners."[4] The *Primitive Hymns*, still in almost universal use among the conservative Primitive Baptists of the region, contains such appeals to the unconverted as:

To-day, if you will hear his voice,
Now is the time to make your choice,
Say, will you to Mount Zion go?
Say, will you have this Christ or no?[5]

In the 1700s, many Baptists and Independents questioned the "free offer" style of preaching implied above, as treated in chapter 1. John Gill, admired by Primitive Baptists as "perhaps the most learned, able, sound, upright, and humble Baptist minister since the days of Paul," strongly opposed the free offer.[6] Toward the end of his life, although considering the "ministry of the word" as "the vehicle in which the Spirit of God conveys himself and his grace into the hearts of men," Gill expressed doubts about its consistency with the rest of his High Calvinism. "Yet this instrumentality of the word in regeneration seems not so agreeable to the principle of grace implanted in the soul in regeneration . . . since that is done by an immediate infusion, and is represented as a creation and . . . as God made no use of any instrument in the first . . . creation, so neither does it seem so agreeable that he should use any in the new creation; wherefore this is rather to be understood of the exertion of the principle of grace, and the drawing forth into act and excercise; which is excited and encouraged by the ministry of the word."[7]

With the missions disputes raging, many Primitives adopted the opinion that regeneration is always the direct act of the Holy Spirit, independent of any instrumentality. The Pulaski Association, located immediately north of the Ochlocknee and Suwannee River associations, expressed the fast spreading opinion on instrumentality in its 1855 circular. "The Savior was far from teaching that the preaching of the gospel or any other labor of man was for the awakening of dead sinners. . . . The life giving power is of God, and of God alone. . . . How absurd then the idea of the preaching of the gospel being the ordinary and extraordinary means in the hands of God of giving life to sinners, it is closely allied to the great mammoth principle of missionism."[8] Although the great majority of Primitive Baptists nationwide adopted the anti-means view, some did not, and among them were several factions in South Georgia and Florida.[9]

The Alabaha River Association disliked the anti-means doctrine from its inception. In 1851, this association proclaimed the gospel the "means of salvation," and the 1852 session lamented dissension among Primitive Baptists "respecting the preaching of the gospel" and "falling out about the way and plan of salvation." Open rupture came in 1860, when Job E. W. Smith, moderator of the Suwannee River Association and soon to be infamous as an advocate of the Two Seed heresy, preached at the Alabaha River Association.

Stating the anti-instrumental doctrine in the baldest terms possible, Smith held up the Bible and said to the congregation, "You have been told that this is the word of God; do you believe it? I say it is not, it is ink and paper." Smith went on to declare that "the gospel had no saving efficacy in it to the awakening of sinners; it was only for the feeding of the flock." Scandalized, the Alabaha River declared Smith's doctrine a "departure from the faith" and dropped correspondence with the Suwannee River "until she becomes reclaimed."[10]

The Suwannee River Association responded by claiming that the "whole ministry stands impeached" by the Alabaha River. Their circular warned of "designing character[s] . . . who . . . have a great zeal for God, but not according to knowledge. These are generally engaged to alarm sinners. . . . By this you may know that it is not of God." The next session declared the salvation through "means" doctrine an "uncertain sound." "We must be made fit subjects before their [*sic*] can be any preparation" for salvation. Finally, in 1869, the Suwannee River Association declared baptism administered by the Alabaha River Association invalid due to differing faith. Isaac Coon, later a Two-Seeder, wrote an extensive circular on the means controversy. "Until [a] child is born . . . it cannot be fed, but when it is born, we feed it, not to make it a child, but to save it, preserve it and make it grow . . . but the food given . . . will not produce . . . the birth." The gospel, said Coon, "saves a believer from all the bogs, dens, swamps, breakers, quick-sands and damnable delusions of false teachers."[11]

Suwannee River's daughter association, the Union, remained in correspondence with the Alabaha River and experienced considerable dissension over the point at issue between the Alabaha River and the Suwannee River associations. Union besought the Alabaha River to negotiate with the Suwannee River, but the offended association thought such heretics unworthy of further admonition. Alabaha River churches dropped correspondence with the Union Association in 1864 because it continued to correspond with the heretical Suwannee River, and in 1865 these churches banned communion with members of either association.[12] After the Crawford-Bennett division in 1871, doctrinal differences assumed a prominent place in the polemics of the Crawfordite faction of the Alabaha River Association. Their 1884 minutes denounced those who had "a form of Godliness, but [denied] the power thereof saying, that the gospel of our Christ, the right arm of God, has no power in it to raise the dead, it can only feed the living after they have been raised by some other power."[13] Free offer preaching remained strong among the Crawfordites. Elder Owen Gibson, ordained in 1898, expressed continued adherence to the doctrine in a poem:

Ye poor careless sinners come hither I pray,
Your souls are exposed and destruction is near,
The way of salvation is offered today,
Take warning from me if the word you will hear.[14]

Recently, I attended a Crawfordite church where the pastor prayed that his hearers might be blessed to "flee from the wrath to come before it is too late," language not used by other Primitives.

Some Primitives went far beyond the Alabaha River in their concern for poor careless sinners. The association dropped John Vickers and a majority of Hebron Church, Coffee County, Georgia, in 1866, on charges of "immorality and heresy." In 1868, the association dropped the minority at Hebron because they continued to interact with Vickers, "who has departed from our faith and advances unscriptural and false doctrine."[15] Pleasant Church, in 1869, dropped correspondence with Brushy Creek Church of Irwin County and with Emmaus and Turner's Meetinghouse churches of Berrien County, all three in Georgia, when they allowed "the faith of the Primitive Baptists as published in the minutes of the Union Association" to be "attacked and publicly denied from the pulpit."[16] The Union Association dropped Emmaus later the same year for the "false or Armenian doctrine" advanced by their pastor, Elder Jacob Young. In later years, this faction became locally known as the "Youngites."[17] The neighboring Pulaski Association also dropped Brushy Creek and Emmaus churches, but not before the Alabaha River Association dropped them "because they sustain a law doctrine among them."[18]

In 1875, Brushy Creek, Emmaus, and Hebron met in a convention that withdrew fellowship from all holding "Calvanistic and Mahometan" fatality and all who held "law salvation." John Vickers defended the convention's action in a tract entitled *An Explanation of the Split between the Hardshell Baptists and the Primitive Baptists*. Vickers argued that election means choice and choice must be made on the basis of distinction. The only distinction among men is that between believers and unbelievers, therefore election is conditional upon foreseen faith in the believer. Vickers seemed blissfully unaware that he stated the classic Arminian theory of election. He roundly condemned other churches as "false" societies and disparaged their "do and live" system. He claimed that all the Primitive Baptists originally believed his theory of election and lamented that "Hardshell" fatalists did great harm to "poor carelesss sinners" by not encouraging them to repent. In spite of his Arminian leanings, Vickers maintained that faith came only through divine gift and that only divine revelation enabled one to believe his doctrine.[19]

The Youngites established a brief contact with other dissident Primitives. Elder J. R. Battle of the Beulah Association, to be considered later, visited Emmaus in 1876, and he and Elder Jacob Young ordained John Vickers and D. N. McMillan to the ministry. Battle favored receiving Missionary Baptists without rebaptism, and in 1878, Emmaus initially received Susan Parr from the Missionaries without rebaptism. Opposition immediately developed and she suddenly discovered a desire to receive Primitive baptism, defusing a potentially volatile situation. Emmaus flirted with Missionism on one other occasion. In 1883, David G. Mathis withdrew from Ramah Church, Clinch County, Georgia, over doctrinal differences and joined nearby Bethel Missionary Baptist Church. Four months later he appeared in the pulpit at Emmaus.[20]

The Youngites soon developed fissures of their own. Vickers served Emmaus as pastor from 1877 to 1880, when a coolness developed between Vickers's Hebron and the Youngites. Emmaus and the Youngites dropped Vickers and Hebron in 1881 for having in some way "incurred the displeasure of the church." The Youngites soon returned to a more conservative position. Emmaus declared the "convention's" acts "null and void" in 1884.[21] The Youngites remained in discouraged isolation for many years; the late Deacon W. H. Paulk of Ocilla (1880–1980) had a childhood memory of his father lamenting their lean condition to an old Sister "Pug" Whitley, who serenely replied that God remained able to raise up children to Abraham from stones. Soon afterward several young preachers appeared among them and several new churches developed.[22] In 1891, the Youngites organized the Brushy Creek Union, an association still in existence today.[23]

Hebron remained in isolation for several years until a new church joined it in organizing the Satilla Primitive Baptist Association in 1889. "Vickersite" being a rather cumbersome term, the locals saddled John "Jack" Vickers's party with the unlovely cognomen "Jackites."[24] The Jackites damned "fatalism and two-seedism" at every opportunity and eventually permitted Sunday schools in their churches, provided that these operated as "moral" and not "religious" institutions.[25] The Jackites—never numerous, and Primitive in nothing but name—survived into the present century, when they became an Independent Baptist body.[26]

Another group, uncomfortable with the strong predestinarian positions dominating the Primitives, appeared in the Ochlocknee Association. The Ochlocknee Association dropped Elder J. R. Battle and Elam Church, Brooks County, Georgia, and Mt. Zion Church, Jefferson County, Florida, in 1872, for wishing to receive Missionary Baptists without rebaptism. The association dropped several more churches for the same cause in 1874. Most of the additional churches were in the Tallahassee area, a region of longstanding Missionary influence.[27] Elder T. W. Stallings expressed the majority Primitive Baptist opinion when he argued that "if the Baptism of the Missionary Baptists is valid, so is their doctrine; and if God does not direct their preaching, he does not direct their baptism."[28]

Eight churches met with Beulah Church, Wakulla County, Florida, in 1874 and organized the Beulah Primitive Baptist Association, protesting that they claimed "no disbelief in the long established doctrines of the old Baptists." They organized for the sole purpose of supporting Mt. Zion and Elam churches, as they thought these churches unjustly charged with "departing from the faith of God's elect." They denounced the Ochlocknee Association's action as "unjustified by FACTS, Associational Constitution, or Scripture." The 1875 Beulah Association, however, did significantly depart from the "doctrines of the old Baptists," at least since the Missionary division. It resolved that the churches should receive Missionary Baptists since "Christ has accepted their baptism, sealing it in their hearts by his spirit." The Beulah Association revealed that doctrinal concerns formed the principal motivation for their stance. Primitive Baptist emphasis on divine sovereignty left them "overwhelmed in a theme so vast" and "may have closed our eyes and ears to the calls or claims of the outer world, and we fear that some of our people have, in this direction, wandered far from original faith and preaching." Missionaries and Primitives had both erred in going "in almost opposite directions since our separation." "But they are all our brethren still, and we love them, and though covered with fratricidal blood, we pray for them and for peace." However, since "to join either of the contestants would but kindle afresh the intestine strife," the Beulah Association chose to remain neutral and refused an offer of correspondence from the Mercer Missionary Baptist Association in South Georgia.[29]

Beulah adopted even more Missionary practices despite its claim to neutrality. The twelfth session, in 1885, invited to seats with the delegates G. W. Hall, Florida Missionary State Evangelist, J. B. Foster of the American Sunday School Union, and E. Trice of the Florida Association. It recognized several other ministers from the Florida Association and sang "Blest Be the Tie That Binds," while giving them the right hand of fellowship. Also, it exchanged official correspondence with the Florida Association, "without making any concessions nor asking any," and would have offered correspondence to the Ochlocknee "if we had any reason to believe it would be accepted." The Beulah Association also recommended prayer meetings and Sabbath schools to its churches and encouraged more preaching, "for it is the power of God to every one that believeth." It profited from its new measures.

From 220 members in eight churches in 1875, it grew to 356 members in the same number of churches in 1885.[30]

This love feast of reconciliation did not last. Elam Church and J. R. Battle took advantage of the thaw in the mid-1880s to move from the Beulah Association to the Mercer Missionary Association. Soon, Battle preached the Missionary sermon for that body, causing its historian, Robert Harris, to rhapsodize almost into incoherence.[31] Old Baptist isolationism remained alive in the Mt. Zion Church, which requested the 1887 Association to stop correspondence with "all other bodies . . . for the peace of our own body." The delegates voted to discontinue official connection with other associations and congratulated themselves for escaping from their "terrible dilemma."[32] The association later engaged in considerable evangelism in the Florida Panhandle and organized the West Florida Primitive Baptist Association there in 1901.[33]

The Crawfordite, Jackite, and Battleite controversies centered around concern over evangelical outreach. The "Coonite" doctrine represented the opposite extreme in Baptist thinking. Emerging during the doctrinal ferment that troubled the Primitive Baptists of South Georgia and Florida during the 1860s and 1870s, it represented the manifestation in that region of the widespread Two Seed doctrine, the most extreme theoretical justification for the Antimissionary position. Elder Daniel Parker, in many ways the very archetype of a frontier Baptist preacher, and the "archenemy of missions on the frontier," popularized the doctrine.[34] Born in Virginia in 1781, he moved with his parents to Georgia when a small child. Like many of his contemporaries in the Baptist ministry, he boasted of his rough ways and limited education."[35]

Ironically, Parker at first was "wonderfully pleased" at the idea of missions. However, when he "compared it with the Lord's way of doing business . . . I was sorry to find that they did not fit or work together." Although Parker kept quiet about his views, he concurred when his association decisively repudiated the missionary program. The next year Luther Rice himself attended Parker's association to promote the cause of missions, and Parker came out publicly against the new measures for the first time.[36]

In 1817, Parker moved to the "Wabash country" of southern Illinois, having found good land and Missionary Baptists and Campbellites to fight. He found the Wabash District Association in a ferment over missions and Isaac McCoy, a prominent pioneer preacher, firmly advocating the new measures. In opposition, he published his first tract, *Address to the Baptist Society,* in 1820. "Although . . . not much in favor of religious periodicals," he recognized their usefulness to the Missionaries and started his own paper, the

Church Advocate, in opposition. His campaign against the Missionaries in southern Illinois and adjacent areas lasted until his emigration to Texas in 1833.[37]

Parker's most distinctive contribution to Baptist history was his popularization of the Two Seed doctrine. Although he claimed he had not "received these principles from man, that makes me an old predestinarian Baptist," he admitted that his most important concept had come to him about 1810 in "a few remarks by an Old Brother." Parker at first rejected the doctrine as heretical and "sharply reproved" the man. Over several years, however, he continued to meditate upon it and reluctantly became convinced that it was the truth. Finally, he began to see the "beauty," "glory," and "God-honouring" nature of the doctrine. With some trepidation, he finally published it in 1826 in a tract entitled *The Doctrine of the Two Seeds.* He later published *A Second Dose of Doctrine on the Two Seeds,* a book of some two hundred pages. The *Church Advocate* also published much of his Two Seed material.[38]

The Two Seed doctrine was essentially an extended and extremely literal commentary on Genesis 3:15–16 and Matthew 13:24–30, 36–43. Other frontier Baptists shared Parker's concern with mysteries from before the foundation of the world. Wilson Thompson, a pioneer preacher in Missouri, recalled his concern with similar points as early as 1812. "My mind was working hard on the doctrine of the union of Christ and His people *before faith.* The preaching I had heard was that God's people became united to Christ by a living faith; but I saw things differently, for I conceived that such an union was indispensable to the legal imputation of our sins to Christ and of His righteousness to us, and that, too, before faith could act upon . . . that mystical union."[39]

Parker interpreted the seed of the woman and the good seed in the texts mentioned as Christ and his members—that is, the elect—and the seed of the serpent as Satan and the souls belonging to him. "Christ and the church are but one seed, and . . . the serpent and the many members composing his body of sin and death are but one seed." Just as the preexisting Christ took upon himself a human body, so the preexisting "seeds," or souls, of Christ and the Serpent are incarnated in human bodies. God provided the bodies for the seed of the serpent when he "multiplied" Eve's "conception," that is, increased her potential offspring. Parker's most startling departure from orthodoxy lay in his revival of Manichean dualism. He asserted the "certainty and self existence of the power of darkness, without which the divine properties of Deity could not be displayed to the glory of God." Satan thus being an outside interloper in God's affairs, He trapped him in the form of his "seed" in human bodies, to punish him for his "rebellion against the rights and government of heaven." According to Parker, Satan "has got into the creation of God . . . and thereby sowed his seed in the soil of nature, which seed being of their father the Devil, is still manifesting the nature of the serpent against God and his children, for which the glory and justice of God will appear in executing his fierce wrath on them as punishment due to the serpent." The presence of the seed of the Serpent in humanity has so corrupted it that "God's family, while unconverted, are by nature the children of wrath, even as others."[40]

Parker anticipated Gregor Mendel with a crude "genetic" theory of salvation. He believed that Israel inherited the good seed, hence the restrictions placed on intermarriage with other people. Through intermarriage with the Gentiles, the Devil's seed got among the Jews, making them "ripe" for "overthrow," and incidentally spreading the good seed among the Gentile nations, preparing the way for their eventual conversion.[41]

Many later Two-Seeders denied a bodily resurrection and eternal punishment. Parker strongly contended for both. He emphasized that the "serpent's seed" did not merely "consist . . . of the wicked nature in man," for in that case "nothing but wicked nature will be burned, and no existing mortals or human beings will suffer the wrath of God forever, and of course the Universalian doctrine is correct." He considered the "tares" (Devil's seed) accountable to God because he had created and sustained their earthly bodies. He even considered them fit objects of gospel address and that repentance and faith should be preached to them. "If they will repent of their sins, believe the gospel, come to, and obey Christ, God will save them. God has appointed no man to eternal destruction, but upon his wickedness." Of course, being direct descendants of the Devil, they do not possess the nature or the grace to repent. Unlike his spiritual descendants, the Coonites, Parker believed in a literal bodily resurrection of the tares, who would be raised "by a display of divine power, something like a curse on them."[42]

While Parker's opposition to missions had numerous supporters, many of the Antimissionary party shared his own initial skepticism about the Two Seed doctrine. He expected opposition from the Missionaries, whose schemes originated with the Devil's seed, but he also admitted that "the first view of the doctrine" had "alarmed" even the "saints." Nonetheless, he almost claimed the prophetic mantle for himself for revealing the true basis of Baptist doctrine. "God's ministers have long been engaged in proclaiming the gospel of Christ, and contending for the necessity of salvation, and that it required the power of God to save. And just as far as this has been done, the doctrine of the two seeds has been employed, or expressed in every gospel sermon, though the preacher himself might not have understood it."

But until Parker came on the scene, "one part of the bible has, as yet, lain silent as a sealed book."[43]

The Two Seed doctrine eventually gave rise to divisions among the Baptists and the formation of separate churches and associations. Although Two-Seeders occurred in some areas where Daniel Parker never preached, most of their associations are like the footprints of his ministry, with their greatest numbers in Tennessee, Illinois, and Texas.[44] Other Two Seed groups seem to have been in contact with the original centers.

The doctrine underwent considerable development during the mid-1800s. A national controversy among Primitive Baptists centered around a milder form of the doctrine espoused by Gilbert Beebe, Samuel Trott, and others. This movement denied the eternal self-subsistence of the Devil and also had Arian tendencies. Controversy over these issues smoldered through the middle years of the nineteenth century and finally died out in the 1880s with the death of the original agitators, Trott, Beebe, and John Clark.[45] There seems to have been little of the Arian controversy in South Georgia and Florida. The only possible indication of it lies in the dropping of the term "persons" from the article of faith on the being of God and the trinity. This occurred in all the associations by 1870. The Primitive Baptists in that area have usually shown a laudable reticence concerning trinitarian mysteries.

Two-Seedism developed in a radical direction in many areas in the generation after Parker. By the 1840s, according to Tennessee Primitive Baptist elder Hosea Preslar, Two-Seeders contended that the gospel was for the elect only, and more important, they now denied the bodily resurrection of either the elect or nonelect. They even expressed doubts as to whether Christ himself actually rose from the dead with the same physical body he had possessed before the crucifixion.[46]

In North Georgia during the late 1850s, Elder Gregg M. Thompson, Wilson Thompson's son, waged war with Missionary Baptist and "Arian Two-Seeder" alike. One suspects that Elder Thompson defined as an Arian Two-Seeder any Primitive Baptist who disagreed with him. Some of his charges were extreme and the men he assailed were often highly respected. However, he offered direct quotations from his opponents' published works, which seem to indicate that their views were indeed unorthodox. Thompson considered the Arian Two-Seeders perhaps the most numerous faction of Primitive Baptists in his time. He admitted that most of them did not believe in an eternal devil, as Daniel Parker had. However, they exceeded Parker in heresy by denying both the bodily resurrection and eternal punishment. Thompson quotes Elder William Mitchell of Alabama as saying that "when the transgressor dies, he has paid the penalty, and that is the end of him." He quotes another spokesman for the group as saying, "These bodies are only adapted as a temporary residence for the Spiritual man to dwell in, and when the spiritual man leaves it, God will have no further use for it; that it will return to the earth, and be destroyed with the earth." Thompson wrote: "I know of none of them in Georgia but what teach that 'the Adam man, soul body, and spirit, dies, and sinks down into the grave.'"[47] Daniel Parker, who loved a whiff of brimstone as well as any Methodist or Missionary Baptist, would have been horrified at such a conclusion drawn from his doctrine, although it is by no means an illogical deduction.

In 1869, Elder Lemuel Potter encountered the mature form of the non-resurrection aspect of the Two Seed doctrine in Daniel Parker country in southern Illinois. An elderly preacher named William Trainer believed that nothing "would ever go to heaven that did not first come down from heaven." Trainer once explained his belief to Potter: "He said he believed there were three generations of people. The generation of Adam, the generation of Jesus Christ, and the generation of vipers. The generation of Adam were made of the dust of the ground, and would go back to the dust where they came from, and remain there forever. The generation of Jesus Christ came down from heaven, took up their abode in the Adam man, and they would finally go back to heaven where they came from. The generation of vipers came from hell, and they also took up their abode in the Adam man, and would go back to hell where they came from." Potter distinguished this nonresurrection doctrine from Two-Seedism proper. Of the latter he wrote, "When I first joined the church and began to preach, there was a great deal said about the Two Seed doctrine, and the most of our preachers of Southern Illinois believed it." Potter also assented to it as a young man, but when "I finally began to study the matter for myself . . . I soon became satisfied that if it was the Baptist doctrine I did not believe it." Potter recognized clearly, however, that Two-Seedism tended toward nonresurrectionism. "If a man admits the doctrine of eternal children, he may as well admit the doctrine of non-resurrection."[48]

The first indication of this complex of ideas in the region of this study surfaced in 1843. Bethel Primitive Baptist Church in South Georgia accused Elder Job Elbert Wilder Smith of believing the body of Christ to be "spiritual" and not "of the seed of the woman." The church went on record as believing that the "suffering body of Christ . . . was made . . . of the Virgin Mary," and that Smith's doctrine constituted a bar to communion. When a group of three elders summoned by the church condemned his views, Smith recanted in somewhat ambiguous terms.[49] In 1845, he moved his church membership to a church in the Suwannee River Association.[50] He remained in that association until the Coonite schism in 1875. Smith pastored many churches and served for many years as moderator of the association.[51] At least one of his churches expressed their confidence in his judgment by granting him authority to take part in ordinations and church constitutions without obtaining the previous consent of the church.[52] Primitive Baptist churches seldom granted such unlimited commissions. Smith's brush with Bethel Church is the first documented appearance in the region of a type of doctrine later associated with "Coonism," but as far as the surviving records show, Smith held his peace for many years. A doctrine similar to Smith's heresy had been disseminated in southern Alabama in the late 1820s by William McKee of the Cahaba Association. "McKeeism" consisted of the belief that "the body of Christ existed anterior to the creation of man, and was not at all, a human body, but a spiritual one. . . . While he possessed flesh and blood, it was spiritual flesh and blood." James H. Wells of the Bethel Association of Alabama wrote a book in support of this doctrine, which also gained support from Willis Whately of the Bethlehem Association in Alabama.[53] Considering that these preachers were active in adjacent parts of Alabama during the period immediately before Smith's entry into the ministry, it seems quite likely that he derived his ideas from the "McKeeites." Their ideas, in turn, seem obviously related to those of the Two-Seeders of Tennessee as described by Preslar. Lemuel Potter encountered in southern Illinois an Elder G. W. Paine who preached the same thing, although not identified with the Two-Seeders.[54]

Isaac Smith Coon, whose name became synonymous with Two-Seedism in South Georgia and Florida, apparently united with Bethany Primitive Baptist Church, Bradford County, Florida, about 1869. He attended the 1869 Suwannee River Association as a delegate and a licensed preacher and presented a circular address condemning the "gospel means" doctrine of the Alabaha River Association. The association elected him clerk, a position which, at least with his own faction, he held for life.[55]

Coon was not a typical Primitive Baptist. Born in Florida in 1836, he graduated from Ogelthorpe Medical College, Savannah, Georgia, in 1859 and began a lifelong career as a doctor.[56] In 1861, he represented New River County, Florida, at the secession convention. There, he made no important motions, but he seems to have viewed secession with alarm and voted for every proposed delay and postponement. He finally voted with the majority on the last day of the convention.[57] He served as a surgeon in the Second Battalion of the Florida Infantry, but apparently not for the duration of the war, as he was Bradford County judge in 1862–63.[58] Coon had a host of friends and was known for his charity. In addition to bringing up eleven children of his own, he took in several orphaned children.[59] J. E. W. Smith may have introduced Coon to the Two Seed doctrine, but references in a letter from Harmony Church, Brooks County, Georgia, to Antioch Church, Thomas County, claims that Coon's theology originated from a pamphlet written by one Mathis, the "doctrin" of which was "advocated by Elder Coon." There appears to have been no minister named Mathis among the local Primitive Baptists at that time, but an Elder G. W. "Mathes," identified as being "of Texas," preached at the 1887 New Hope Association in Illinois, the first Two Seed association the Coonites approached for correspondence.[60] Coon himself proposed New Hope as a possible corresponding association, indicating that he had probably had previous contact with them.[61]

Whatever its exact origins, the first appearance and progress of Coonism are well documented, mainly by the Coonites themselves. In 1871, an Elder Hodges declared in a sermon at a general meeting of the Suwannee River Association that "part of the sacrifice for sins [i.e., Christ's physical body, which suffered and died] came from Adam." J. E. W. Smith, a senior minister and moderator of the association, reproved Hodges with the support of Coon and Elder John M. Mott. Elder Andrew G. Connell also soon came around to their views. The controversy simmered until 1875, when Elder Jeremiah B. Smith, J. E. W. Smith's twin brother and fellow minister, refused to visit Hebron, his brother's and Connell's home church, on account of their heretical opinions.[62]

Into this tense situation intruded Elder Timothy Stallings, pastor of Wayfare Church, located a few miles inside Georgia and belonging to the Union Association. J. E. W. Smith and Andrew Connell, although members of a church in Florida, lived in the neighborhood of Wayfare and seem to have become well known to Stallings.[63] Elder Stallings's combative and unhappy temperament caused him to treat his long ministry as basically the Civil War continued on other fields. Stallings managed to figure in every major controversy within his reach, and his mercurial temperament often made a bad situation worse.

In the early stages of the controversy, Stallings supposedly expressed great friendship for Coon and supported his party.[64] Suddenly, as was his wont, Stallings reversed himself, called a special conference at Wayfare in July 1875, and demanded that a council be called from other churches to investigate doctrinal deviations there. The council met in October and declared that "in our judgement . . . they have erred from what we believe . . . to be sound doctrin." Wayfare expelled six members for heresy concerning the resurrection and last judgment.[65]

Not content with cleaning his own house, Stallings visited the 1875 Suwannee River Association and debated Coon on the disputed doctrines, and then left the grounds with the delegates of three churches.[66] Early in 1876, Hebron Church expelled Andrew G. Connell, J. E. W. Smith, and four others.[67] In the same year the Union and Ochlocknee associations dropped fellowship with the Suwannee River on account of Coonism.[68]

The controversy spread to the Ochlocknee Association, where Bethlehem Church, Brooks County, dropped Elder William Smith, Deacon A. M. D. Simpson, and eight others as "unsound in faith and sustaining this new doctrin that has divided us," identified in one place as the "Coon principle."[69] At the same time, Harmony and Antioch churches entered into a controversy over Elder Allison Dekle, sometime moderator of the association and then a member at Antioch and serving as pastor at Harmony. Harmony dismissed him for "endorsing the Mathis Doctrin advocated by Elder Coon." After a council meeting in which Dekle equivocated masterfully, Harmony continued him as their pastor; but they soon accused him of still maintaining heresy.[70] They dropped him as pastor and expelled twelve of his followers.[71] The 1876 Ochlocknee Association dropped Antioch along with Mt. Zion Church of Thomas County, Georgia, and Mt. Moriah Church, Nancy Hagan's old foes, "for advocating the two seed doctrine, as held by one Mathis."[72] After equivocating for some time, Mt. Moriah, Antioch, and part of Mt. Zion returned to the Ochlocknee Association in 1879, Antioch having declared the "Coon doctrin" to be "grose heresee."[73] Allison Dekle disappeared from all records by 1880.

Coon seems to have been the originator of the doctrinal dispute in the Ochlocknee Association. However, another prominent figure in that association may have opened the way for the doctrine. Gregg Thompson denounced Elder Haley G. Fuller as "a prominent member of this sect in Georgia." He quoted Fuller as saying that "all the human family are nothing but Adam in a state of multiplication, or expansion: and the church, or elect of God, are nothing but Christ in a state of multiplication or expansion." Fuller joined Bethsaida Church in the Ochlocknee Association by late 1865, perhaps a refugee from war-torn northern Georgia.[74] He soon moved his membership to Harmony Church and remained there for the rest of his life.[75] He served as clerk of the Ochlocknee Association from 1868 until his death.[76] Although he may have played a role in predisposing some to accept the radical Two-Seedism of Isaac Coon, Fuller himself died in February 1875, in full fellowship with the church, his orthodoxy unquestioned. His obituary in the Harmony minutes called him "a bold and fearless defender of the doctrine of Christ and his apostles; uncompromising in the last degree touching the doctrines of grace which caused him to have some enemies."[77]

Only three of its original churches sent delegates to the 1876 Suwannee River Association presided over by Elders Smith and Coon, and one of them dropped out the next year. On the credit side, four tiny churches joined. The expelled members of Wayfare Church formed Pilgrim's Rest Church in Clinch County. Members expelled from the Ochlocknee Association formed Sarepta and Primrose churches in Brooks County, Georgia. The handful excluded from Hebron formed Mars Hill Church, Hamilton County, Florida. Only Cedar Creek Church in Baker County and Bethany Church in Bradford County, both in Florida, adhered as a body to the Coon faction. By 1880, Sarepta had ceased to report to the association, but in that year Mt. Zion of Thomas County, Georgia, joined, being made up of those members of that church who continued to hold Coonite principles and did not return to the Ochlocknee Association. Bethlehem Church in Baker County, Florida, which had been consolidated with Cedar Creek, "went back to keep house" in 1876. The early Coonites suffered no lack of preachers, having five to serve seven churches, a very good ratio among Primitive Baptists.[78] The anti-Coon churches of the association reorganized themselves as the Suwannee River Predestinarian Baptist Association. They obtained the recognition of the neighboring associations as the orthodox body and in 1877 had nine churches, with 227 members compared to the Coon faction's seven churches and 114 members.[79] Their faithful being scattered, as well as few in number, the Coonites lamented in their 1881 minutes: "The extremes of this association are now 150 miles apart."

Once free of their orthodox critics, the Coonite branch of the Suwannee River Association condemned the "natural construction" their opponents placed on the Scriptures and the articles of faith.[80] The old associational articles plainly asserted eternal damnation and the resurrection of the dead, so in 1877, the Coonites declared that "their language do not convey the doctrine as taught in scripture, and they also admit of two constructions." They were replaced by one article: "We believe that the Scriptures of the Old and New Testaments are all given by inspiration of God, and contain all things necessary to a perfect rule of Doctrine, Faith and Practice to the Christian." At the same time they repudiated as invalid all baptisms performed by "so-called Primitive Baptist Churches differing from us."[81]

The Coonites faced a major problem not only in being isolated from one another other but also in being far from others of their faith. The nearest Two Seed association, Lookout Mountain Primitive Baptist Association, was located in extreme northwestern Georgia and northeastern Alabama.[82] The Coonites immediately petitioned the New Hope Association of Illinois for correspondence and, in 1877, received a visit from Elder E. D. "Herod" of that body, one of the few actual visits they ever received from their distant coreligionists.[83] Lemuel Potter knew "Herod," actually Hearde. They debated in 1873, when Hearde was in his sixties. Potter called him a "very shrewd man. . . . His advantages as to education, perhaps were limited."[84] Usually, Two Seed associations only mailed their minutes. The Coonite Suwannee River eventually corresponded with associations in Tennessee, Kentucky, Illinois, Indiana, Arkansas, and Texas. The Caney Fork and Richland Creek associations in Tennessee corresponded the most regularly and, after 1900, occasionally sent messengers as well as minutes.[85] Most of their corresponding associations were small also, but sometimes larger than they were. In 1911, the Caney Fork had 133 members in nine churches, while the Coonites had thirty-six in five churches.[86]

From their inception as a separate body, the Coonites dwindled steadily. From a total membership of 114 in 1877, they declined to seventy-five in 1890 and thirty in 1916. After the latter year, they apparently decided not to expose the weakness of their cause to a mocking world by publishing a statistical table with their minutes. They soon began to lose their original leadership, most of whom were elderly at the inception of their movement. Elder William Smith died in 1881. In the same year they lost their moderator, Elder J. E. W. Smith, to whom they paid this tribute: "No man in South Georgia ever made more sacrifice or manifested more energy in the cause of Christ than did Job Elbert Wilder Smith, and though most of his time he was assaulted by persecution; but he stood as a firm pillow [pillar] in [that] building of new timbers, never willing to compromise on anything short of what he believed to be Bible truth." The two Smiths were followed in 1884 by Andrew G. Connell, who had served as moderator since Smith's death. Then, in 1891, Isaac Coon and J. M. Mott both died, the latter having served as moderator since Connell's death.[87]

Isaac Coon's death marked an epoch in the history of the people named after him. Although he had never held any associational office except that of clerk, Coon had served as the ideologue of the movement, always able to express their doctrines as clearly as their nature permitted. The circular addresses after his death were weak rehashes of his writings. The association mourned him and Mott as "probably the brightest lights in this association," who "in the dark days of 1876–7 . . . fought the battles."[88]

In the 1890s, the association began to lose churches as well as members. In 1895, Bethlehem ceased to meet. In 1898, the association dropped Mt. Zion for "disorder and unchristian conduct." In 1911, Pilgrim's Rest folded, having declined to only two members. In 1919, the minutes declare Mars Hill "in disorder." The minutes grew ever shorter and more cheaply printed. In 1919, the association agreed to discontinue the printing of circular addresses. The last one, however, true to form, criticized belief in a literal resurrection and last judgment as "the devil's scarecrow."[89] The remaining three churches, Primrose, Bethany, and Cedar Creek, held two more associational meetings, but after 1921, the only surviving Coonite church minutes, those of Cedar Creek, show no further associational meetings.[90] The Richland Creek Association heard nothing further from the Coonites after 1920.[91] In 1923, Primrose Church sold some property, an act which likely marked the end of services there.[92]

Scarcity of members gave Coonite laymen and women opportunities they seldom enjoyed in other Primitive Baptist groups.[93] Women served as delegates to the association and in several instances as church clerks.[94] One layman, John F. Smith, son of Elder J. E. W. Smith, even served as moderator of the association.[95]

There seem to have been no black members in these churches. Black membership in white Primitive Baptist churches in the region was never large and declined after the Civil War. However, since minutes of only one Coonite church, Cedar Creek, still survive, there may have been a few black members, but if so they never appear on the associational level. As the benches emptied, so did the pulpit. Although the Coonites ordained six preachers after the division of 1875, only three remained in 1900, and after 1909, only Elder Matthew O. Touchstone remained, serving as pastor of the remaining churches and moderator of the association.[96]

Church decline mirrored that of the association. Cedar Creek Church, organized in 1851, had eighty-three members in 1864, and twenty-one in 1876. Its steady shrinkage thereafter matched that of the association as a whole. In 1890, twelve members remained, declining to six in 1899. In 1901, the last male member left. During the entire Coonite period, only ten people were baptized by Cedar Creek Church.[97] Conferences became more and more intermittent. The church met only twice in 1905, and after 1909, M. O. Touchstone attended the church once a year to hold conference and communion. In 1923–24, no meetings at all occurred. As far as can be determined from the minutes, two women made up the entire membership in the last several years of the church. After 1936, Cedar Creek never met again, and as far as available records show, the Coonite movement came to an end.[98]

Coonite relations with other denominations, especially the orthodox Primitive Baptists, displayed the usual bitterness and rancor of sectarian disputes. The Coonites seemed simultaneously worried about and proud of their small numbers and isolation. One minute commented on correspondence with other associations: "It is a source of pleasure to us to know that we are not the only little despised flock, but that we can feel that we have fellow sufferers in other localities." They nonetheless felt envious of the prosperity of other churches: "Brethren, look at our enemy's churches. . . . What a great time and preparations are made by the world to meet them in their feast." The prosperous churches seemed so enticing that Coonite minutes frequently exhorted their members not to go "near the door of her house." Despite such apprehensions, the Coonites looked forward to a time when "Babylon will fall . . . and then [this] . . . doctrine will be adhered to and seen as the only truth." Despite mutual hostility, some cross-fertilization took place. The 1913 minute refers to the concept of a "time salvation" that became current among the Primitive Baptists long after the Coonite secession.[99] This doctrinal development is dealt with at length in chapter 8.

The Coonites constructed a strangely liberal theology out of the harsh material provided by frontier Calvinism. Although nearly every associational minute contains a lengthy doctrinal exposition, their beliefs exhibit a complexity that makes them hard to summarize. Coonite scriptural exegesis, characterized by allegorizing or "spiritualizing" virtually everything in the Bible, made their unusual conclusions possible. All Primitive Baptists loved "type and shadow"—that is, allegorical—preaching, but the Two-Seeders raised it to apotheosis. Isaac Coon wrote: "We take the scriptures as they apply to the man of God, and firmly believe that none can feel, see or know the truth as it is in Christ unless it is by the revelation of Christ."[100] A good example of such exegesis, or eisegesis, is Coon's handling of the passage: "The hour is coming and now is in the which all that are in their graves shall come forth, they that have done good to the resurrection of life, and they that have done evil to the resurrection of damnation." He interpreted the graves as being the bodies of men, the good as being the spiritual children of God in them, and the evil as being the spiritual children of the devil, both of which kinds of spiritual children must leave their tenement in a person when he or she dies.[101] Here Coon allegorizes away a passage of obviously literal meaning. Allison Dekle went even further and reportedly claimed an extra scriptural revelation, claiming that he knew the mysterious utterance of the seven thunders in Revelation 10:4, which the Apostle John was told to "seal up" and "write them not," "as plain as if a man had slapped him on the shoulder."[102] He believed "these things are being revealed to the children of God."[103] Coon also placed a surprising emphasis on reason as an aid to discovering truth: "I am sometimes astonished that men will not reason, but when I remember what I am myself I can excuse anyone else."[104]

Like Daniel Parker, many Two-Seeders believed Satan to be an eternal, self-existent being, although paradoxically, they did not consider him God's equal in power. Coon wrote that "God is the condemner of his enemies, and like those of old they must obey although it is torment."[105] The Coonites did not emphasize this doctrine, but the Lookout Association, with which they corresponded, stated in its articles of faith: "We believe that good and evil proceed from opposite causes; that all good comes from God and all evil from the devil, and there is no relation between the two."[106] The Coonites criticized other articles held by the Lookout Association but not this one, so it must have met with their approbation.[107]

Denying a bodily resurrection, the Coonites had to come up with some rationale for the event the Christian Scriptures insist upon most strongly: the bodily resurrection of Christ. They achieved this by asserting that Christ's body and blood came from heaven. J. E. W. Smith's doctrine on this point has been referred to already. Harmony Church accused Allison Dekle of preaching that "Christ's flesh did actually come from heaven and that there was no humanity about him" and that consequently, Christ was no more the Virgin's son than was Dekle himself.[108]

The doctrine of eternal children and of time as merely the manifestation of events that had taken place before the foundation of the world formed the cornerstones of Coonite theology. God's children "existed before time," and the "transgression of the church was a fact before time," and "Christ was slain for the offense of the church before time"; "all earthly things are only patterns of the heavenly things." The biblical account of the fall of man reflected events in heaven previous to and explanatory of the creation of the world: "The same devil that entered the garden, entered the heavenly Jerusalem and as he defiled Eve in the garden, he defiled the Bride, the Lamb's wife, and brought sin and death on the generation of God, and as God drove Adam and Eve out of the garden, he drove the Bride . . . out of the heavenly Jerusalem down here in the wilderness, a place prepared for her."[109]

Coon explained the crucial doctrine of the two seeds as follows: "If Christ is eternal, his children . . . are as eternal as he is. . . . The generation of Christ is a spiritual generation, and the generation of the devil is spiritual. . . . God puts his child into the Adam man, and it is his secret how he does it. The devil introduced his spirit in the garden, and all of Adam's family are the common heirs of that introduction. When God calls his child in the Adam man the war between the two spirits begins and never ends until the death of the Adam man."[110]

Human beings, or "Adam men," serve only as a battleground for the two seeds in Coonite theology. "Adam's children are of the earth, and return to the earth as they were." The Coonites denied that Adam's transgression in the garden merited him and his descendants any more punishment than physical death. Not even the new birth could change Adam: "The new birth does not change the substance of anything . . . but it is the manifestation of God's child in the earthy man." When those "earthy" humans not fortunate enough to have been chosen as vessels for the eternal children die, "the devil that is in them goes to the lake of fire and brimstone, and the earthy man returns to the earth as he was. The devil is no part of the man that God made nor is the spiritual man."[111] Much of the Coonite insistence on the doom of the "earthy man" was based on those passages of Ecclesiastes and other parts of the Old Testament that seem to deny a life after death.[112]

Coon and his followers interpreted the resurrection entirely in spiritual if not figurative terms. Certainly the "Adam man" had no resurrection coming. Coon apparently believed that a "spiritual body" existed in heaven waiting for the child of God to return to it. He based this on 2 Corinthians 5:1, which does seem to contain such an idea. He summarized the resurrection of God's people as "a change . . . in their situation not their substance."[113]

Although they did not believe in freedom of the will, the Coonites blasted the Calvinistic theory of election as fiercely as did rabid Methodists. Coon summed up their objections: "The man is without power to prepare for heaven, and then because he does not do so he is to burn forever. It destroys mercy. . . . I would ask myself the question why did God choose and ordain one man to joy and leave out another of the same sort to suffer eternal woe, and then say he did not respect persons." Other Coonites declared that such a doctrine made God the "best friend that the devil has got" and God the "chief of devils." Election for them meant no more than God's love for His own eternally existing children. "God's choice is a nation, a generation, and not part of it."[114] This represents a remarkable departure from the original doctrine of Daniel Parker, who believed firmly in eternal damnation.

People in Baker County, Florida, habitually referred to the Coonites as "No-hell" Baptists.[115] The Coonites condemned as a "doctrine of devils" the idea "that for sin we shall suffer eternal misery and torture." To them of course, only the devil and his children suffered torment, and while they might live in people, they were not part of people. They believed the last judgment to be going on all the time as the children of God were being manifested. "A Christian that believes in a future resurrection of the earthly or Adamic family, or any part thereof, is a Babylonian and one of the family of Babylon, the great whore spoken of in the text."[116]

The Coonite movement was an unconscious recapitulation of some aspects of the ancient Manichean heresy, with its belief in an eternal evil god and its suspicion of the "flesh." This curious example of parallel evolution constitutes the movement's greatest point of interest in the history of religious ideas. An Arkansas Two Seed association in correspondence with the Coonites dropped members for advocating the abolition of baptism and communion, a move also taken by the medieval Albigensian Manicheans.[117] Their mode of interpreting Scripture on this as well as other points had remarkable affinities with that of the early Quakers.

The Coonites emerged for some of the same reasons other small sects appear. They had little money or education and lived for the most part in remote, backward areas. Such people needed a psychological boost, and theirs came from seeing themselves as the possessors of a secret doctrine unknown to the world, which made them especially favored of God. Matthew Touchstone described those outside his true church as "those who are not far advanced in the . . . school of Christ and whom it is . . . the will of God to reveal but little to."[118] Their corresponding association Lookout expressed the effect of this conviction on them: "Though you cannot boast of illustrious ancestors or of noble blood, having been born of God, the blood royal of heaven runs in your veins and purifies you . . . though ever so lowly."[119]

While this explains much about sectarian religion in general, it does not entirely explain this particular sect. Some of the Coonites appear to have been of the backwoods aristocracy. John F. Smith, mentioned previously, served as a Florida state senator.[120] T. B. Willaford, a prominent Coonite layman, "was well read and defended the cause every time it was needed."[121] Coon's acquirements have been noted. It is easy to see how intelligent, devout, but sketchily educated people such as these might have felt compelled to rework a grim theology into a more humane form. Coon wrote that before his conversion to Two-Seedism, he had but to think of judgment, damnation, and arbitrary election "and all my comforts fled." He wrote of his children: "I am not afraid that one of them will burn forever in the lake, for God did not make anything for the devil." He also wrote: "Many of God's dear children are kept in bondage through fear of death, and never enjoy the freedom that belongs to them."[122] Anyone familiar with the relentless bellowing of hellfire that constituted most preaching at that time can understand what a bitter bondage of fear he meant. In a community with more intellectual opportunities, the Coonites might have become Unitarians or Freethinkers.

Paradoxically, the very feature that attracted adherents to Coonism also probably contributed to its failure. As already noted, hard people and hard lands breed hard doctrines. The Crawfordites exemplify this pattern. As seen in chapter 5, the Crawford faction of Primitive Baptists recoiled in horror from J. E. W. Smith's doctrines from the first, and they became totally isolated from the other Primitive Baptists only a short time before the Coonites found themselves in a similar state. Geographically, the bounds of the two groups overlapped. Unlike the Coonites, the Crawfordites distinguished themselves by the strictness of their discipline and doctrine. Perhaps by thus offering a more secure rock to cling to, they not only survived but grew in numbers and still survive with considerable vigor at the present time.

Although the Coonites disappeared as a separate entity in the 1930s, much of their doctrine is held, more or less secretly, among local Primitive Baptists. The Coonites noted that there were those who believed their doctrine but would not confess it publicly for fear of being "turned out of the synagogues."[123] If one knows where to go and what to listen for, one can still occasionally hear the "grose heresee" of Isaac Coon.

8

"Seeking the Old Paths"

The Progressive and Peace Movements

The isolation of southern Georgia and northern Florida began to lessen in the 1890s. Railroads and the lumber and turpentine industries opened many remote areas to outsiders. Increased availability of commercial fertilizer made the cut-over land left behind by the sawmills attractive to new settlers.[1] With new people came new ideas and attitudes.

At first, the Primitive Baptist Church prospered from the boom. During the 1870s, the Union Association did not grow at all; however, in the 1880s, membership rose from about 600 to 832. The Ochlocknee Association increased during the 1890s from eleven churches with 385 members to sixteen with 735. The Union Association expanded from eighteen churches with 832 members to twenty-two with 1,154 during the same period. A. V. Simms noted in 1894 that "some of our churches in South Georgia and Florida are receiving members in a manner almost unprecedented in their history."[2]

Despite general growth, the mid-1890s were hard years in the Wiregrass country, as elsewhere. Political agitation and falling cotton prices reverberated even within the walls of Primitive meetinghouses. Members came under the displeasure of the church for voting Populist and joining the Farmer's Alliance. Some of the rapid growth experienced during the 1890s probably resulted from people turning to an older and stricter faith during a time of change and stress. The *Pilgrim's Banner,* a Primitive Baptist paper published in Valdosta, frequently reported conversion of Missionary Baptists and Methodists to the Primitive faith. One Missionary preacher, J. H. Chitty, united with the Primitive Baptists during this period.[3]

On the whole, the Missionary Baptists experienced greater growth in the 1890s than the Primitives. In the areas under consideration, only Clinch County, Georgia, still had more Primitives than Missionaries in 1890, and this was only true of white Missionary Baptists.[4] The Primitives did not react gracefully to Missionary expansion. Elder Lee Hanks, in a September 1, 1894,

Pilgrim's Banner, attacked the doctrine and practice of the Missionary Baptists as heretical and unscriptural. Hanks exhorted all sincere Christians to withdraw from Missionary churches. The local Mercer Missionary Baptist Association, in turn, attacked Hanks's article for having "willfully, grossly, and maliciously misrepresented" their position.[5]

J. F. Eden, pastor of the Quitman Baptist Church, remarked in an 1894 sermon that "there is a denomination which has a great deal to say against paying preachers and against mission boards. But do we not see 'Ichabod' clearly written over against this people? They are dying of starvation and dry rot." Encouraged by the great revival then going on among the Primitives, the editors of the *Pilgrim's Banner* gleefully butchered Eden's sermon.[6]

The Methodists came in for relatively little criticism, Old Baptist wrath usually being reserved for the Missionaries. Although aggressive pioneer Methodists, such as Simon Peter Richardson, aroused the Old Baptists, most Primitives in South Georgia seem always to have regarded the Methodists as pitiful and unworthy of serious attack. Elder Henry W. Parrish of Berrien County, Georgia, allowed his daughter to attend a Methodist college. A rumor circulated in the community that she intended to join the Methodists. Asked whether he would allow such a thing, Elder Parrish replied, "Why not? She joined all the other little clubs in school."[7]

A new doctrinal development appeared during the 1890s. The London Confession declared that "God hath decreed in Himself from all eternity . . . all things whatsoever come to pass; yet so as thereby God is neither the author of sin, nor hath fellowship with any therein."[8] John Gill declared the "decrees and purposes of God" to "reach to all things that come to pass in the world."[9] Tired Creek Church's articles expressed belief in absolute predestination. Other Primitives stood in some doubt of the doctrine. Owen Smith of the Suwannee River Association wrote to Gilbert Beebe in regard to the expression "The absolute predestination of all things" in the prospectus of the *Signs of the Times*. Smith admitted that "I do not understand your meaning as well as I wish to."[10]

Some Primitive preachers became apprehensive concerning the moral inertia this doctrine seemed to breed in their people, especially in light of the improvement mania of the Progressive era. Without abandoning belief in the unconditional predestination of the elect to eternal salvation, some preachers began to assert a "conditional time salvation" gained by obedience to God's commandments. This "timely salvation" consisted of a sense of communion with God and freedom from the guilty pangs resulting from neglected duty. A. V. Simms, clerk of the Union Association and editor of the *Pilgrim's Banner,* strongly advocated the new doctrine. In a critical review of an article by Elder David Bartley of Indiana, Simms disagreed with the statement that "our salvation now, or in period of time is not conditional, and does not depend upon ourselves." Although Simms conceded that "there is a sense in which 'all things are of God,'" he denied that "the gospel works procuring our time salvation is [sic] unconditional or the sure gift and work of God." On the contrary, he continued, obedience "is conditional and we . . . may or may not resist the Spirit prompting to obedience." He concluded that the old doctrine "creates too many willing, passive . . . drones in the church."[11] This new doctrine gained a good reception from many Primitive Baptists. Simms noted that "our preachers . . . seem to understand that God has required more of them than simply to preach predestination and election."[12] He noted with approval that local preachers were "denouncing" the "sentiment" that "the spiritual enjoyments of the Lord's people is [sic] not contingent on their works and obedience. All maintained that the eternal salvation of God's people was unconditional, but that the time, or gospel salvation here on earth . . . was conditional."[13] In fact, the purpose of the "conditional" doctrine apparently served as an antidote to the free will preaching of the Missionary Baptists. Apprehensive of continued Missionary growth, some Primitive leaders perhaps hoped to beat them at their own game of rousing exhortation.

The new doctrine created a schism in the Mt. Enon Association, whose founders had nurtured their faith on the *Signs of the Times*. Preachers from South Georgia began to criticize the doctrine of absolute predestination in the 1890s, claiming that the doctrine made God the author of sin and stifled godly living. David Bartley, an absolute predestinarian from Ohio, visited the Mt. Enon Association in 1904 and encouraged the predestinarians. The association adopted the London Confession statement on predestination in 1906, which provoked a division. E. I. Wiggins, the historian of the Mt. Enon "Absoluters," proudly declared: "We believe in the doctrine of God's unlimited predestination of all things whatsoever comes to pass. We believe that God's predestination reaches all the way down the line from salvation to damnation."[14] While other associations in the region did not divide specifically over this issue, doctrinal concerns played a part in the Progressive controversy, as they had in the case of the Missionary controversy.[15]

Railroads led to increased communications between churches and associations, but the results were not always positive. Such communication caused at least one minor local dispute to jeopardize the peace and fellowship of all the associations in South Georgia and Florida. The Primitive Pulaski Association occupied territory in Dooly, Irwin, Wilcox, and Worth counties, in Georgia, directly north of the Union and Ochlocknee associations.

For many years these three bodies had enjoyed close and cordial relations. With increased contact among them, however, the possibility of discord grew.

In 1891, such a controversy arose in Mt. Beazor Church, Dooly County, Georgia. Deacon Hall prevailed on Perry G. McDonald to acknowledge an unspecified fault to the church. He later claimed that McDonald's statement to the church fell far short of what he had promised. Deacon Hall protested, and the church expelled the McDonald adherents, who then organized themselves and claimed to be Mt. Beazor church "in order." Both factions sent delegations to the next session of the Primitive Pulaski Association. After an abortive attempt at reconciliation at the associational meeting, the McDonald party called a council of elders and deacons from the Primitive Pulaski and Union associations to settle the dispute. Elder T. W. Stallings, moderator of the Union Association, presided over the council. In the absence of any witnesses from the Hall faction of Mt. Beazor, the council not only found in McDonald's favor but also ordained him to the ministry. At the next session of the Primitive Pulaski Association, both factions again presented their cases. Elder Stallings, again present, proposed that each faction call two representatives from three churches, who would in turn call representatives from a seventh church. Further, he proposed that the decision of these representatives was to be binding on all concerned. Yet, on the last day of the associational meeting, for some unknown reason, Stallings suddenly withdrew his own suggestion and threw his support to the McDonald party. The new tack caused a turmoil resulting in the creation of two hostile factions, each asserting its claim as the true Primitive Pulaski Association.[16]

The Union Association subsequently endorsed its moderator's preference by recognizing the McDonald faction, provoking criticism throughout its neighboring associations. The Ochlocknee and Alabaha River associations suspended relations with the Union, and the San Pedro Association accused the Union of causing the division and acting with undue haste. The Union replied by asking them "to meet us at our next annual session, in the spirit of love, and to name the parties guilty of this grave charge, with all the 'facts' in their possession; and if 'facts' establish their guilt, we promise peace. . . . But if, upon examination she finds she cannot sustain the charges with 'facts,' we ask her to lay down her sword, and let her failure to do so appear in her minutes."[17]

By 1894, the Ochlocknee, San Pedro, and Alabaha had all adopted the Union's position on the Pulaski problem.[18] This senseless wrangle and others like it led several preachers in South Georgia to question certain basic practices of the Primitive Baptist Church. A number of young preachers in the

Union and Ochlocknee associations, led by A. V. Simms, editor of the *Pilgrim's Banner*, Robert Barwick, Lee Hanks, and J. B. "Toad" Luke, became increasingly critical of the old order. In a denomination that regarded the least punctilio of immemorial custom as sacrosanct, this eventually generated a major controversy. The Progressive Primitives, as they became known, imbibed much of the reform spirit abroad in the United States at the time. They centered their program around three longstanding Primitive Baptist institutions: associations, correspondence, and ministerial nonsupport.

Associational constitutions never claimed any power to "lord it over God's heritage, nor by which she can infringe on the internal rights of the churches." Associations claimed the power to "recognize the gospel discipline of the churches, and drop from our list any church or churches from which sister churches may have withdrawn," implying the right to judge disputes between churches. Associations also had authority to "correspond" by means of letters and messengers with other associations "of our faith and order."[19] The last items gave associational meetings vast discretion in recognizing other Primitive Baptist bodies, since to "drop correspondence" usually meant to discontinue fellowship and recognition as well. From the earliest settlement in the region, associations had acted as supreme tribunals for the churches, even hearing complaints from individual members against the churches that had disciplined them.[20]

In addition to associational correspondence, the regional churches also corresponded among themselves. The churches in the Piedmont Association adopted the custom of exchanging letters and messengers on an annual basis in 1823.[21] In a practice unique to South Georgia and Florida, Primitive Baptists intended correspondence to form a closer bond between isolated churches. It also provided a means for churches to examine one another for "missionary" tendencies. Correspondence eventually became a potentially divisive test of fellowship. Refusal to send or receive a church letter became the ecclesiastical equivalent of breaking off diplomatic relations.

In September 1897, the *Pilgrim's Banner* published a long letter from I. J. Taylor of Texas, deploring associational power over the churches. After condemning associations in general as tyrannical and unscriptural, Taylor added: "The most general, powerful, disasterous [sic] and unscriptural evil in the machinery of modern Associations is developing to be the apparently lamb like and harmless formal correspondence between Associations, by which errors and troubles, otherwise local and transitory, are spread and perpetuated."[22]

Commenting on the Taylor letter, A. V. Simms wrote: "we have . . . been in line with Brother Taylor and others for quite a while on the associational question. Yet I am at the feet of my brethren and want us all to see together, before we suspend the associations."[23] A move to suspend associational correspondence in 1897 failed in the Union Association.[24] Shortly thereafter, Simms's home church, Columbia, applied for dismission from the Union Association to return to the Ochlocknee, from which it had come originally in 1863 and where Progressive sentiments were stronger. The business committee ruled that a church, being an independent body, did not require a letter of dismission to go from one association to another. However, association delegates nonetheless overruled the committee and dismissed Columbia by letter anyway.

Advocacy of ministerial support touched a sore point of long standing. Primitive Baptist indifference to their preachers' financial needs was noted in chapter 5. By the late 1800s, most Old Baptists, preachers included, ceased even theoretically advocating assistance for their elders. Most Primitive Baptist preachers took pride in serving without pay. The tombstone of Elder Aaron Knight of the Union Association states that "because of the labor of his own hands, like the Apostle Paul, [he] was never chargeable to the churches whom he faithfully served to the day of his death."[25] Generous support, especially in the form of a stated salary, branded a preacher as a hireling, like the despised Missionaries and Methodists.

Wilson Johnson, moderator of the Ochlocknee Association in the early 1890s, expressed the attitude of most of his brethren in an exchange with a Missionary pastor in Quitman, Georgia. Being asked "what the Hardshells paid him for preaching?" Johnson replied, "Fifty cents or a pocket handkerchief. Generally nothing." "I get 1000 dollars a year," the Missionary informed him. "Preacher, you ain't paid enough," said Johnson. "Why not?" asked the Quitman pastor. "Because I wouldn't preach what you do for 10,000 dollars a year."[26]

Robert Barwick and Allen Simms attended the Suwannee River Association during the 1890s. After traveling through a vast wilderness to a church near the Okefenokee Swamp, they saw more horse carts than they had ever seen before. Barwick, writing in the 1940s, remarked that this traditional conveyance of the flatwoods did not ride like a Buick. After a long service in which Barwick preached the "Introductory Sermon," a great honor, the services adjourned for lunch. The visiting preachers discovered that everyone had brought their own provisions. As no one invited them to dine, Barwick swallowed his pride and begged a piece of beef and a sweet potato.

Famished, he devoured his alms before getting back to Simms, who remarked that the Bible must not be true, since he had seen "the righteous forsaken and his seed begging bread." A good "conditionalist," Barwick concluded that they must not have been sufficiently righteous. During the afternoon service, they shared the pulpit with an intruding deer hound.[27] With such attitudes prevalent among Primitive Baptists, no proposal would have met with a colder reception than insistence on ministerial support.

In 1896, rumors circulated that R. H. Barwick advocated a salaried ministry and had demanded a salary from his home church, Harmony, Brooks County, in the Ochlocknee Association. The church denounced the reports as "false" and "scandalous" and sent the *Pilgrim's Banner* a statement that "no such claims have been made upon us but to the contrary."[28]

In the Union Association, several preachers appointed a meeting for December 15, 1897, at Cat Creek Church near Bemiss, Lowndes County, Georgia, to hear charges and complaints against A. V. Simms for preaching ministerial support. As a result, in January 1898, T. W. Stallings, A. V. Simms, A. A. Knight, Lee Hanks, E. S. Ward, and R. H. Barwick signed a *Basis of Agreement* on ministerial support. It emphasised the duty of preachers to serve churches whether supported or not and the church's duty to contribute toward their pastor's expenses. It denied, however, that a church should pay their minster a stated salary. Elder Stallings later withdrew his support from the settlement because mistaken impressions of it had circulated.[29]

In January 1899, Simms and twenty-two others organized the Valdosta Primitive Baptist Church. The new church purchased the old Missionary Baptist church building in Valdosta, thus becoming the only Primitive Church in South Georgia with a steeple.[30] Robert H. Barwick and others in 1898 organized the Pavo Primitive Baptist Church.[31] Simms and Barwick founded these churches to obtain a greater measure of independence and also a degree of protection from the increasingly hostile Old Line.

Elder J. F. McCann of Harmony Church emerged about 1898 as the champion of orthodoxy in the Ochlocknee Association. McCann, at Harmony Church's 1899 annual meeting, moved that they refuse messengers who "did not believe in Associations and letter writing at communion meetings, and those who did believe in church sovereignty."[32] At the next meeting, the church charged McCann with "unchristian conduct" and then divided, with thirteen in favor of McCann and seventeen against him. Expelled from the house, the minority met under the shade trees in the churchyard, declared themselves the "Church in order," and excommunicated the majority on a charge of "Unchristian Conduct in departing from the regular faith order and practice of the Church of Christ." More specifically, they charged the majority with favoring "new things and professed improvements . . . principally ministerial support and the independent sovereignty of the churches to do away with organized associations and to do away with formal correspondence of the churches."[33]

The Barwick party attended the 1899 Ochlocknee Association at Bethel Church, Brooks County, Georgia. However, the delegates were wasting their time. The Old Line party controlled the associational meeting and dropped the Barwick faction of Harmony and two other churches on the same charges that the minority at Harmony had brought against the majority. J. F. McCann, incidentally, served as clerk of that session of the association.[34] The fiery Elder Lee Hanks, furious at the McCann faction, rose from his seat at the association and left the building yelling, "All orderly Baptists, follow me."[35] Hanks did not enhance his reputation among the Old Liners by this action. In 1911, the Bennettite faction of the Alabaha River Association confirmed an Anti-Progressive resolution of the previous year by witholding "correspondence from all associations that are contaminated with Elder Lee Hanks."[36]

The Barwick faction met at Harmony Church in November 1899 and conducted their own version of the Ochlocknee Association, which Barwick's Pavo Church and Simms's Valdosta Church, previously unassociated, joined. The Barwick faction adopted a resolution sharply curtailing its authority:

> Whereas Associational dictatorial rulings have, in our judgement, been a fruitful source of confusion among our people, and this question having been extensively discussed and considered by our brethren for several years, and believing the church, in her organized capacity, to be the only Ecclesiastical body authorized in the Scriptures; Therefore, we suggest that it is the sense of this body to leave all disciplinary government to the churches, to be directed and executed by them in their regular conferences. And we further suggest the propriety of leaving off all constitutional rules of the Association, and continued rules of decorum, and submit to the general regulations and government of the church with which the Association meets.
>
> In thus speaking, we beg to say that we mean no declaration of non-fellowship for our brethren who do not see fit to make the same announcement, but humbly ask for a continuation of your sweet fellowship.[37]

The association printed lengthy rebuttal to their opponent's charges. Claiming that they had never advocated a salaried ministry and regarded such a concept as heretical, they admitted to advocating the duty of churches to make a contribution to their minster's assistance. Also, they declared correspondence to be without biblical authority, unknown to "the Baptist family at large," and a "dry useless formality," but claimed that they "did not dream" speaking against it would cause "such grave offense." Regarding church sovereignty, the delegates pointed out that every Primitive Baptist church covenant plainly asserted the principle.[38]

In 1903, the Barwick wing of the Ochlocknee went a step further and abolished interassociational correspondence: "As official correspondence between sister associations has proven in the past a fruitful source of confusion—designing men having taken advantage of it to the furtherance of their pernicious work in declaring non-fellowship for many of the Lord's faithful followers, we have, in our present session, thought it best to suspend all official correspondence with sister associations."[39]

The Ochlocknee schism affected almost immediately the Suwannee River Association, where Simms pastored Bethel Church located near Jennings, Florida. At least one member of Bethel Church did not sympathize with Simms's views on ministerial support. The late Elder Otto Hill recalled his father's disgust when Simms announced that the church would have to give him more money as he had several children to put through school. Hill pointed out that he had childen of his own to educate and called for his letter of dismission.[40] In 1900, the Suwannee dropped Bethel for "departing from the old line of practice by choosing one . . . as pastor not in line with the churches of this association, or sister corresponding associations."[41] Later the same year, Bethel joined the Barwick faction of the Ochlocknee Association.[42]

Matters in the Union Association were somewhat more complex. After the Simms faction withdrew to form the Valdosta Church, Cat Creek Church voted to "sustain Elder McCan [sic] and those that stood with him as Harmony church in gospel order and at the same time declare a non-fellowship for the . . . Barwick side and all that are in simpathy with them." The membership went on to condemn the Barwick position on associations, correspondence, and their contention "that a preacher and his family should be supported by the Baptist [sic]."[43] Pleasant Church, Berrien County, Georgia, adopted an almost identical resolution in January 1900, only denying, however, that a preacher should be "entirely" supported by the church.[44] Pleasant Grove Church, also in Berrien County and the home church of Elder J. B. "Toad" Luke, adopted an anti-Barwick resolution in May 1900 but repealed it the next day, claiming "the sentiment we endorse, but the act itself we regard as new."[45] Salem Church of Adel, Georgia, took no action.

According to a tradition current among South Georgia Primitive Baptists, personal animosity between Elder J. B. Luke and Elder Timothy W. Stallings contributed to the 1901 schism in the Union Association. It was a typical example of the concealed reasons often underlying the official statements. Many of the "Progressives" reflected a "new breed" of Primitive Baptist, often town dwellers and nonfarmers. Allen Vincent Simms served as probate judge of Lowndes County from 1904 to 1911.[46] He took a prominent part in the prohibition movement, which culminated in Georgia going "dry" in 1908. Robert H. Barwick attained sufficient prominence for the Brooks County village of Barwick, Georgia, to be named after him. Toad Luke sold insurance, a most novel occupation for a Primitive Baptist, since many Primitives had strong scruples about taking out insurance.[47]

Elder Timothy W. Stallings had been preaching before J. B. Luke's birth. Sylvester Hassell considered him the "most prominent" of the Anti-Progressive preachers in South Georgia.[48] An impecunious backwoods farmer, "Uncle Tim," wounded during the Civil War, never entirely recovered. His son wrote in 1899, "He received a severe wound in his right arm and has been a great sufferer ever since the war."[49] Possibly because of his physical sufferings, Stallings manifested an abrupt, mercurial temperament throughout his ministry. Some of his temperament probably was natural and hereditary, for when his son Jim entered the Primitive Baptist ministry, he manifested such talent as a troublemaker that when he moved his membership from Pleasant Church to Cat Creek, the clerk at Pleasant wrote in the margin of the minutebook, "We hope he keeps it there."[50] T. W. Stallings participated in almost every ecclesiastical vendetta of the era. As treated in the preceding chapter, he played a major role in inciting controversy over Elder Isaac Coon, for whom he had professed great affection. Stallings's role in the Hall-MacDonald schism was typical of his ability to jump from one side of a question to another.

By the time of his confrontation with Luke, Stallings was in his sixties and in increasingly poor physical and emotional health. In 1895, he wrote, "I have not been entirely free from pain for along time, and sometimes my sufferings seems more than I can bear. I have also discovered that my afflictions and sufferings are weakening my mind. No one could be more despondent than I have been of late. I do not now hope for relief this side of the grave."[51]

In 1899 Stallings lost his wife, who had cared for him for many years both as a nurse and as a secretary, "writing, reading and hunting scriptures for him as he was uneducated." His son wrote of him, "It does seem that he is bereaved of all, and that it will bring his gray hairs with sorrow to the grave."[52]

Old age, rather than sorrow, brought Elder Stallings to his grave. He lived until 1923, dying at the ripe age of eighty-seven. Unfortunately, grief and pain brought him to the bottle rather than the grave. In November 1900, Stallings confessed to his home church that he had been "drinking." They forgave him.[53] Primitive Baptists had long considered lapses relative to alchohol fairly venial sins.

The Progressives, on the other hand, considered sobriety inseparable from godliness.[54] According to a local tradition, a hotel keeper in Nashville, Georgia, hailed J. B. Luke, then a newly fledged elder, and showed him Elder Stallings, the venerable moderator of the Union Association, stretched out in a back room, attended only by a swarm of flies and thoroughly disguised in liquor. From that point, according to the traditional account, Luke "had it in" for Stallings.[55] In any event, the Union Association, with Stallings as moderator, soon expelled Luke and his supporters in connection with the Barwick controversy.

The Barwick controversy reached the Union Association in 1901. In July 1901, Cat Creek Church sent a committee to Salem and Pleasant Grove to demand that they "fall in line with us by an official act of the church against the Sims [sic] and Barwick faction on ministerial support."[56] During July and August, Salem, Pleasant Grove, New Hope, Mt. Paran, and Concord churches either divided over the demands of Cat Creek and other churches or solidly refused them.[57]

In October 1901, the Union Association sustained the anti-Luke factions of Salem, Pleasant Grove, New Hope, and Concord and dropped Mt. Paran entirely. In the case of Pleasant Grove, the association recognized a minority faction composed of only one third of the membership. It also declared Elders William Luke, J. B. Luke, C. W. Stallings (T. W. Stallings's son), and R. T. Hall "unsound in practice."[58] Four of the Luke churches organized in 1903 as the Union Association and established fellowship with the Barwick faction of the Ochlocknee Association.[59] The main body of the Union Association responded by adding "Old Line" to its title.[60]

This division left the anti-Barwick associations of South Georgia and Florida isolated from the main body of Primitive Baptists. Sylvester Hassell estimated that Barwick had about twenty-five hundred followers and his opponent McCann about eight thousand. The Progressives claimed that the Old Line Primitive Baptists not only opposed ministerial support, church sovereignty, and religious periodicals but also that they insisted on the sole use of the Lloyd's hymnal and required their preachers to dress poorly. The Old Line denied this and laid the blame upon advocacy of a salaried ministry and "a modern mission spirit." The Old Line also declared, in connection with the conditional time salvation controversy, that "the real cause of the divisions among us is opposition to God's sovereign and eternal purpose and . . . worldly doctrines of free will and conditional salvation."[61]

Progressives soon discovered that revolutions are started more easily than they are controlled. In 1900, the Valdosta Church decided to buy an organ. When this act called up a storm of protest, the church sold the organ in October 1901. Apparently, the church later obtained another, for in February 1906, A. V. Simms offered a resolution to discontinue the use of the organ. The church resumed use of the organ in July 1907 because dissension with other churches had not ceased with its discontinuance, and Valdosta Church ignored several protests that arrived during the ensuing year.[62] At Brushy Creek Church in Irwin County, Georgia, those in favor of an organ sought to present the church with a fait accompli. The musical party purchased the instrument and secretly installed it on Saturday night. On Sunday morning the congregation gathered and stood about pondering the innovation, a small cabinet-style pump organ on casters. One zealous old pillar of orthodoxy advanced to it as though struck with admiration, and when he saw a clear path, shot it toward the back door of the meetinghouse, where a steep set of steps would have disminished its value to the going rate of kindling and brass scrap. Only a last-minute flying tackle by some of the organ party saved it.[63]

Antebellum Baptist churches in the South did not generally use musical instruments. As noted, hymns were "lined out" from a book containing only lyrics. After the Civil War, a few Missionary churches began to use pump organs.[64] Hickory Head Baptist Church in Brooks County, Georgia, obtained an organ in 1882.[65] Since the Primitives had long felt that distance from the Missionaries was closeness to God, instrumental music and hymnals with musical notation had little chance of acceptance among them.

In 1909, Concord, Bethsaida, and Bethlehem churches sent letters to Salem demanding that they take a stand against the organ, which they called a "Babylonian" and "barbarian" innovation without warrant in the Bible. Salem refused and so lost their fellowship, even though they did not adopt the organ for their own use.[66] The organ controversy disrupted the Luke faction of the Union Association so badly that it never met again. At one conference at Pleasant Grove Church, Luke became so incensed as to rise from the moderator's seat and walk out of the meetinghouse, saying, "Boys, you can take this and go to hell with it."[67]

The anti-instrumental Progressives of the Luke and Barwick factions met in 1910 and formed the Mt. Olive Association. Evincing a reaction against Progressivism, they adopted the order of business of the 1889 Ochlocknee

Association. They condemned "all modern attempts to reform or babylonize the church of God to make her more popular with the world." To justify not returning to the Old Line, Mt. Olive criticised the handling of the Barwick-McCann affair and reasserted the early Progressive position on associations and correspondence as things indifferent.[68]

The Mt. Olive founders handled their Old Line brethren with courtesy. On the other hand, their denunciations of the organ-playing Progressives fill more than a page of fine print, accusing the Progressives of lax discipline, false doctrine, and worldly innovations, in excruciating detail. Further, Mt. Olive even condemned church barbecues as heretical.[69] However, the Mt. Olive brethren found one another as hard to deal with as the organ people and Old Liners. The association split into two factions in 1916, apparently as a result of personality conflicts between two preachers.[70] A similar divison took place in 1923.[71] These small factions became something of a "Cave of Adullam," with tiny dissident groups and individuals finding refuge with one or another of them. Even T. W. Stallings, excommunicated from Cat Creek Church for his support of the Joseph Newbern faction of Wayfare Church, Echols County, Georgia, found his final home in a tiny offshoot of the Mt. Olive Association.[72]

Toad Luke's stay with the Progressives ended in 1913. Salem Church could tolerate the organ but not the despised Youngites of the Brushy Creek Union. After 1900, they began to receive overtures from the Progressives. In June 1913, Salem realized that they were "indirectly connected" to the detested heretics through their fellow Progressives and dropped all connection with them.[73] In July the church split over the issue, with the majority in favor of dropping fellowship with the Progressives.[74] Salem Church began to mend fences with Concord and other Mt. Olive Association churches and repudiated and readministered every baptism it had performed since the instrumental music controversy began.[75]

The Luke faction initiated peace overtures to the Old Line as early as 1905, with no results.[76] By the mid-1920s, the multiplicity of Primitive Baptist factions caused alarm among many of the brethren. Many prominent ministers had come into the Old Line associations since the schisms of 1899–1901, and in several cases the old animosities had been defused. Unfortunately, the peace party in the Union Association underestimated the strength of conservative sentiment, especially out in the flatwoods country in the eastern bounds of the association.

Two churches represented the symbolic key to reunion. The Old Line faction of Concord Church had merged with the Old Line side at Salem and had later organized Spring Hill Church. From January to April 1927, Spring

Hill and Concord negotiated a settlement between themselves.[77] At Salem, a peace proposal from the Luke side went unheeded in 1926, but in April 1927 both sides met in a joint conference and "united by forming a line and giving the right hand of fellowship one to the other." As its first official act, the united church expelled the Old Line dissidents who declared "the hole preceeding . . . out of order & church felow ship withdrawn from apposin side."[78]

The churches hotly debated the "Peace Move" from April to June. Events at Cat Creek followed a course typical in all the churches that divided over the issue. Deacon H. J. McMillan moved in June that the church declare nonfellowship for "all these new things they have put upon us." His motion lost by a narrow margin. Cat Creek endorsed the Spring Hill–Concord Settlement on July 1. The same day, the Old Line dissidents held a conference and "declared a non fellowship for all churches and faction of churches receiving and endorsing the action of Spring Hill Church with her present order, Together with Elder J. B. Luke and his official worke." The July conference lasted so long that a funeral scheduled for that afternoon had to be held under a tree in the churchyard because the bickering factions refused to relinquish the meetinghouse. In the ensuing months, both sides quarreled over the meeting day, the treasury, the deeds to the property, and any other subject that occurred to either of them.[79]

Much of the Old Line opposition to the Peace movement centered on dislike of Elder Toad Luke. His long flirtation with Progressivism did nothing to endear him to the conservatives. Many Primitives simply did not care for Luke himself. He was a short, dumpy, redheaded man, his head barely appearing above the "bookboard" of the pulpits. When preaching, he turned red in the face and bounced up and down with his heavy jowls flapping. He displayed considerable dexterity in the pulpit. At Wayfare Church, Echols County, Georgia, his upper plate flew out during a sermon. He caught it in midair and slapped it back in his mouth, not pausing an instant in his delivery. After church, he would amuse his companions by mocking the other preachers in the service. Coming home once in an automobile, he told his driver, "Be careful Launcie, I'd rather not die mocking preachers." Even members of his own faction did not care for him. One stern old sister, whose descendants would doubtless prefer that she remain anonymous, referred to him as "That son a bitch Toad Luke." Within the writer's lifetime, his name remained a virtual obscenity in the Original Union Association.[80]

The 1927 Union Association met with Wayfare Church, Coffee County, Georgia, in a session unrivaled for bitterness and acrimony since the Missionary Controversy of the 1840s. When the "Toady Frogs," as the Old line called them, arrived, the deacons of Wayfare Church, in an action reminiscent of "Pride's Purge" during the English Interregnum, refused to allow them into the meetinghouse.[81] The Old Line delegates then expelled "all churches and factions of churches that have received and endorsed the act of Spring Hill Church, or the factions of Elder J. B. Luke." They also "dropped from our list all associations and parts of associations who have partaken of the disorders named above."[82]

The Peace faction met in an adjacent forest to discuss their plight, but its Old Line owner, Jesse McKinnon, ordered them away before they could do more than decide on a place to meet. They reconvened at Pleasant Grove Church in November 1927 and organized as the Union Association.[83] The Old Liners then added "Original" to their own title.[84]

The Peace side made one abortive attempt to reunite the association. Elder Luke went to the 1928 Old Line Association meeting and tried to get a hearing. The delegates referred him back to the minority faction of Pleasant Grove Church, where he was technically an excluded member.[85] Deacon J. M. Cook stood in Luke's face, shaking his finger, and said, "All you are saying is not worth the flip of my finger."[86] Neither side made any further attempts at reunion.

The Old Line Union recognized only the Bennettite Alabaha River Association and an Old Line faction of the Suwannee River, together with tiny splinter groups of the Pulaski and Upatoie associations, all of whom shared their detestation of Toad Luke. These factions still stand aloof from all other Primitive Baptists.[87]

9

"I Have Given You an Example"

The Footwashing Controversy and Related Issues

The footwashing controversy of the 1930s represented the high point of the reaction from Progressivism. It revealed the insularity and particularism of the southeastern Primitive Baptists and the limitations of the Peace movement. It resulted in as extensive a disruption as the Progressive and Peace movements, and similarly, its results lingered for many years, generating a new round of divisions. It also demonstrated the extent to which the Primitive Baptist reverence for denominational history in fact extended no further back than living memory.

Originally, the Primitives had taken a tolerant attitude toward differences about the practice and status of footwashing. As seen in a previous chapter, the rite had become widespread among Baptists in relatively recent times, becoming an integral part of the Primitive Baptist communion service only after the 1850s. Reflecting this tolerance, the *Primitive Hymns* proclaimed:

And we who do this duty see,
With others we'll not disagree;
In lowest stoop we will them greet,
We'll eat our herbs and they their meat.[1]

By the late 1800s, however, they began to advocate a more uniform diet, as footwashing assumed sacrosanct status in Georgia and Florida.

As with any religious practice, a body of traditional stories, ranging from the tenderly affecting to the sacrilegiously hilarious, surrounds foot washing. A wealthy white landowner, a sometime state legislator, and a poor black man were both members at Unity Church, Lowndes County, Georgia, toward the end of the last century. At Big Meeting the black man walked to church barefooted, wearing only a well-laundered shirt and overalls. The landowner arrived in a fine conveyance and elegant clothes. During preaching he thought, "I don't believe the Lord could make me wash that old Nigger's feet," which were large, black, and dusty. Soon, however, he began to experience what Old Baptists call "the rod of correction": the assault of conscience. When footwashing came on, the landowner washed the dusty black feet with tears as well as water.[2]

At the other end of the spectrum, Elder T. W. Stallings's son Tony, a classic example of the genus "preacher's kid," turned the old man's socks wrong way to and swept a foot or so of chimney with them on the eve of Big Meeting. Elder Stallings and his partner at footwashing were much astonished to discover what a practical necessity it had become in his case. Tony camped out in the swamp for two weeks after Big Meeting.[3]

Footwashing often powerfully affected those witnessing it. The late Elder James Mahue Young remarked that one of his first serious religious impressions occurred while watching a footwashing at Pleasant Grove Church, Berrien County, Georgia, when a tedious ritual witnessed many times before suddenly assumed for him a supernatural beauty. The late Elder Lamar Carter said that as a young man watching the deacons throw out water from the footwashing, he had felt that along with the water, they were throwing out all the spites and hard feelings of the last year.[4]

Rumblings among Georgia Primitive Baptists over lack of footwashing among northern Old Baptists came as early as 1872. In that year the Echeconnee Association in Middle Georgia wrote to the Kehukee Association:

> Dear Brethren, we have been informed that you omit the duty of washing the saint's feet: this we practice, from the fact we believe the Bible to be the Word of God [and] the only rule for the Kingdom of Christ here on earth. We find this duty recorded by one of the servants of the King and the example set forth by the King Himself. Lest they and we might not understand, He said, 'If I then, your Lord and Master, have washed your feet; ye also ought to wash one another's feet.' Brethren, do you do this? If not, in this plain injunction, how can you admonish the brethren and sisters to other Christian duties? Suffer us your sister, who feels to be less than the least, but who loves you in Christ our Spiritual Head, to repeat the language of Him we love, to you; 'If ye know these things, happy are ye if ye do them.'[5]

In 1878, *Gospel Messenger* editor T. J. Bazemore ominously intoned: "It really does seem to me that all should attend to [footwashing] literally in a church capacity or all should not."[6] The entire 1896 volume of the *Pilgrim's Banner* carried installments of an involved debate between R. Anna Phillips, a footwashing Primitive Baptist, and Elder John Downey of Illinois, a non-footwasher. Over time, feeling intensified on the footwashing issue. The Euharlee Association in northwest Georgia corresponded with the Warwick Old School Baptist Association of New York and the Delaware River Association of Delaware and New Jersey from 1840 until 1920, when they discontinued correspondence with the northerners "on account of their being non-footwashing Baptists."[7] As communication and travel improved and Virginians and other non-footwashers began to appear more often in the Deep South, a collision on the subject became inevitable. One might argue that Henry Ford and the highway department had as much to do with the footwashing schism as anyone.

As the Progressive movement reflected the spirit of the Progressive era, and the Peace movement emerged during the optimistic, pacifist 1920s, the footwashing schism represented a conservative backlash fueled by the anxieties of the Depression. As with other rural areas, South Georgia and inner Florida experienced the Depression as an intensification of the rural recession following the end of the First World War. The San Pedro Association lost the $22.80 in its treasury when the Madison State Bank of Madison, Florida, closed in 1926.[8] With times increasingly difficult, members began to "take the Homestead" in defiance of the longstanding rule against bankruptcy. In 1931, the Original Union Association dropped the Refuge and Red Bluff churches of Atkinson County, Georgia, and part of Pleasant Church, Berrien County, Georgia, (not to be confused with Pleasant Grove Church or Mt. Pleasant Church) for "receiving and carrying in their fellowship a member who had taken advantage of the bankruptcy law."[9] In 1934, their Business Committee composed a list of "disorders as we see them," noting that they "yet [seem] to be prevalent with some and we have ever stood against them." Against the backdrop of the creative economics of the New Deal, they reacted with stern simplicity to the greatest economic crisis in American history: "We do not hold with any that take advantage of the Bankrupt Law."[10]

Most Primitive Baptists seem to have responded to the Depression by tightening their belts, and often by simply letting their property go for debts. W. E. Redding, a member of Cat Creek Church, Lowndes County, Georgia, eventually allowed the bank to take his farm for the crushing debt on it and actually fared better by renting it for a fixed sum instead of paying all he made for interest. During the Depression, he and his family ate well, although store-bought food items became rare treats, and clothing had to be made from feed sacks. He resumed the ancient practice of sweetening his coffee with cane syrup and put his automobile up in a shed until times improved.[11] In the sand hills of North Florida, others were not so fortunate. Elder J. R. "Uncle Bob" Dukes of the Original Suwannee Association received an invitation to "eat a piece of bread" from a widow with several children. On arriving at her home, he found that she had not spoken metaphorically. The entire meal consisted of one "pone" of hoecake and a pitcher of water.[12] Under such pressing circumstances, the naturally combative Primitive Baptist temper became even more frayed than usual.

Ironically, the Peace movement caused as many breaches as it healed. In the 1930s, its promoters disastrously overreached themselves in extending fellowship not only to "Optional Footwashers" but also to the Towaliga Association in Middle Georgia, a body which had been out of the Primitive Baptist mainstream for nearly eighty years. The resulting shock waves caused tremendous dislocation throughout Georgia, Alabama, and Florida.

The Towaliga Association represented the Primitive wing of the Flint River Baptist Association and had divided from the main body in 1838. However, a tolerant attitude toward Masonry soon strained Towaliga's relationship with the Primitive Western Association to the breaking point. In 1854, the Towaliga Association declared that it did not disfellowship Masons if they remained "orthodox and orderly."[13] As a result, most Georgia associations refused to associate with the Towaliga after the mid-1850s.[14]

The Towaliga's subsequent history for many years did nothing to restore their former brethren's confidence in them. In 1861, the Missionary Flint River Association made a peace overture to the Towaliga, which actually flirted with the proposition for several years. The Towaliga went so far as to repeal an article denouncing the Missionary institutions but expected in return that the Flint River Association would discard most of the institutions themselves.[15] As might have been expected, the peace overtures went nowhere, but they doubtless had a chilling effect on other Primitives observing the flirtation.

For several years in the mid-1800s, the Towaligans departed from Primitive Baptist practice by receiving Missionary Baptists as members without rebaptism, a position that made them even more controversial than their stand on Masonry. In 1875, however, a majority of the churches declared Missionary baptism invalid; but the association tabled a resolution demanding no more reception of Missionary baptism and rebaptism of those previously received.[16] Even this moderate position generated a division within the association. One church "saw nothing in either [the] faith or practice of [the] Missionaries in our midst, that should debar them from becoming members of our churches."[17] The Towaliga Association offered a couple of irrelevant, if not sophistical, defenses of their membership policy. They first argued that the local Missionary baptism remained valid until 1858, because until then the Flint River Association had not officially endorsed Sunday schools. They denied receiving Missionary baptism since then.[18] Considering that the Flint River Association became a charter member of the Southern Baptist Convention in 1845, one wonders who the Towaligans thought they were fooling.[19] The association actually seems to have ruled Missionary baptism valid up until 1858 because about that time the wife of one Nichols, a prominent minister in the Towaliga, had come in from the Missionaries and apparently did not wish to be rebaptized. The Towaliga further argued that churches, not associations, determined their admission standards, as though the association could somehow distance itself from the acts of its constituent churches.[20] Other Primitive Baptists appear to have ignored these arguments as mere sophistries.

Like many isolated Old Baptist factions, the Towaliga frequently accepted excluded churches and ministers from surrounding Primitive Baptist associations, including one elder turned out for adultery.[21] None of this improved relations with their former coreligionists.

In addition to their unorthodox practices, the Towaligans held to the type of general call evangelism being repudiated by most other Primitive Baptists in the late nineteenth century. Their 1893 Circular Address lambasted their less evangelical opponents: "We well remember, not many years ago able divines claimed that they were not called to preach to sinners, but to feed the sheep. That, with fatality, two seedism, and many other errors that are God-dishonoring, was held by those who called us Armenians [sic]. And poor little lambs who had been made alive by the holy spirit were left for years to wander in this wilderness of sin without a word of encouragement to take up the cross and follow their loving Savior."[22]

The same circular declared it the duty of ministers to preach "salvation to a lost and ruined world, telling poor sinners to repent." The 1896 minutes contained a lengthy statement of principles, which sidestepped the issue of valid baptism, strongly expressed church sovereignty, and declared footwashing "inseparably connected with the Lord's Supper." It also clearly expressed belief in gospel regeneration and maintained that the gospel should be preached to all that providence brings within its range. The Towaligans avoided the Missionary pitfall by arguing that if there were no gospel in a country, there were none of the elect there either, as the purpose of the gospel is to call the chosen. It would therefore be presumptuous to try and send it where it is not.[23] The main body of Primitive Baptists had moved far away from these views by the 1890s.

Unlike many isolated Primitive Baptist factions, the Towaliga did not retreat into a pessimistic lethargy. In the late 1890s, the Towaliga seemed poised to spread its unwelcome variant of the faith beyond the confines of

Middle Georgia. In 1888, the association began to publish the *Towaliga Messenger,* which carried on its masthead the apt quotation: "for as concerning this sect, we know that everywhere it is spoken against." In the 1890s, the hated Youngites in Georgia's Irwin and Berrien counties formed themselves into the Brushy Creek Union, in order to correspond with the Towaliga.[24] Worse, the Towaligans began to make converts outside their original range. In 1893 and 1894, Liberty Church in distant Wayne County, Georgia, and Philippi Church in Bulloch County, Georgia, joined the association.[25] To the orthodox Primitive Baptists of Georgia, the Towaliga Association must indeed at this point have seemed "the habitation of devils, and the hold of every foul spirit, and a cage of every unclean and hateful bird."[26]

With the rise of the Progressive movement, the Towaligans began efforts to reestablish contacts with other Georgia Primitive Baptists. In 1897 they "freely" admitted "that some of our churches committed gross errors years ago in recognizing Missionary baptism," but they claimed to have repudiated Missionary correspondence in 1867 and their baptism in 1875.[27] The Progressives responded well to these overtures. The Towaliga received an invitation to attend the 1900 Fulton Convention, sponsored by the Progressives, and sent W. T. Godard.[28] By 1902 they were in correspondence with the main Progressive association, the Lower Canoochee.[29]

Once the Towaliga began to move in a more conservative direction, the movement developed considerable momentum. The instrumental music split among the Progressives eventually led to a division in the Towaliga also. In 1910, the association repudiated the Brushy Creek Union churches for using instrumental music, which they declared to be "wholly contrary to the word of God in the New Testament and . . . very grievous to our churches."[30] Half the Towaliga churches affiliated with those Progressives using musical instruments.[31] The Old Line party condemned "all modern innovations of every kind including the use of instrumental music and as a body we deem it wise to refuse affiliation with any church, brother, or sister so long as they are associated with it." The circular address for that year thanked God for "keeping the old ship from sinking amid the storms and waves of Progressivism." By 1928, the Old Line Towaliga had definitely adopted the anti-instrumental theology of the other Primitive Baptists as well, declaring that "the object of [the] ministry is not to give eternal life." Also in 1928, they declared their intention of "denying all the worldly institutions of men, such as masonry, oddfellowship and all attendant orders of the day."[32]

By 1930, many Old Line Primitive Baptists, bursting with Christian charity as a result of the Peace movement, regarded the Old Line Towaliga As-

sociation as completely reformed and prepared to take it back to their collective bosom as a group of long lost brethren for the first time since the 1850s. In 1931, the Towaliga formally reestablished connection with the mainline Ocmulgee Association. In the early 1930s, representatives from many Geor-
... and others from as far afield as Virginia appeared at the
... ckoned with the long memories of
... Association alone constituted too
... t the appearance about 1930 in the
... tive Baptist elders from the upper
... mbers due to Ford and Macadam

... s and non-footwashers exploded in
... Bethel, Euharlee, and Lott's Creek
... nnee and Ebenezer declaring against
... .[35] Ephesus Church, Bulloch County,
... Association, expressed the conserva-

> ... owaliga Association was alienated
> ... s since 1866, and that they were a
> ... secret-orderism, alien-baptism, and receiving excluded members from orderly churches has been handed down to us by our forefathers. They received excluded members from some of our churches for such disorders as fornication, falsifying and secret-orderism. Such acts were little noticed as they stood alienated. The Towaliga association remained alienated from all orderly Old Line Baptists until the fall of 1931, at which time the Ocmulgee Association had an interview with her for reconciliation which resulted in taking her up, recognizing her official works for all the time she had been in disorder or alienated. The Towaliga being incapacitated to make amends to the Lott's Creek churches by way of acknowledgements, the inevitable was to reject the encroachment of such disorder.[36]

The acceptance of the Towaligans "official works," such as baptism and ordination, constituted the chief stumbling block to the conservatives. They held that the association had departed sufficiently far from orthodoxy to invalidate all its "official work," such as baptism and ordination. While pre-1854 validly baptized members remained among them, the Towaligans could have repudiated their errors, redone their "official work," and rejoined the main body of Primitive Baptists. With the death of that generation, however, the Towaliga became officially extinct in the eyes of the conservatives and could only have reentered the main body of Primitive Baptists by baptism and reorganization at the hands of ministers acting on behalf of "orderly" churches. Commenting on this principle, Elder Charles Wells of the anti-Towaliga faction of the Ebenezer Association wrote, "It is true that church can make a mistake in excluding a member, or members; but it is equally true that she (not her grandchildren) can correct those mistakes."[37] The more liberal Primitive Baptists assumed that current sound faith and practice outweighed past derelictions.

The Beulah and Hillabee associations in Alabama declared against optional footwashing, and the Pilgrim's Rest and Mt. Enon associations in southern Florida divided on the issue, with minority factions taking a strong anti-Towaliga/anti–optional footwashing stance.[38] In a leaflet inserted in their 1936 minutes, the Pilgrim's Rest anti-Towaligans swooped down on their opponents: "We also declare ourselves opposed to and not in fellowship with any of the so-called peace move Baptists or any of their affiliations or alignments, or any other progressive movements, as non-Feetwashing, unjustifiable divorces, secret orders, Bible class, Ministerial support, or alien baptism. We detest these things and maintain that they belong to the world."[39]

Meanwhile, in South Georgia, apprehension over the Towaliga Association and optional footwashing became evident as early as 1933.[40] Tension mounted in the Flint River, Ochlocknee, and Union associations until they attained "critical mass" in 1936–37 and exploded. Elder T. J. "Josh" Davis, the moderator of the Flint River Association, had heard that their northern visitors did not wash feet but could not prevail on any of the brethren in his acquaintance to question them on the subject. He shared a fateful automobile ride to the Lott's Creek Association with Elder R. H. Pittman, a nationally known Primitive Baptist minister from Virginia and sometime editor of the *Gospel Messenger.* Davis worked up his courage and asked Pittman if he knew of any "orthodox, old-line Primitive Baptist associations" that did not wash feet. Pittman replied that his own association did not. Horrified, Davis returned home and rallied the anti-Towaliga/anti–optional footwashing forces in his home association.[41] The Flint River Association divided in 1936, the anti-Towaliga party claiming that "some of our people engaged in and favored certain forward and misleading acts, evidently having been influenced by a prevailing spirit of Progressiveness."[42] They went on to express their nonfellowship for "those who affiliate with and refuse to put into practice the commandments, ordinances and examples of our Lord and Savior, Jesus Christ."[43]

In 1938, after several years of confusion, the Ochlocknee Association dropped the Union, San Pedro, and Pulaski associations "on the grounds of their affiliation directly or indirectly with Tiologia [sic] Association and the non-footwashing people."[44] In the previous year they had clearly aligned themselves against the optional footwashers:

> We deeply deplore the sad condition of our Zion everywhere. Slackness and many sicklings with optional and non-footwashers to the bleeding and sorrow of many hearts. Our forefathers more than one hundred years ago as faithful, humble servants to God drew up by the guiding hand of God Scriptural articles founded upon the written word, and our churches were constituted upon them and we have ever stood upon and by them and [are] still desiring to do so. . . .
>
> Now let us, the Ochlocknee association, assert ourselves plainly that all Baptists may know where we stand.
>
> Brethren, we hold that Jesus made a test of fellowship with Peter when he (Peter) objected to Christ's washing his feet, saying, "If I wash thee not, thou hast no part with me . . ."
>
> Brethren, declare to us your attitude and stand as to your willingness to fellowship or affiliate with optional or non-footwashers directly or non-directly, as we are aware that some are advocating that footwashing should be excluded from our service.[45]

As one venerable Primitive said, "There used to be some in that Ochlocknee Association that was so stiff, they leaned over backwards." Their stiff stand lost them two churches but gained them five others from more wishy-washy associations.[46] Ironically, the stiff-backed Ochlockneans apparently had none of their own early minutes in their possession, or they would have made the horrifying discovery that footwashing had not been listed as an ordinance in their articles of faith for much more than sixty years.

One of the more supple bodies was the Union Association of central South Georgia. The association tried to take a neutral stance in the Towaliga controversy, suspending correspondence with the hotly partisan Lott's Creek Association in 1934, "for the time being."[47] Once again, as in 1901 and 1927 Elder J. B. "Toad" Luke helped controversy along, this time by agitating for the reception of non-footwashers. Luke died during the footwashing controversy, thus ending his ministerial career in a storm of controversy similar to the one in which it had commenced.[48]

Elder H. A. Byington also generated trouble on this subject. Elder Byington often wrote for church papers, and his son Barney recalled getting up deep in the night many times as a boy to find his father writing furiously by lamplight. Byington traveled considerably and many Primitive Baptists gladly put him up in their homes for the benefit of his deep knowledge of the Scriptures and his interesting conversation on religious topics. W. E. Redding's daughters recalled their father's glad welcome of Elder Byington whenever he came through the Hahira, Georgia, area. Flue-cured tobacco had become a major crop in South Georgia in the early 1920s, and Redding and Byington would sit up all night together, firing tobacco barns and discussing spiritual matters. Although an excellent "fireside" preacher, Byington performed lamentably in the pulpit, having a weak voice that seldom carried beyond the pulpit and the first couple of pews.[49] At the annual meeting at Salem Church, Adel, Georgia, in April of 1937, Elder Byington stated in a churchyard conversation that he had equal fellowship for footwashing and non-footwashing Baptists. As a result, Caulie Bennett, the messenger from New Friendship Church of Hahira, Georgia, refused to hand in that church's corresponding letter. This action provoked a split at New Friendship.[50] About the same time, Elder Pat Byrd of Virginia, a non-footwasher, began to be much in evidence in the Union Association. This horrified two prominent elders, John Harris and Duncan McCranie.[51]

Harris began preaching about 1915 and had taken a prominent part in the Peace movement.[52] Peace with Towaligans and non-footwashers went further than he had bargained for. Like most initiators of revolution, he found his movement going further than he did. Harris was a tall, dark, commanding man with a noticeable dash of reputedly Indian blood and a trace of rule or ruin in his personality. "Brother John was longheaded [i.e., stubborn]," a former parishioner recalled. He had a better education than the average Primitive Baptist preacher of his day, and although a powerful preacher, he did not "jump the rabbit," or chant, his sermons.[53] He enjoyed a fair degree of affluence, being the president of the Valdosta Nehi Bottling Company. The Old Baptists tolerated his education, and even admired it at times, but the Nehi Company nearly got him "jerked up" before the church. The Nehi logo consisted of a pulchritudinous drum majorette in a very brief skirt with a "knee high." Harris thoughtlessly slapped one of his stickers on his car bumper. Suffice it to say that after the logo's first trip to church, it never returned.[54]

Duncan McCranie, Harris's good friend, began his ministry riding to church on horseback and continued preaching into the 1960s. Stories still circulate about "Uncle Duncan," or just "Dunc." He loathed weddings and once, sporting no more than a shirt over his long johns, married a couple out of his bedroom window, saying only, "Will you have this woman to be your

Elder Duncan McCranie at New Friendship Church, Hahira, Ga. Circa 1955. Courtesy of Fred E. Blanton.

lawfully wedded wife, will you have this man, etc. I now pronounce you man and wife." When his scandalized wife doubted the validity of such cavalier proceedings, he simply signed the license and observed, "When this gets to the ordinary's office with my John Henry on it, it'll take 'em a lot longer to get unhitched than it did to get hitched."[55] As might be expected, he was a strong predestinarian. Two of his still repeated aphorisms are: "The Bible was written to the children of God,"[56] and "The more men you have together, the more devils you have together."[57] "He should have known," one critic remarked. He enjoyed puncturing the exalted opinions entertained by many people of preachers. He once told Elder Fred Blanton, then a young layman, that he would tell him the kind of holy thoughts preachers had in the pulpit. A fellow preacher had the odd habit of praying on all fours, facing the front of the pulpit. Kneeling at the pulpit bench behind the elder, Duncan caught a sidelong glance at his huge fundament sticking up at a tempting angle. He thought, "If I had a pin to goose that old man with, he'd go through the front of this stand."[58]

Among McCranie's possessions was a well-thumbed copy of the *Black Rock Address,* with its jeremiads against Sunday schools, Mission societies, seminaries, and so forth. Duncan not only despised seminaries and by extension written, polished sermons; he even detested recordings of sermons. After tape recorders came into general use, he kept a sharp lookout for them, saying he had no use for "canned preaching." He refused to preach at one church until thoroughly convinced that the goose-necked lamp on the pulpit was not a microphone.[59]

Duncan's brutal sense of humor left a lasting impression on his victims. He once wished a vain young girl would get a boil on the end of her nose.

Although Duncan had a Celtic marauder's face suitable for frightening small children, on one occasion he approached Elder Henry Rhoden, a visiting preacher to whom he had not so much as been introduced, and asked, "Is your name Henry Rhoden? " "Yes, sir," replied the hapless victim. "Well, Henry Rhoden, you ain't two faced, for if you'd a-had another face, you'd a-wore it."[60] The late Zuma Kelly, a member at New Friendship Church, recalled that "Duncan was a good old man, but he had a *big mouth.*"[61] Elder Fred Blanton said of him, "Duncan had an explosive personality. He exploded first and surveyed the damage afterward."[62]

McCranie had another side to his personality. Deacon Edwin Johnson of New Friendship Church recalled that as a young man he endured such spiritual distress relative to his conversion that he would plow a field and then have to look at it again immediately thereafter to see if he had been over it. In this state of mind he attended worship at New Friendship on a day when Duncan was the only preacher present. During the sermon, Johnson's feelings so overpowered him that he left the church and went into the woods across the road to pray. Soon he felt a huge hand on his shoulder and found that Duncan had broken off his sermon and left the ninety and nine to seek the one that was lost. "I figured I'd do more good out here," he told Johnson.[63]

Through most of his life a misogynistic bachelor, Duncan often boasted that the woman he would marry had never been born. Late in life, however, he did marry, but his wife later became deranged. All who knew his irascible temper were amazed at his endless patience and tenderness in caring for her. He refused all assistance and insisted on performing the most humble offices for her himself, even to washing her clothes. To any offer of help he indignantly replied, "I'll take care of Annie."[64] But he remained Duncan to the end. Old, near death, and heavily drugged, he lay in the hospital cursing like a longshoreman, and his nurse tried to calm him with "Such talk and you a preacher!" He instantly fixed her with a lucid glare and growled, "A preacher ain't nothin' but a man."[65]

Harris and McCranie were not the sort to tolerate the hordes of optional footwashers they envisioned descending on them to uproot immemorial customs. In 1937, Pleasant Church in Berrien County, Georgia, Duncan's home church at the time, stood almost solidly against the Union Association on the footwashing question. New Friendship and Cat Creek churches, both in Lowndes County, Georgia, divided on the issue, New Friendship losing twenty-two of its fifty-four members.[66] Cat Creek lost Elder Harris and eight others, not enough to sustain a rival faction there.[67] Refuge Church, Atkinson County, left the "Peace Folks" and returned to its former allegiance with the Original Union Association.[68] Mt. Pleasant Church in the flatwoods of Clinch

County, Georgia, also left the association over the footwashing controversy.[69] As usual with such splits, considerable confusion resulted. Pleasant Church appointed a committee to visit Maxie Simpson and Ellie Clanton and "explain to them that this church did not expell them as we understand they thought we did."[70]

At the 1937 session, the Peace faction of the Union Association dropped Pleasant, Mt. Pleasant, and Refuge for "denouncing our order." However, the association tried to conciliate the conservatives by authorizing their delegates to other associations to inquire whether some of their ministers "endorse optional footwashing." The association also adopted a resolution that they would not "knowingly affiliate with any association whose churches do not practice footwashing as it is taught in the scripture." The next year, they reiterated their stand: "When we joined the Primitive Baptist church, it practiced foot washing. We liked it then and we like it yet, and will not depart from it. We get a joy out of it that we would not get if we leave it off. Then how can we walk together hand in hand and see eye to eye and speak the self same thing. We furthermore humbly beg and admonish primitive Baptists all, here and everywhere that if they feel footwashing is a duty, for them to practice it one hundred percent. If for any reason any Primitive Baptist anywhere desires to leave it off, we the Union Association prefer not to affiliate with you or bid you God speed."[71]

This argument shows clearly the extreme present-mindedness characteristic of the footwashing controversy. From an occasional practice in the eighteenth and nineteenth centuries, footwashing had burgeoned into a major article of faith over which communion could be sacrificed. The standard of proof for the conservatives consisted of a literal reading of Scripture, combined with a sense of tradition that extended no further back than living recollection. This resolution of the Union Association extended only to non-footwashers, of which there were none in Georgia. It did not repudiate the equally controversial Towaligans, and relations with them continued.[72] If this resolution attempted to quell the fears of conservatives and lure them back into the association, it failed. Pleasant, New Friendship (including the seceders from Cat Creek, Harris among them), and Mt. Pleasant joined the Ochlocknee Association in 1939, effectively ending the footwashing controversy.[73]

Duncan McCranie did not long remain in "The West," as he called the Ochlocknee Association. After a falling out with one of his deacons at Pleasant Church, he returned to the Union Association, joining Cat Creek Church in 1943.[74] For the most part, his former brethren received him warmly. A few, however, such as Sister Mary Blanton of Unity Church, never forgot and barely forgave his defection. Sister Blanton was a Baptist woman in the Nancy Hagan and "Grandma" Alderman tradition, what George Washington Harris called an "ole obsarvin' she pillar of the church."[75] McCranie had served Unity Church as pastor when he "went west," and whenever he and Sister Blanton met thereafter, their eyes would lock and it would seem as though a stream of fire jumped along their glance.[76]

The anti-Towaligans experienced several bitter schisms after 1950, to the point of near extinction as a distinct party. Most of these resulted from new pressures on the traditional way of life associated with Primitive Baptists and are dealt with in the next chapter.

10

"The Shadows of the Evening"

1945 to the Present

In 1977, the late Elder W. F. Bethea of Nashville, Georgia, preached Elder J. L. Rowan's ordination sermon at Pleasant Grove Church, Berrien County, Georgia. He took for his text the latter clause of Jeremiah 6:4, "Woe unto us! for the day goeth away, for the shadows of the evening are stretched out." He warned the ordinand never to expect the great crowds and prosperous churches remembered from his youth. Further, as the world drew to its close, the shadows would lengthen, and the truth would become increasingly dim and unsought. Nor was Elder Bethea alone in his pessimism, for Elder Frank Lee of the Crawfordite Alabaha River Association, in a 1974 sermon at Piney Grove Church, Ware County, Georgia, had declared the last days of time at hand, signified by the dwindling of the true faith. Deacon W. Hardeman Paulk (1880–1980) often greeted his visiting pastor with the words, "I may be wrong, brother, but it seems to me we are living in the evening of the last days."[1] Elder Elisha Roberts of the Original Union Association believed he had been called to the ministry for little other purpose than to assist in the dissolution of old, dying churches.[2]

Statistically, these Primitive Baptists had good cause for their pessimism. Although the proportion of Primitive Baptists to the general population had declined sharply from their glory days in the 1840s and 1890s, their absolute numbers tended to remain stable and sometimes to grow. After World War II, however, the combined effects of desertion of the southern countryside where their main strength lay, the pressures of town and city life, aggressive proselytizing by other denominations, competing worldly entertainments, and their own divisiveness resulted in a sharp and accelerating decline in numbers. As might be expected, many Primitive Baptists saw this as merely a manifestation of the inscrutable will of God, while a few sought by various means to counteract the trend.

William Nathaniel Redding. 1866. Courtesy of John G. Crowley.

Esther Caroline Newton Redding, wife of William Nathaniel Redding. 1866. Courtesy of John G. Crowley.

The statistics indeed painted a gloomy picture throughout the various factions. Between 1944 and 1992, the Original Union Association declined from 489 members in nineteen churches to 112 in eleven churches.[3] The main faction of the Mt. Enon Association decreased from 912 in twenty-two churches in 1933 to 529 in thirteen churches in 1981.[4] The Crawfordite Alabaha River Association dropped from 596 members and thirteen churches in 1941 to six churches with eighty-seven members in 1993.[5] Between 1945 and 1989, the Peace faction of the Union Association fell from 756 members and twenty-three churches to eight churches with ninety-three members.[6] The Progressives fared little better, with their faction of the Ochlocknee Association declining from ten churches and 474 members in 1945 to six churches with 187 in 1993.[7]

The Redding family of Lowndes County, Georgia, once strongly Primitive Baptist, typifies the process of decline. William Nathaniel Redding (1824–93), nephew of Elder Henry Milton, a leading Antimissionary in the Ochlocknee Association, married Esther Caroline Newton Dukes (1840–81).[8] He and his wife joined Cat Creek Church, Lowndes County.[9] Two of their daughters joined the Missionary Baptists and those daughters' children remained largely of that faith. Two Redding sons joined no church and married

Methodists, although inclined to the Primitive faith. John, the eldest, once remarked that the Methodists were "plumb pitiful. I ain't got no religion, and they ain't either, but they think they do, and its plumb pitiful." Thomas, the younger unchurched brother, once remarked that there would have to be "a side door cut in hell" to accommodate a certain large, ostentatiously pious Missionary family. John's children followed their mother into the Methodist Church, and Thomas's offspring left their maternal Methodism for Pentecostalism.[10]

Two of W. N. and Caroline Redding's children joined the Primitive Baptists. Their daughter Belle Moore united with Cat Creek Church, but although some of her children and grandchildren attended there, none of them ever sought baptism, and none of her descendants attend Primitive worship today. William Elhanon (1874–1937), W. N. Redding's second son, joined Cat Creek Church in 1905. As a young boy, he felt strong religious impressions, which, however, his father dismissed, telling him that young children did not have genuine religious experiences. In his thirties, William Elhanon found that his religious impressions had returned, and his eldest sister, a Missionary Baptist, persuaded him to join the Bethany Missionary Baptist Church near Hahira. However, he refused baptism and became distraught from having apostatized from the Primitive religion his conscience dictated. Convinced he was becoming insane, his family had him committed to the State Insane Asylum at Milledgeville. The director of the institution soon discerned that nothing ailed him except religious conflict and sent him home with instructions to his family to leave him to his own choice in the matter. He soon joined the Primitive Baptists, where he remained for the remainder of his life, being regarded as something of a martyr for the true faith. He married Mayme Turner, descended from a Primitive Baptist family. She never sought baptism although she believed in the doctrines of the church and attended it throughout her life. Of their five children who survived to adulthood, none joined the Primitive Church, although four of them strongly adhered to its doctrines. The youngest daughter of the family married into a family traditionally identified with the Church of Christ, or Campbellites, and she and her children remained in that faith. James Hanon, the only son, married first a Missionary Baptist and later a Methodist, and his two children never shared his Primitive faith. The three remaining daughters believed strongly in the Primitive faith, although only one of them had a child. That child, a son, joined the Primitive Baptists in 1973 and is a member at present. Thus, of the more than one hundred descendants of William Nathaniel and Caroline Redding, a century after their deaths, only one remains a Primitive Baptist. This account could be multiplied endlessly in

William Elhanon and Mayme Turner Redding, Hahira, Ga. Circa 1925. Courtesy of John G. Crowley.

South Georgia and Florida, where virtually every family of the old settler stock has Primitive Baptist ancestors, but very few members profess that faith today.[11]

Several factors emerge from the foregoing account and from the experiences of other Primitive Baptist families. William Nathaniel Redding's dismissal of his young son's impressions indicates the severe scrutiny purported conversions received and which doubtless discouraged many who inclined toward the Primitive Baptists from making a public profession of faith. William Elhanon Redding's daughters and son who adhered to the Primitive faith never offered to (sought membership in) the church. They held that one had to be "changed" to join the church, and one would know when the requisite change had taken place, and that to receive baptism without such evidence constituted a grave sin. Although most Primitive Baptist churches have grown increasingly lax in receiving members, many older people remember the experiences formerly required and do not wish to suffer the fate of the unfortunate Mary Baxley, refused as a candidate for baptism by Beard's Creek Church because "she could relate nothing of a work of grace upon her soul."[12] As a result, most Primitive Baptist congregations have an entourage of "Dry Baptists" who never join but spend their lives "eating through the crack," an unlovely reference to razorback hogs pulling corn from between the logs of a crib.[13]

The Primitive emphasis upon salvation as an unconditional covenant transaction before the foundation of the world makes church membership absolutely unnecessary for salvation in their view; consequently there is little imperative for one to join the church. This gave rise to a sort of antinomianism with respect to religious profession. When a descendant of the Redding clan turned Catholic for a brief time, his family drily observed that if he was elected, he would be saved no matter what church he joined, and if he was not elected, he could join them all and would still be damned. Belief in regeneration as a prerequisite to understanding Primitive doctrine made proselytizing, even of one's children, seem presumptuous, if not useless. Children's questions about the faith frequently got short shrift from older relatives, who only opened to the subject when the young showed a sustained interest in the matter.[14]

Although considerable hostility toward other denominations lurks close to the surface among Primitives, most of them now subscribe to a "there's good people in all churches" attitude, which eases social interactions but further weakens their platform for proselytizing. The Crawfordites formed for many years one notable exception to this temporizing attitude, holding that an unrepented heretical religious profession indicated nonelection. When the late Deacon John Royce Proctor of Brantley County, Georgia, joined the Missionary Baptists as a youth in the 1920s, his Crawfordite father flatly informed him he was on a fast track to hell.[15]

The growing closeness of the outside world with its allurements and distractions contributed to the alienation of the rising generation from their ancestral tradition. The Primitive Baptists of the twentieth century, except for the Progressives, have had no more organized indoctrination for their children than their forebears had in the preceding century. Children accompanied their parents to church and were required to sit through one of the several sermons likely to be preached. Afterward they got permission to play in the churchyard.[16]

W. E. Redding read the Bible aloud to his wife on many evenings, while his children listened with half an ear, unconsciously absorbing the family's Primitive doctrines. His daughters recall him commenting so extensively on what he read that it took him quite some time to work through only a few verses. When his aged mother-in-law could no longer attend meetings, she seldom requested their church to hold services in her home, preferring for Redding to read and elaborate on the Scriptures for her. In his latter days, however, he purchased a battery-powered radio and thereafter read the Bible to himself and his wife while the children listened to the radio. Perhaps not coincidentally, the older children retained the Primitive Baptist faith, while the youngest daughter did not.[17]

The introduction of television accelerated the process of alienation. Many older Primitive Baptists remained dubious of radio and television as worldly amusements, and some of them refused to attend theaters, but their example had little influence on the rising generations. Their children and grandchildren quickly acquired a taste for such things, permanently short-circuiting in many homes the old process of learning the faith through osmosis as the older people discussed it on quiet rural evenings. This was not universally the case, however, as some children continued to absorb the faith in the old manner, despite the absence of formal religious instruction. In the 1970s, the seven-year-old daughter of a young Primitive Baptist couple at Bethel Church, Echols County, Georgia, attended a Bible camp conducted by another denomination. She soon asked to come home because the "crazy" preacher directing the camp, in her already decidedly Primitive eyes, "did not know how people were saved." In many cases radio, television, and other distractions prevented the transmission of the faith, leaving descendants of Primitive Baptists easy game for the aggressive proselytizing of the Missionary Baptists and younger and even more aggressive denominations such as the Pentecostals and Churches of Christ. The Crawfordites forbade their members to own radios and televisions, and while their internal divisions have greatly reduced their numbers, they do still have, for Primitive Baptists, a remarkable number of young people who at least attend their churches, if they do not often join them.[18]

Most Primitives, like Elder Henry Parrish when his daughter wished to join the Methodists, failed to take competing religions seriously enough to regard them as a threat. W. E. Redding's children yawned through school devotionals and attended Missionary Baptist revivals mainly to laugh at their playmates' terrified weeping under the hellfire preaching, which seemed absurd in their predestinarian context. Levi Bennett of Salem Church, Cook County, Georgia, took his children to the early Pentecostal tent revivals because they were as amusing as a circus and did not charge admission.[19] Nonetheless, six of his eight children remained true to the faith.[20] Elder Henry Rhoden, of Pleasant Grove Church, Baker County, Florida, recalled how a female Pentecostal evangelist conducted meetings in Baker County during his youth. She played hot gospel tunes on a piano and encouraged all the young people to shout and gyrate, much to their delight. She left the community convinced she had founded a flourishing Pentecostal congregation—blissfully unaware that none of her young proselytes believed anything she had said or that they returned to Primitive worship as soon as the piano was gone. In earlier days, when the faith had great momentum from generation to generation, this cavalier attitude probably allowed only for a healthy culling among the rising generation. In later times, however, the combination of fear and glitter they encountered in other churches enticed many children. In at least one instance, a member supposedly left Pleasant Primitive Baptist Church because he had young children and the Primitives had "nothing for young people." Elder I. B. Hall of the Original Union Association summed up the usual Primitive response to such concerns while waiting for inspiration from on high in the pulpit at Bethany Church, Clinch County, Georgia. Referring to the young man's concern, he added that "unless the Lord comes on the scene, I have nothing for the old people either."[21]

Primitive Baptist leaders believed more than a century ago that town life had a deleterious effect on Primitive Baptist churches. Sylvester and Cushing Biggs Hassell noted in the 1880s that "genuine [i.e., Primitive] Baptists Churches are seldom found in cities, and, when found in such localities, are apt to be in a sickly condition. The forms and fashions, the parades and shows of city life, are very uncongenial to the staid habits and to the faith and practice of old-fashioned Baptists."[22] With abandonment of farm life, school consolidation, increased mobility, and the development of more places of recreation for young people, children of Primitive Baptists often found future mates in places other than church meetings. When, as was often the case, the husbands or wives so met belonged to other denominations, if they did not succeed in converting an Old Baptist spouse to their faith, they raised their children in it. Unlike the Mennonites, Amish, and other ultraconservative sects, the Primitives have never officially discouraged outmarriage into other religious traditions, although the practice has cost them dearly from an early period. Mary Knight, excommunicated by Union Church in 1832 for joining the Methodists, probably did so because her husband was a Methodist preacher.[23] The history of the decline of the Primitive faith in the Redding family is largely a story of the results of marriage into other denominations. Actual Primitive Baptist church members, however, seldom apostatized as a result of such marriages. Elder John Harris, a major actor in the foot-washing schism of the 1930s, married a Methodist. On Sunday she went her way and he his, and a judicious silence by both parties on the subject of religion maintained domestic peace.[24]

From the early 1800s onward, Primitive Baptists tended to be old. Lillian Crowley recalled that in her youth, during the 1910s and 1920s, most church members were middle aged or older. This trend became more pronounced. For many years past there have been few young members in Primitive Baptist churches, and the few exceptions often caused astonishment. In the early

1980s, a man in his twenties pastored the "second Sunday side" of Cat Creek Church, Lowndes County, Georgia. Before a funeral where he was to officiate, a bystander asked where the Primitive preacher was. When he was pointed out to her, she said, "He can't be a Hardshell. He's young!" With a gap of an entire unchurched or other-churched generation developing between the bearers of the faith and their youngest descendants, the informal process of instruction became ever more fragile and ineffective. While many descendants of Primitive Baptists left the faith, relatively few outsiders joined it. On rare occasions, however, the process of outmarriage worked to bring non-Primitives into the fold. Elder Fred Bethea's daughter, Kinnette, married Earl James, a staunch Missionary Baptist, in the early 1970s. She refused to give up her religious allegiance, and he often attended Primitive worship with her. After presenting all his objections to the Primitive Faith during a trip to a distant church, James found the sermon he heard there answering his criticisms point by point. Struck by the coincidence, he began to examine his wife's belief with a more open mind. He then noticed an apparent contradiction in Missionary preaching, produced by emphasis on salvation by grace, yet coupling the proclamation of grace alone with the necessity of human effort. He soon thereafter united with the Primitive Baptists and remained a firm believer.[25]

Many twentieth-century social trends conflicted with basic Primitive beliefs, generating damaging divisions. Lillian Crowley, a descendant of many generations of Old Baptists, observed that the agony of her ancestral faith stemmed from the attempt to maintain a seventeenth-century church in the twentieth century.[26] By midcentury, the tension became unbearable in some places. The Ochlocknee Association divided in 1952 over a divorce case arising in Indian Creek Church, Colquitt County, Georgia. A member had been expelled for nonattendance and rebellion. His wife left him and obtained a divorce on the grounds of nonsupport. While excluded from the church, he remarried. This circumstance generated controversy over the issue of divorce and remarriage, resulting in a three-way division in the association.[27] The Indian Creek faction reestablished fellowship with the Peace faction of the Union Association, first dropping Elder John Harris and his faction of New Friendship Church as a sacrificial offering. The Ochlocknee's moderator, Elder J. W. Rogers, later claimed that he knew Harris had been in disorder from the time of the 1937 footwashing schism. One disgruntled Harris follower observed that if he knew such a thing, it had taken him a remarkably long time to voice his opinion.[28] Five churches seceded from the Ochlocknee and joined the anti-Towaliga, or "Josh Davis," faction of the Flint River Association.[29] Three Ochlocknee churches reorganized as the Original

Ochlocknee Association, resolving not to "fellowship members who are divorced and remarried with all parties still living, and where such bill of divorce was granted for other reasons except adultery or fornication."[30] Harris returned to the Old Line side at Cat Creek, which had demanded his credentials in 1927 and finally got them in 1956. He remained with the Original Union Association for the remainder of his life.[31]

When divorces and subsequent remarriage seldom occurred, the churches could afford to take a strict line in regard to them. After "deliberately weighing the subject in the balance of the sanctuary," the Georgia Association in 1804 ruled "pretty unanimously" that a divorced husband or wife might not remarry during the lifetime of the former spouse.[32] The Suwannee River Association seconded this opinion in 1847.[33] Elder Gilbert Beebe in 1840 proclaimed remarriage after divorce sinful under any circumstances, enactments of human legislatures to the contrary notwithstanding. "We could as soon extend our fellowship and approbation to the direct crime of adultery, where no separation has taken place between the husband and wife, as where such separation has taken place, a divorce obtained and the new connection legalized by the marriage of parties where one or both have a living wife or husband." He hoped "never to hear of an instance among the Old School Baptists; nor can we hold any as Old School Baptists who would thus live in adultery."[34] Frequent divorce, however, eventually appeared among the Primitives. Elder W. G. Hunter of the Ochlocknee Association separated from his wife in 1855, although apparently neither remarried. Considering that Mrs. Hunter's alimony settlement consisted of fourteen slaves, a mule, five cattle, three hundred bushels of corn, and two hundred acres of land, poverty as well as his sixty years rendered Elder Hunter an unlikely suitor.[35] Empire Church in Berrien County, Georgia, expelled Jethro and Francenia Patten in 1896 for separating from each other. Patten returned to the church in 1899, but his wife never did.[36]

As long as the churches maintained an absolute ban on divorce, little question arose on their proper course of action in such cases. By the 1930s, however, some Primitives interpreted the "exceptive clause" in Matthew 5:32 as allowing divorce and remarriage in the case of adultery. The Bennett faction of the Alabaha River Association sanctioned remarriage after divorce on the grounds of adultery in 1932. "We agree that fornication is the only legal cause for any man or woman to divorce their husband or wife . . . and marry another and be an eligible subject for reception into the church by water baptism. If such person should come seeking admission, a thorough investigation must be made before reception and baptism; neither shall any church or churches be held in our fellowship that receives or retains such persons among them."[37] As divorce became more common, especially among the young, the Original Union and its sister associations adopted the view that if individuals remarried after divorce on nonbiblical grounds before conversion, when they were in the "stock of nature" and unregenerate, then they could be received into the church, but not otherwise. The Peace churches adopted the somewhat more liberal view of taking no account of divorce or remarriage before baptism. But some brethren took exception to these liberalizing trends. Deacon Russell Register of Providence Church in the Peace Union Association remained an adamant opponent of divorce until his death in the 1970s, and Deacon J. A. Sapp of Cat Creek Church in the Original Union Association dissuaded his own son from offering as a candidate for baptism at Cat Creek because of his remarriage after a divorce. The son then joined the Peace faction at Cat Creek.[38]

Elder O. J. Rives, for many years moderator of the Peace Union Association, strongly opposed divorce until the experience of his own children convinced him that in some cases it might be the best course. Nonetheless, despite an officially liberal policy in this regard, divorced and remarried potential members were quietly discouraged from offering as candidates for baptism in some churches. The anti-Towaligan churches of southwest Georgia continued to refuse all candidates for membership who had previously divorced and remarried for reasons other than adultery. The Original Flint River Association once faced the vexed question of a possible candidate for membership who had remarried after a teenage marriage had been annulled. Fortunately for the peace of the association, the person in question never actually offered for membership. Only the Crawfordites maintain the ancient total ban on membership for any persons divorced and remarried in the lifetime of the previous spouse. Elder Tollie D. Lee, of the Crawford faction of the Alabaha River Association, in a sermon at Piney Grove Church, Ware County, Georgia, in January 1995, warned members that if divorced and remarried relatives and their spouses slept together at their houses, members owed the church an acknowledgment for conniving at adultery. However, laxity among the main body of Primitives extended only so far. In the 1970s the principal faction of the Mt. Enon Association in central Florida divided over divorce and remarriage in the ministry.[39]

In the late 1960s, the "do your own thing" spirit of the era reached the Old Baptists in the form of the Independent movement, which greatly diminished the San Pedro Association and the Peace factions of the Union and Suwannee River associations. The Independent movement basically reasserted the sovereignty of the individual church against the authority of associations, in a manner reminiscent of the early Progressive movement of the 1890s. The Peace faction of the Suwannee River Association assumed great authority over its constituent churches, thought by many to be in excess of what its constitution allowed. Macclenny Primitive Baptist Church withdrew from the association because of this. A member of Macclenny Church, Elder James Land, pastored Midway Church, Pierce County, in the Peace Union. The 1969 Union Association was scheduled to meet at Midway Church, and a move developed to change the meeting to a more acceptable location, lest they alienate the Suwannee River Association.[40]

In a called meeting at Pleasant Grove Church, Berrien County, Georgia, most of the churches decided to move the association to Refuge Church, Atkinson County. Nine churches, favoring the Independence movement, under the general leadership of Elder Varn Marshall of Salem Church, Cook County, Georgia, did not go to the Refuge meeting and were in effect dropped from the rolls. At the same session—on the testimony of one elder, who later defected himself—the Union dropped correspondence with virtually all its former corresponding associations, excepting only the Suwannee River and San Pedro. Three years later the Union dropped the Suwannee River Association because of various accusations against one of its ministers.[41] The Suwannee River subsequently dwindled as churches defected, finally leaving only three in the isolated association.[42]

The Union and San Pedro also dwindled as churches left for various causes.[43] With their relatively more liberal fellowship policies, the Independent churches became another refuge for any dissident church or faction. The associated churches adopted a total nonrecognition policy toward the Independents, even to the point of rebaptizing members baptized by them subsequent to the division. The seceding churches of the San Pedro Association attempted holding a factional associational meeting for a few years but soon abandoned the plan.[44] The antipathy toward associations became very strong among the Independent churches. Rather than claim to be an association, the seceding churches of the Suwannee River Association organized a North Florida Fellowship Meeting in 1972. The Fellowship Meeting published a pamphlet listing the churches attending, the ministers preaching, and the old associational articles of faith. Eventually the North Florida Meeting began to publish church statistics, but it made no further steps toward reproducing associational practices.[45] The churches formerly identified with the Peace Union Association in South Georgia attempted a fellowship meeting for a few years, but associations met with such disfavor among them that they soon discontinued the practice.[46]

The outside world, always distant, grew ever more so in the latter part of the present century. The Civil War generated enough friction to cause a few blips in the church records, but the Spanish American War, First and Second World wars, Korean and Vietnam wars might as well not have happened as far as the official records of the Primitive Baptists were concerned. The civil rights movement elicited no official comment either, although some white Primitive Baptists are as hostile to blacks in general as are most other southern whites of similar background. However, their traditional dislike of political intermeddling and membership in extraecclesial organizations kept most of them out of the Ku Klux Klan, citizens' councils, and other similar organizations. The most extreme racial views seemed unacceptable among them. A case in point concerns a preacher from Middle Georgia, highly recommended by some brethren in that area, who filled an appointment at Zion's Rest Church, Waycross, Georgia. The church's deacons, Stonewall Jackson Raulerson and Tommy Driggers, soon discovered the reason for his popularity in the black belt: the doctrine that blacks did not possess souls. After one sermon, the deacons bundled the segregationist fanatic on board a northbound train with no invitation to return. At that time, one black man attended Zion's Rest with some regularity, and Deacon Driggers always expressed his thankfulness that the man chanced not to come to that particular meeting.[47]

For the most part, interchurch visitation between black and white Primitive Baptists had largely ceased by the era of the Civil Rights movement. Elder M. T. Sheppard of the Original Ochlocknee Association knew several black Primitive Baptists during the volatile 1950s and lamented that the tense times did not allow fellowship between believers whose only difference was that of color.[48] His apprehensions were well founded.

During the 1970s several members of the white Peace Union Association attended a service at St. Luke's Primitive Baptist Church, Valdosta, Georgia, of the black Union Association. The "integrationists" received a storm of criticism from several members who dreaded a return visit from their black brethren.[49] Since Primitive Baptist churches are usually in obscure locations and have little social significance in their communities, they were never targeted by civil rights demonstrators for integrationist activity. Nonetheless, *Goodwill,* a small Primitive Baptist magazine published in Florida—with Elder O. J. Rives, moderator of the Peace Union Association, as an assistant editor—carried a tirade by Samuel Middlebrooks, Jr., in 1964 condemning forced integration as dictatorship and predicting as its end result that "in the years ahead there are going to be many white granddaddies bouncing little colored babies on their knees." Elder Tom Crawford of Orlando, Florida, the editor and a man of a fine sour wit, observed that while the brother's predictions were "gruesome," the outcome of the race question as of all others lay entirely in the hands of God.[50] For many white Primitive Baptists, as for other southerners, Martin Luther King, Jr., represented the fiend incarnate. A young pastor of the Second Sunday Side at Cat Creek Church during the early 1980s often quoted the reformer Martin Luther's saying, "No one ever yet prayed, not being in trouble," attributing it to Luther by name. King being the only "Martin Luther" familiar to most of them, one of the deacons informed him that his reference to the black leader upset some of the congregation.[51] When asked about white Primitive Baptists' treatment of blacks in general, Deacon Lucius Bennett of Providence Church, Valdosta, Georgia, reflected and at length weakly replied that they treated them "pretty well."[52] Elder Fred E. Blanton, moderator of the Peace Union Association, believed white Primitive Baptists generally tolerant of blacks.[53] Elder Lamar Carter recalled that his Primitive Baptist father indignantly refused to attend a lynching in the 1920s.[54]

Labor unions, rare in the South, nonetheless generated a small degree of friction among the stricter Primitive Baptists, presumably because they represented a worldly combination with overtones of the hated secret societies of the eighteenth and nineteenth centuries, or perhaps just because they were something new. The anti-Towaligan faction of the Pilgrim's Rest Association in south Florida grimly agreed to "bear with" its sister associations that "has the labor unions" for the ensuing year, since "they are laboring to get rid of same." Their business committee reported the Flint River and Lott's Creek associations, near Albany and Savannah, respectively, to be contaminated with trade unionism, and that the rural Ochlocknee Association "has not got the labor unions." The Pilgrim's Rest warned the infected associations that it would be "compelled to deal with the same . . . in another year as patience will cease to be a virtue."[55] The corresponding associations apparently did not pass muster on the union question within the allotted year, as the Pilgrim's Rest discontinued correspondence with the Flint River, Lott's Creek, and Ochlocknee associations at its 1948 session "because of labor unions" and declared its opposition to "all secret institutions of men that carry oath-bound obligations and hold meetings behind closed doors."[56] As late as 1985, the Independent churches in South Georgia withdrew fellowship from Oakey Grove Church, Berrien County, Irene Church, Lanier County, and Damsacus Church, Bacon County, because they held Masons in membership.[57] However, secret Masonic affiliation is more widespread among Primitive Baptists than most of them care to admit, and most churches in practice pursue a "don't ask, don't tell" policy in regard to the lodge.

Controversy over the doctrine of absolute predestination revived in 1951, when the anti–labor union faction of the Pilgrim's Rest Association proclaimed themselves "Old Line Predestinarians" and declared their belief that "Almighty God in His unlimited wisdom . . . decreed . . . all things . . . and events . . . therefore all things were foreordained and predestinated by him according to His own will and purpose."[58] Although this neo-"Absoluter" association contained only three churches, three elders, and a total of thirty-five members, its determinist ideology spread in south and central Florida. A ministers' meeting at Ft. Pierce, Florida, in 1965, condemned "the heretical doctrine of absolute predestination of all things."[59] Four south Florida ministers, S. P. Jones, C. Cromer Crawford, A. D. Cook, and C. T. Morris, signed a document on the nature of good works, reasserting the "Conditional Time Salvation" doctrine.

> We believe that all Gospel obedience that is acceptable to God is the ultimate result of the inward influence of the Spirit. Yet, we believe that the influence of the Spirit may be quenched so that disobedience is possible. We cannot by our best works merit anything from God, as these works though rendered by the Spirit are mixed with the imperfections and weaknesses of the flesh. Yet, it is the sovereign right of God to accept our works (in the person of his son) and reward that which is sincere, although accompanied with weakness and imperfection. But, this reward is according to the pleasure of the Father and not because our works have obligated him in any degree. Let us conclude, that we believe the sinner is passive in regeneration, but active in maintaining good works, being activated by a true and lively faith. . . . We believe that all men of sound mind are morally obligated to God. That they should strive to live honorably and upright before their fellow man, we maintain they are capacitated to this end.[60]

Repercussions from the Absoluter revival reached northern Florida and South Georgia. Sharon Church of Madison County, Florida, expelled Elder Cleveland Blanton for supporting Elder Percy Ming of Ocala, Florida, a minister influenced by this neo-Absoluter movement. Blanton, in turn, persuaded the Pulaski Association that his exclusion was unjust, whereupon they dropped fellowship with the San Pedro Association and the Peace Union Association.[61] Few associations in the area went so far as to adopt official anti-Absoluter resolutions like that of the Original Ochlocknee: "We will not fellowship those who preach or contend for the doctrine that God predestinated all things that come to pass, good, bad, and indifferent."[62] However, commitment to the conditional time salvation doctrine remained strong. Elder Fred E. Blanton of the Peace Union condemned belief "in the absolute predestination of all things, good, bad, and indifferent." He asserted the predestination of the elect to salvation but not of all events, the common conditionalist Primitive Baptist position.[63] Absolutism, or something very like it, is common among the more conservative factions. Elder T. A. Wasdin of the Suwannee River Association once had a fellow preacher call him into question for giving God "all the credit" for everything. Elder J. E. Griffis, an Independent Primitive preacher, dismissed Wasdin's doctrine as entirely too "salty" for his taste. Not all conservative Primitives incline toward Absolutism. Elder Robert Register and Elder James Hortman of the Original Union Association firmly oppose the doctrine of absolute predestination.[64]

Other ancient doctrinal disputes remained alive. The eternal children and nonresurrection doctrines associated with the Coonites remained alive in the anti-Towaligan faction of the Flint River Association and in the Original Union Association. The Crawfordites continued to proclaim the doctrines of gospel instrumentality and the free offer.[65]

The Progressive churches, most of which were still located in South Georgia, adopted more and more Missionary trappings. To instrumental music and ministerial support, they added during the postwar period Sunday schools, a denominational college, a host of benevolent institutions, and greatly elaborated services, with robed choirs and other innovations, none of which saved them from the pervasive denominational decline.[66] Several elders revived the issue of gospel regeneration and free offer preaching, with the result that a schism in the Waycross Primitive Baptist Church resulted in the formation of a Sovereign Grace Baptist Church, which affiliated with the rising Calvinistic movement among Independent Baptists. The most shocking deviation among the Progressives, however, occurred when Elder Charles Carrin of the Delray Beach, Florida, churches embraced the charismatic movement and started holding revival meetings accompanied with speaking in tongues and claims of miraculous healing. Needless to say, the Progressives soon closed all their pulpits to him. Few other Primitive Baptists manifested much of an interest in the charismatic movement.[67]

Belief in miracles remains strong among Primitives, however. The Beulah Association expressly stated its belief in divine healing in its articles of faith.[68] While preaching, Elder Fred Bethea once had a case of apparently spontaneous healing of a severe back disorder in one of his hearers. Elder Walter

Barnard of the Bennett faction of the Alabaha River Association recently stated in a sermon that he had cured a neighbor's hemorrhage by reciting the "blood verse," Ezekiel 16:6, over him, and earlier a Primitive preacher cured Elder Fred Blanton of a severe childhood nosebleed by the same means. Visions and dreams, while not as common as in the past, still occur among Primitives and are highly regarded. Usually, the more conservative the faction, the greater the number of instances of such things and the greater reliance placed upon them. Others dismiss most of them as "collard fits." Some members have dreams and visions and divine interviews that seem too facile and convenient to their less favored brethren. A brother once detained Deacon Kit Parker of Little Phebe Church, Charlton County, Georgia, with a long rendition of a series of revelations that validated the speaker's position on a current controversy. Seeing Parker skeptical, the dreamer asked him if the Lord ever spoke to him in a similar manner. "No," barked Parker, "and now I know why. He spends all his time talking to you."[69]

The modernist-fundamentalist controversy never disturbed the Primitive Baptists. Few of them being well educated, they remained largely unaware of Darwin, the higher criticism of the Bible, and similar developments. Elder Fred E. Blanton of the Peace Union Association spoke for most of his brethren when he said, "I don't argue with science. I ignore it." Indeed, several Primitive Baptists, including one minister still living and active, deny the heliocentric theory and the sphericity of the earth. With Copernicus and Magellan disowned, Darwin hardly got a hearing.[70]

Services and preaching have changed little among the Primitive Baptists from the days of their Separate Baptist ancestors. Except for the Progressives, most of them still sing ancient hymns from the Great Awakening in a slow, minor-sounding style, which either captivates or repels those who hear it. A few churches still line out some of the hymns, and some churches have adopted a more modern hymnbook, with musical notation and a selection of modern hymns. The degree of conservatism in the various factions can usually be determined by the speed with which they sing. Churches using the songbooks that include music often sing in a fast, sprightly style, reminiscent of the Southern Baptists in all but the absence of a choir and instrumental accompaniment, both of which are present in Progressive churches. At the other end of the spectrum, the Crawfordites sing in a slow, melancholy style of great beauty, with most hymns lined out. Black Primitive Baptists use the *Primitive Hymns* in common with conservative white churches but practice a type of call and response lining, reminiscent of early African American work chants.[71]

Many Primitive preachers still chant their sermons in the style of their Separate forebears. Virtually all ministers among the black churches and the more conservative white churches still do so and never dream of preparing a sermon beforehand. These churches and ministers believe that the chanted delivery is indicative of divine inspiration, and they entertain some suspicion of polished, well-organized sermons as being mere human contrivances, destitute of sacred authority.[72] Elder Elisha Roberts of the Original Union Association always prefaced his sermons with the observation, "I haven't brought a thing with me, and if I had, you wouldn't have it."[73] Elder John Harris of the Old Line Suwannee River Association said that rather than his taking a text, the text took him, and some Primitive preachers described entering an almost trancelike state while preaching. Elders Marcus Peavy of the Original Union Association and Fred Bethea of the Peace Union said that they underwent something similar to a visionary experience while preaching, as though they saw their subject unrolling before their eyes. Elder Bethea, in particular, often did not recall anything he had said during this condition. Among the Progressives, such preaching has long been actively discouraged, and many younger ministers now preach in a more polished manner, similar to the delivery of the Missionary Baptists but often lacking the power of the old style. One elder, formerly of the Peace Union Association, sang his sermons in the ancient fashion but, upon hearing a more polished visiting minister, deliberately broke himself of chanting in the pulpit. "And he broke himself of preaching, too," remarked one adamant defender of the old style. No Primitive Baptist preacher of any faction, however, would dare write out a sermon, although some of them heavily annotate their Bibles as an aid in speaking. Elder Fred Bethea, once a Progressive himself, recalled with amusement how unnerved a Progressive preacher became if his personal Bible was mislaid. Among the most conservative Old Baptists, a minister often does not even read a text but simply begins to talk "as his mind leads him." Elder Bethea believed firmly in inspired sermons, even though he taught school and had, for a Primitive Baptist, a remarkable education. Although he often preached in the entranced manner of other Primitive preachers, his delivery remained fluid and devoid of "jumping the rabbit." Soon after his defection from the Progressives to the Old Line Primitives, he delivered an excellent sermon, in grammatical English. A sarcastic hearer remarked to Elder Lamar Carter, "Well, we have us a *educated* preacher now." Elder Carter replied, "If he'd had all that in his head, it would have burst."[74]

The ritual of footwashing remains universally observed among the Primitives of the region under consideration, although few churches now make its nonobservance a test of fellowship.[75] A subject of some controversy has been the use of individual cups during communion. Traditionally, two cups of homemade wine were handed about the congregation by the deacons. A few of the more liberal churches adopted the individual tray of cups, ostensibly out of fear of AIDS and other diseases, a concern their more conservative brethren regard with inexpressible contempt.[76] The use of fermented wine, usually made by the deacons, is unquestioned among the Primitives. Elder Bob Dickerson of Cat Creek Church, Lowndes County, Georgia, once remarked that the Missionary and Methodist use of grape juice in communion was quite appropriate, since their doctrines bore the same resemblance to truth as grape juice bore to wine. The communion bread consists of large unleavened disks prepared by the deacons' wives, known as deaconesses. The more conservative churches still exchange formal correspondence at "Big Meeting," or communion time, although some have discarded the practice. Although many churches have left associations, many others remain in such organizations, but few associations exert their former power over their constituent churches.[77]

The fabric of the meetinghouses represents the most obvious change among the Primitive Baptists during the twentieth century. The interior layout of the churches remains virtually identical to that of the early 1800s. However, beginning in the 1940s, most Primitive Baptist meetinghouses saw the addition of tin and asbestos-shingle siding. Glass windows replaced wooden shutters, and the interiors were ceiled and eventually painted. In the 1960s, a misguided desire for improvement led to painting the walls and furnishing most meeting places, greatly diminishing their austere beauty. Gas space heaters began to replace wood-burning heaters; electric lights made evening services possible in many places, and churches began to build restrooms onto the meetinghouses. In the late nineteenth century, some conservatives had opposed the replacement of crumbling log chapels with frame buildings, and the same spirit opposed more recent improvements. The Crawfordites resisted the entire program. Their meetinghouses are still unlighted, unceiled, unpainted, and completely unheated. In the warm climate of South Georgia and northeastern Florida, such buildings are quite comfortable except during winter cold snaps, when worship with the spiritual descendants of Reuben Crawford requires considerable fortitude.[78]

Among other Primitives, improvements arrived, but slowly. Changes produced sparks most often where the church was "split," with two factions using the same building. Invariably, one "side" is more conservative than the other, and disapproves, sometimes vehemently, of all changes. Cat Creek Church in Lowndes County, Georgia, provides an excellent case in point. The church split in April 1927, over the Peace movement, and the two factions have glowered at each other for nearly seventy years, one meeting on the first Sunday each month and the other on the third, and both equally convinced that it alone represents Cat Creek Church "in order." When the "Peace folks" installed restrooms, the "Old Liners" obstinately continued to use the crumbling privies at the edge of the woods. Gradually, most Old Liners succumbed to the temptation of indoor plumbing, which all of them had at home by that time. Deacon Jack A. Sapp, however, continued to hold out against the cloacal heresy until quite old and feeble. During a driving rainstorm, he asked another brother to help him to the privy, but that brother flatly refused to get them both drenched. Deacon Sapp surrendered to the inevitable and bowed his arthritic knee to the Baal of modern sanitation. Sapp left the Peace folks with an enduring reminder of his ire at innovation. In the late 1960s, they replaced the church's old plank benches with varnished, factory-built pews. The Old Liners had always scrubbed down the old benches in preparation for Big Meeting. When the Old Line annual meeting came around, Deacon Sapp, implacable as Juggernaut, hauled the new benches out and scrubbed their fine varnish, imparting a curious zebralike effect that may still be seen. Eventually, all churches that could afford them installed restrooms, although the Crawfordites compromised by building completely separate structures to house the innovations. These neat, modern structures juxtaposed with antique unpainted meetinghouses present an odd disjunction.[79]

Previous to the late 1940s and 1950s, visitors at a Primitive Baptist church accompanied the various members home to eat after the service. At annual Big Meetings especially, this imposed a dreadful burden on those living closest to the church. After World War II, they adopted the practice of taking food to church and eating after services or during an intermission. The Crawfordites alone retained the old practice, with members who have made preparations issuing a general invitation to the congregation. At first, they spread "dinner" on a section of fence wire mounted on rows of posts. After rainstorms destroyed several dinners, churches erected open-sided shelters over the rude tables. These soon acquired poured concrete floors, and finally walls, completing their evolution into what the Primitives would call a "social hall" if the detested Missionaries and Methodists had not preempted the name.[80]

Even these humble and useful structures managed to generate controversy at pugnacious Cat Creek. The first-Sunday side at Cat Creek split in 1977 over an attempt to heal the Independent-associational schism of 1969. The associational minority commenced meeting on the second Sunday.

Sometime later, the dining shelter burned. The first-Sunday side had insured the structure and built a huge replacement, finer in many respects than the aging meetinghouse. Old Liners and second-Sunday people made the traditional offerings of labor and small sums of money. When the new facility was completed, the first-Sunday side invited the other two factions to a conference. They first proposed a reunion of the factions, a rather quixotic project in view of the decades of bad blood between all parties. Then the first-Sunday faction declared the new building theirs and offered its use to the others on what they considered insulting terms. The two minority factions left the meeting with reunion further away than ever. Not to be outdone, they constructed a considerably more modest dining hall of their own, behind the new one. Lest Cat Creek should be thought odd in having three factions, let it be known that Pleasant Grove Church of Berrien County, Georgia, had three factions for several years, and Mt. Enon Church of Plant City, Florida, split four times, with each faction building a meetinghouse on a different corner of the churchyard, to the scandal of the faithful and the amusement of unbelievers.[81]

Their declining numbers and numerous divisions made many Primitives increasingly uneasy that they were seeing the fulfillment of St. Paul's warning: "But if ye bite and devour one another, take heed that ye be not consumed one of another." The tendency to divide bitterly over minor issues continued well after 1945, alienating some who might otherwise have been inclined to unite with the Primitives. To detail all the schisms that have afflicted the Primitive Baptists during the postwar period would be tedious and all but impossible. A brief overview of the denomination's increasing friability must suffice. The Crawfordites split in 1921 over whether Sunday was the first or seventh day of the week. They divided in 1952, 1960, and again in 1968, in all three cases over jealousy between prominent ministers.[82] The Original Ochlocknee Association disintegrated in 1963.[83] The Bennett faction of the Alabaha River Association divided in 1948 and the Old Line Suwannee River Association soon after.[84] The minority factions in both cases found their way into other associations after a few years.[85] In 1977, the Old Line Suwannee River split, with a minority following the moderator, Elder Perry Harris.[86] The Original Union and Alabaha River associations then dropped correspondence with both factions. Simultaneously, the Original Union reached it highest pitch of isolationism, briefly adopting a resolution against "outside preachers" saying grace at their church dinners. When the Alabaha River recognized one of the Suwannee River factions, the Original Union dropped correspondence with them as well. The Original Union recognized the Harris faction in 1981, and in 1982, dropped that group and resumed correpondence with the Alabaha River Association and the other Suwannee River faction.[87] The Harris churches eventually joined the Independent Primitive Baptists.[88] In 1977, the Peace Union split over a proposal to recognize and fellowship the Independent churches.[89] Virtually all these ecclesiastical games of musical chairs grew entirely out of personality conflicts, family feuds, and minor disciplinary questions.

Finally, the lengthening shadows began to drive the shrinking factions together. In 1982, the anti-Towaligan faction of the Flint River Association, with the exception of four small churches, dropped their "bars" and recognized their long estranged brethren in the other faction of the association and the main body of Primitive Baptists in general.[90] The two factions of the Suwannee River Association, divided since 1928 and both verging on extinction, reunited in 1985.[91] The Original Union Association and the Bennett faction of the Alabaha River Association, though remaining aloof from the main body of Primitive Baptists, modified their stance to receive members from other "orthodox, old line" Primitive Baptists without demanding rebaptism as a prerequisite.[92] In 1991, the Peace Union and San Pedro associations "let down the bars" between them and the Independent Primitive Baptists. The last remnants of the Original Ochlocknee Association, later reorganized as the Pleasant Union Association, dissolved into the main body of Primitives, leaving the Crawfordites as the main opponents of divorce in the local branches of the denomination.[93]

Several obscure factions contributed to denominational reunification by becoming extinct. The Old Line factions of the Pulaski and Upatoie associations died out in the 1950s.[94] The Absoluter factions of the Mt. Enon and Pilgrim's Rest associations and the anti-Towaligan faction of the Mt. Enon descended into the dust of death, leaving only two known factions of that often divided body. A Crawfordite faction emanating from the 1968 split, the Satilla River Association, hovers near extinction, and all other Crawfordite offshoots have long since folded. The St. Mary's River Association, which contains Pigeon Creek Church, the oldest Protestant Church in Florida, totters on the brink of nonexistence. The St. Mary's River, a very small association throughout its history, is remarkable for having survived at all. Totally isolated since 1910, it has often had only one minister within its bounds.

At the present time, most Primitive Baptists in the region of this study are in communion with one another, a remarkable development. Even the two factions of the divided Mt. Enon Association are recognized by other Primitive Baptists, although they do not recognize each other. However, several factions still stand aloof. The Original Union, Bennett Alabaha River, and Suwannee River associations commune with one another and no one else.

The Crawfordites refuse all recognition to other factions and until recently did not own insurance policies or attend weddings, funerals, commencements, or any other gatherings involving other denominations. They never allowed members of other persuasions, even "Bennettite" Primitives, to pray in their homes. And they believed until recently that all who died in the profession of any other faith suggested reprobation by that fact. Recently, they allowed their members to wear neckties while employed by businesses that demanded these. Women still avoid pants, short hair, jewelry, and make-up. As noted, they strongly condemn radio, television, and other worldly amusements, although those of them married to nonmembers often bow to the inevitable to secure domestic harmony. Remarkably, perhaps because of their uncompromising stance and theology, Crawfordite churches usually have a noticeable number of young members and attendants. Of all Primitive Baptists in the region, they most resemble the doctrine and practices of the Baptists of the pioneer age.[95]

The Beulah Association has accepted musical instruments and more and more Missionary Baptist practices and doctrines during the twentieth century. After growing to a considerable size at mid-century and organizing a daughter association, the West Florida, in the Panhandle and South Alabama, they succumbed to the logic of their position when most of their churches and members became nondenominational Arminians or Freewill Baptists. The West Florida Association is now extinct, and the Beulah has dwindled to four small churches in Wakulla County, Florida, essentially indistinguishable from Southern Baptists.[96]

The liberal black Primitive Baptists of the Tallahassee area now belong to the Old West Florida Association, a large body of churches centered on Leon and adjacent counties. Like the Beulah Association, they retain little in the way of distinctively Primitive Baptist doctrine or practice.[97] The Old Line black Primitives of the Union Association retain the belief and ritual of their white counterparts and share in their decline. Between 1973 and 1990, the black Union declined from thirty-two churches with 453 members to twenty-six churches with 295 members.[98] Few young people attend. Recently, a deacon of the tiny St. Luke's Church, Valdosta, Georgia, attended a service at the even tinier Providence Church, a white Primitive congregation in the same city. Both parties seem to have found the visit enjoyable.[99]

A science fiction buff of my acquaintance recently compared the local Primitives to figures in Jack Vance's macabre *The Dying Earth,* depicting a far future in which ingrown remnants of humanity skulk through vast ruins, engaged in Byzantine intrigues as they wait for the sun to burn out and plunge the world into everlasting night. While I must reluctantly grant the aptness of the unflattering comparison, there are a few exceptions. Eureka Primitive Baptist Church in Irwin County, Georgia, and of the Pulaski Association, constitutes a startling and controversial one. The pastor, Elder L. Jeff Harris, an energetic and charismatic young native of New Mexico, is supported by the church, although by free offerings rather than a salary. The church holds morning and evening services each Sunday and has discarded the *Primitive Hymns* in favor of a hymnal with notes and newer songs. Each Wednesday evening, the church holds a prayer meeting at which Elder Harris preaches an expository sermon, systematically working his way through the books of the Bible. In 1994, Eureka baptized seventeen new members, an astounding rate of growth for a Primitive church. The total membership stands at ninety-six, making it one of the largest Primitive Baptist churches in the area.[100] An astonishing number of young people not only faithfully attend but actually join Eureka Church. Although keeping within the bounds of orthodox Primitive Baptist theology, Elder Harris emphasizes the duty of preaching repentance and faith and is considerably more evangelical than most other Primitive preachers. In another remarkable departure, he supports conservative political organizations, such as the Christian Coalition.[101]

Most Old Baptists have always hated Arminans worse than homosexuals and abortionists and so ignore conservative action groups that concern themselves overly with the "weak and beggarly elements of this world." A few Primitive preachers oppose abortion in their sermons; however, given the age of their congregations, it could hardly be called a pertinent issue among them. A few others vaguely support prayer in school, although Elder

Eureka Church. Courtesy of Elder L. Jeff Harris.

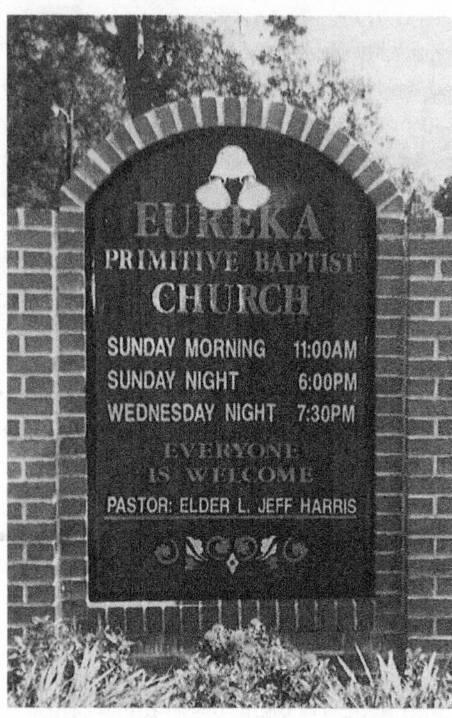

Above: Elder L. Jeff Harris, pastor, Eureka Primitive Baptist Church, Tifton, Ga. 1998.

Left: Eureka Church's controversial sign, deemed too elaborate for an Old Line church. Both photos courtesy of Elder L. Jeff Harris.

Bob Dickerson of Cat Creek Church spoke for most of them when he said that unregenerate little brats babbling the Lord's Prayer might as well be saying:

> The boy stood on the burning deck,
> Eatin' taters by the peck.

Elder Dickerson, incidentally, edits a local Primitive paper, the *Gospel Appeal,* and strongly opposes innovations such as those adopted at Eureka, which many hold to violate the spirit if not the letter of Primitive belief.[102]

All Eureka's departures pale into insignificance beside its "mission" work in the Philippines. Actually, like other practices fostered by Elder Harris, the Philippines outreach technically violates no Primitive canons, but it is still a concept to set their teeth on edge. The American Baptist Association, or "Landmarkers," supported mission work on Mindanao for decades. Landmarkers believe in a Baptist "apostolic succession," an unbroken chain of baptisms, ordinations, doctrines, and practices extending back to Christ and the Apostles. This belief is all but universal among Primitive Baptists. In 1991, a Landmarker minister from California, Lawrence Crawford, preached throughout Mindanao. A decided Calvinist, Crawford also taught that regeneration precedes conversion, a tenet held by most Primitive Baptists. Crawford's Filipino followers, often disfellowshipped by their former churches, became dubious of the validity of their baptisms and ordinations, conferred by ministers they now regarded as heretical. Learning of the Primitive Baptists in America, the Filipino proto-Primitives established contact with several American preachers, one of whom brought them to Elder Harris's attention. In February 1994, Harris and Elder Norval Mann of Statesboro, Georgia, clothed with the authority of Eureka Church, went to Mindanao, baptized more than forty ex-Landmarkers, and ordained seven of their preachers to the Primitive Baptist ministry. On a subsequent trip in July, Harris and Elder Gus Harter of Bethany Church, Atlanta, Georgia, ordained more Filipino ministers and constituted two churches. Harris, Harter, and two other preachers made a third journey to the Philippines in January 1995. As of March 1995, there were 450 Filipino Primitive Baptists meeting in thirty places.[103]

Rumblings already reverberate over the Filipino brethren, and if such a development does not breed at least a local—and probably a denomination-wide—schism, then the Primitive Baptists have changed out of all recognition. Although Harris provided the neophyte ministers with copies of

Baptism of Filipino Primitive Baptists by Elders L. Jeff Harris and Gus Harter, Davao City, Philippine Republic. 1995. Courtesy of Elder L. Jeff Harris.

Filipino Primitive Baptist Church, Davao City, Philippine Republic. 1995. Courtesy of Elder L. Jeff Harris.

Hassell and Hassell's *History of the Church of God* and Gill's *Body of Divinity,* transplantation of Old Baptist doctrine and practice to the other side of the world will inevitably produce highly diverting changes.[104] Considering that the nineteenth-century South in which the Primitive faith originally flourished was even more a frontier than Mindanao is today, the faith of Isham Peacock and Duncan McCranie may be proclaimed in Cebuano long after it has been forgotten in English.

Conclusion

The Good Part

A Primitive Baptist who read an earlier draft of this work asked, "Where is the good part?" Unfortunately, conflict makes better copy than peace, and interesting times are often violent. A reader unfamiliar with Primitive Baptists might wonder how such a fractious people could survive and how anyone could tolerate membership with them.

Yet there is a "good part," and for Primitive Baptists it far outweighs the bad. They often remark that the best conferences and associations are those where nothing happens but worship and preaching. Old minute books often contained the entry, "Nothing appearing, came to a close in order." Churches and associations often experience decades of peaceful worship between periods of controversy and bitterness. Many remember Reuben Crawford for his conflict with Richard Bennett but forget the fifty years of peace over which he presided at Shiloh Church. Some of the greatest Primitive Baptist preachers in South Georgia and Florida figure little in this work because they lived in such peace that there is little to write about them. Ansel Parrish and Isham Wetherington together presided as moderators of the Union Association for thirty-five peaceful years. After the bitter schism of 1927, Elder C. A. Vickers and Elder O. J. Rives quietly led the Original Union and Peace Union associations for decades. Many controversies erupt in the vacuum left by the death of such gifted leaders.

What is the "good part?" Primitive Baptists wish not to change the world but to escape from it. Preachers often pray that they and their hearers might be lifted for a little while above the "weak and beggarly elements of this world." They often refer to their churches as "little heavenly places," where they escape out of time and mundane concerns. One friend offered me this explanation of his faith: "I can't prove that this is all true, but I know it helps me get through the week better."

Primitive worship, especially in the more conservative congregations, conveys a sense of awe and timelessness rare in the modern American religious experience. A Catholic priest who attended a funeral at New Ramah Church, Ray City, Georgia, remarked to me, "That place was like a time tunnel!" For those from families long associated with the faith, there often come moments in Primitive services when doubts cease, and generations roll away. It seems as if Old Father Peacock, or Reuben Crawford, or one's great grandmother might be sitting nearby.

Those who attend Primitive churches for the first time are often moved by this sense of timelessness. One Presbyterian told me, "It is so refreshing to hear predestination preached without apology." An agnostic found delight in the evident sincerity of the emphasis on the next world; in the old hymns, unretouched for political correctness; and in the plain meetinghouse.

Most communities in the area of this study contain many descendants of Primitive Baptists. While most of these people no longer profess the faith or attend its worship, they seem to derive comfort from the continued presence of their grandparents' faith. When Union Church in Lakeland, Georgia, finally disbanded in 1996, people in the community seemed grief stricken. Many descendants of Old Baptists entertain a sense of the old faith as the "real thing." For them, the worship conducted in the old meetinghouses seems one of the pillars of the world. Even when churches disband, communities sometimes treasure the places where the worship went on. Many people in Quitman, Georgia, quickly formed a preservation society when a suggestion came forward to dismantle the old Bethlehem meetinghouse. At Lakeland, the community lovingly restored the dilapidated Union meetinghouse, after the church disbanded. On a grimmer note, when a hunting club established its headquarters and revelries in the Olive Leaf meetinghouse in Clinch County, Georgia, the building mysteriously burned.

In times of personal crisis, descendants of the Primitive faith often turn back to it. Primitive preachers often conduct funerals for those not of their faith. The grimmer the circumstances of death, the more comfort the bereaved seem to derive from the solidity of predestination.

One Primitive Baptist commented that I had virtually preached the denomination's funeral in the last chapter. Although the future prospects of the Primitive Baptists seem grim now, several hopeful factors may be at work. The Primitives seem to be gradually healing many of their old schisms. They presently enjoy a greater degree of unity and mutual toleration than at any time in the recent past. Also, the revival of conservative values generally may work in their favor. Predestinarian doctrine enjoys a revival among many Southern and Independent Baptists. While most of these advocates of the "doctrines of grace" hold to Fuller's free offer theology, a few of them incline to the High Calvinism of John Gill. Several "Sovereign Grace" Baptist preachers have united with the Progressive Primitive Baptists. They may represent the pioneers in a movement back to the old doctrines and the denomination that preserved them during the ascendancy of freewill. Modern communication technology may help the Primitives, ironic as that may seem. The individualism of the Internet fits in perfectly with the independent, personal nature of Primitive Baptist evangelism. The World Wide Web now has several Primitive Baptist sites, and more are in contemplation.

The Primitive faith, like some desert-adapted plant, may be only dormant, rather than dying. Indeed, a revival may well occur among Primitive Baptists. A period of great stress and uncertainty could drive people away from the "cheap grace" offered by popular denominations and back to the inscrutable yet comforting God of their ancestors. Critics of the Primitive faith have been preaching its funeral since the 1830s, and today even its friends feel concern. But, like the bush Moses saw, though always burning, it is never quite consumed.

NOTES

Chapter 1. Origins of Primitive Baptist Doctrine and Practice

1. Suwannee River Association, *Minutes,* 1838.
2. Shurden, *Associationalism,* 14–15, 22–24.
3. Ibid., 5–6.
4. Ibid., 7–8.
5. Quoted in Ibid., 9.
6. Gillette, *Philadelphia Association,* 60–62.
7. Ibid., 83–84.
8. Shurden, *Associationalism,* 63.
9. Furman, *Charleston Association,* 1–8.
10. Benedict, *General History,* 2:96–100.
11. Mosteller, *Kiokee Church,* 8.
12. Benedict, *General History,* 2:99. The words *mene tekel* appear in the Book of Daniel 5:25–27 AV.
13. Ibid., 2:100.
14. Paschal, *North Carolina Baptists,* 1:217–18.
15. Toon, *Hyper-Calvinism,* 143–44.
16. Hassell and Hassell, *Church of God,* 525.
17. Toon, *Hyper-Calvinism,* 70–74, 79–83.
18. "Book and Bible List," *Old Faith Contender* 56 (October-December 1978), 125.
19. Hassell and Hassell, *Church of God,* 651. The appellation Arminianism is derived from the name Jacobus Arminius, a Dutch theologian who asserted the freedom of man's will, a universal atonement, and the possibility of final apostasy.
20. Gill, *Body of Divinity,* 387–88.
21. Hassell and Hassell, *Church of God,* 569–70.
22. Benedict, *Fifty Years among the Baptists,* in Hanks, *The Church of God,* 118–19.
23. Toon, *Hyper-Calvinism,* 131–132.
24. Benedict, *General History,* 1:274.
25. Ibid., 1:274, 520.
26. Purefoy, *Sandy Creek Association,* 45.

27. Benedict, *General History,* 2:27, 37–38.
28. Ibid., 2:38.
29. Hooker, ed., *Woodmason,* 23, 31–32.
30. Edwards, *Tour,* 6–9, quoted in Paschal, *North Carolina Baptists,* 1:227–28.
31. Benedict, *General History,* 2:39–40.
32. Asplund, *Register,* 6.
33. Quoted in Shurden, *Associationalism,* 29; Benedict, *General History,* 2:308.
34. Benedict, *General History,* 2:50–51.
35. Hooker, ed., *Woodmason,* 102.
36. Gillette, *Philadelphia Association,* 70.
37. Benedict, *General History,* 2:38.
38. Hassell and Hassell, *Church of God,* 697–98.
39. Crowley, "Notes," 21.
40. Hooker, ed., *Woodmason,* 102–3.
41. Ibid., 109.
42. Benedict, *General History,* 2:56–58.
43. Gillette, *Phildelphia Association,* 68–69.
44. Hooker, ed., *Woodmason,* 114.
45. Mallary, *Edmund Botsford,* 36–39.
46. Leland, "Virginia Chronicle," in Greene, ed., *Writings,* 115.
47. Quoted in Ninde, *American Hymn,* 98–99.
48. Rippon, *Hymns,* xi, xii, passim.
49. Upper Black Creek Church, Minutes, August 1823; Jackson, "Story of the Sacred Harp," in White and King, *Sacred Harp, Facsimile,* vi.
50. Jackson, "Story of the Sacred Harp," vi, vii.
51. Benedict, *Fifty Years among the Baptists,* 206, quoted in Hanks, *The Church of God,* 120.
52. Quoted in Ninde, *American Hymn,* 94, 100, 103.
53. Benedict, *General History,* 2:101.
54. Furman, *Charleston Association,* 71.
55. Leland, "Virginia Chronicle," in Greene, ed., *Writings,* 117.
56. Benedict, *General History,* 2:54–56, 107.
57. Furman, *Charleston Association,* 71.
58. Ibid., 120–24.
59. Benedict, *General History,* 2:39, 63.
60. Asplund, *Register,* 7.
61. Benedict, *General History,* 2:457–58.
62. Leland, "Virginia Chronicle," in Greene, ed., *Writings,* 116n.
63. Benedict, *General History,* 2:291–92.
64. Ibid., 2:94.
65. Furman, *Charleston Association,* 119.
66. Benedict, *General History,* 2:60–62.
67. Ibid., 2:136, 156–57.
68. John Leland, "Valediction," in Greene, ed., *Writings,* 172.

69. Benedict, *General History,* 2: 172–74, 2:350–55.
70. Mallary, *Edmund Botsford,* 39–40.
71. Ibid., 41–42.
72. Mallary, *Jesse Mercer,* 201–2, quoted in Mosteller, *Kiokee Baptist Church,* 23.
73. Benedict, *General History,* 2:357–58.
74. Hervey to Gill, quoted in "Memoir," in Gill, *Body of Divinity,* xiii.
75. Phillips' Mill Church to Georgia Association, 1787, by Silas Mercer, in Mercer, *Georgia Association,* 140–42.
76. Mercer, *Georgia Association,* 385–86.
77. Quoted in Mercer, *Georgia Association,* 128.
78. Georgia Baptist Association, Minutes, 1790.
79. Benedict, *General History,* 2:188.
80. Ibid., 2:178; Georgia Association, Minutes, 1793; Kilpatrick, *Hephzibah Centennial,* 13–15; Mercer, *Georgia Association,* 385.
81. Benedict, *General History,* 2:178.
82. Kilpatrick, *Hephzibah Centennial,* 28.
83. Hephzibah Association, *Minutes,* 1814, in Kilpatrick, *Hephzibah Centennial,* 32.
84. Savannah Baptist Association, Minutes, 1802.
85. Kirkland and Kirkland, eds., *Confession of Faith,* 54.
86. Savannah River Association, *Minutes,* 1817.
87. Benedict, *General History,* 2:251–56.
88. Savannah Association, *Minutes,* 1803.

Chapter 2. The Baptist Expansion into South Georgia and Florida

1. Coulter, *History of Georgia,* 225.
2. Paisley, *Red Hills of Florida,* 71, 95.
3. Hall, *Travels,* 3:255–56.
4. Quoted in Huxford, *Brooks County,* 5.
5. Abrahamson and Harnett, "Pine Flatwoods and Dry Prairies," and Myers, "Scrub and High Pine," in Myers and Ewel, *Ecosystems of Florida,* 106.
6. Rambo, "The 1820 Land Lottery in Georgia," 23, 25–26.
7. Johnson and Perdigao, "Pioneers of Old Lowndes County," 3, 6, 7.
8. "Detailed Report of General Brisbane," in Keily, *Statistical Sketch of Georgia,* 26, quoted in Crawford, "Cotton, Land, and Sustenance," 221–22.
9. Smith, *Georgia Methodism,* 82, 139, 143, 150.
10. Richardson, *Lights and Shadows,* 26–27, 84–85.
11. Bryant, *Indian Springs,* 15.
12. Union Church, Minutes, June 1832.
13. Richardson, *Lights and Shadows,* 10, 28–29, 33–34.
14. Huxford Society, *Pioneers,* 1:11, 15, 39, 55, 90–91, 153, 159, 2:42.
15. Suwannee River Association, *Minutes,* 1841.
16. Gannon, *The Cross in the Sand,* 89, 101–2.
17. Smith, *Georgia Methodism,* 63–64.
18. Union Church, Minutes, June 1831.

19. Revolutionary War Pension File, Peacock.
20. Pierce, *Peacocks,* 4, 15.
21. Huxford Society, *Pioneers,* 6:207.
22. Revolutionary War Pension File, Peacock.
23. Huxford Society, *Pioneers,* 6:207, 7:553.
24. *Analytical Repository* 1 (September-October 1802), 124.
25. Parker, *Jones Creek Baptist Church,* 1n.
26. Ibid.
27. Savannah Association, *Minutes,* 1803.
28. Pigeon Creek Church, Minutes, January 1821.
29. Union Church, Minutes, June 1831.
30. Suwannee River Assocation, *Minutes,* 1839.
31. Piedmont Association, Minutes, 1823.
32. Savannah Association, *Minutes,* November 1804.
33. Beard's Creek Church, Minutes, March–April, 1811.
34. Huxford Society, *Pioneers,* 1:2–3.
35. Hassell and Hassell, *Church of God,* 894; Upper Black Creek Church, Minutes, June 1819, March 1821.
36. Beard's Creek Church, Minutes, December 1804, April 1811.
37. Alabaha River Association, Minutes, Introductory notes on the early churches.
38. Pigeon Creek Church, Minutes, January 1821.
39. Beard's Creek Church, Minutes, June–July 1831.
40. Union Church, Minutes, June 1831.
41. Huxford Society, *Pioneers,* 6:208.
42. Ibid.; Peacock Obituary, *Christian Index* 18 (June 14, 1851): 95.
43. Revolutionary War Pension File, Peacock; Alabaha River Association, Minutes, 1843.
44. Adiel Sherwood, *Memoirs,* quoted in Christian Index, *Baptist Denomination in Georgia,* 166.
45. Piedmont Association, Minutes, 1815.
46. Adiel Sherwood, *Memoirs,* quoted in Christian Index, *Baptist Denomination in Georgia,* 166.
47. Piedmont Association, Minutes, 1817, 1818, 1819; Hephzibah Baptist Association, *Minutes,* 1819.
48. Beard's Creek Church, Minutes, April 1810.
49. Ibid., July–September, 1807.
50. Asplund, *Universal Register,* 83–86.
51. Beard's Creek Church, Minutes, 23.
52. McElvey to *Primitive Baptist,* September 20, 1839.
53. Parker, *Jones Creek Baptist Church,* 12, 14, 49.
54. Rosser, *Florida Baptists,* 5.
55. Piedmont Association, Minutes, 1817.
56. Huxford Society, *Pioneers,* 3:50, 6:309, 7:500.
57. Piedmont Association, Minutes, 1817, 1819–21, 1823–25.

58. Ibid., 1817.
59. Alabaha Assocation, Minutes, Introductory notes.
60. Piedmont Association, Minutes, 1819.
61. Ibid., 1820, 1821, 1823, 1824, 1825.
62. Ibid., 1826.
63. Beard's Creek Church, Minutes, passim.
64. Allen, *Baptist Annual Register 1833,* 165.
65. Piedmont Association, Minutes, 1845.
66. Isaac D. Hutto, "Experience," 5.
67. Union Church, Minutes, October 1825.
68. Huxford, "Fleming Bates," n.p.
69. Garner, et. al., *Georgia Association,* 84, 107.
70. Kirkpatrick, *Hephzibah Centennial,* 54; Huxford, "Fleming Bates," n.p.
71. Piedmont Association, Minutes, 1818, 1821, 1825, 1827.
72. Union Church, Minutes, February, November 1827, February 1829.
73. Union Church, Minutes, July 1827, November 1829, February 1830, July 1831, August 1830, March 1831.
74. Tucker to *Christian Index,* February 28, 1845.
75. Union Church, Minutes, July 1831.
76. Ibid., August 1831.
77. Huxford, "Fleming Bates," n.p.
78. Huxford Society, *Pioneers,* 1:2–4, 3:357.
79. Upper Black Creek Church, Minutes, July 1823.
80. Union Church, Minutes, January 1828.
81. Hephzibah Church, Minutes, June 1824.
82. Ibid., January 1825.
83. Allen, *Baptist Annual Register 1833,* 168.
84. Hephzibah Church, Minutes, January 1825.
85. McElvey to *Primitive Baptist,* September 20, 1839; McElvey to *Primitive Baptist,* May 25, 1838.
86. McElvey to *Primitive Baptist,* May 25, 1838.
87. McElvey to *Primitive Baptist,* September 20, 1839.
88. William Hawthorn to *Primitive Baptist,* May 20, 1839.
89. Perry, *Early County,* cited in Jones, *Decatur County,* 277; Hassell and Hassell, *Church of God,* 708.
90. Mayfield, *Calvary, Georgia Heritage,* 2.
91. Jones, *Decatur County,* 277.
92. Union Church, Minutes, June, August 1826.
93. Ibid., September 1827.
94. Ochlocknee Association, *Minutes,* 1833; Union Church, Minutes, January, May, 1834.
95. Piedmont Association, Minutes, 1827.
96. Union Church, Minutes, November 1827.
97. Ochlocknee Association Corresponding Letter, 1829.

98. Hassell and Hassell, *Church of God*, 893–94.
99. Union Church, Minutes, August 1827.
100. Ibid., December 1827; Prior Lewis to *Primitive Baptist*, December 30, 1841.
101. Union Association, *Minutes*, 1855, in Union Association, *Minutes*, 1876.
102. Hassell and Hassell, *Church of God*, 893–94.
103. Hassell and Hassell, *Church of God*, 894. Extrapolated from list of churches in Ochlocknee Association, *Minutes*, 1833; Union Church was in Lowndes/ Lanier County and should not be confused with Union Church in Appling County.
104. Resolution of 1834 Ochlocknee Association as recorded in Union Church, Minutes, November 1834.
105. Union Church, Minutes, December 1834.
106. Ibid., October 1835.
107. Suwannee River Association, *Minutes*, 1838–49.
108. Union Church, Minutes, October 1836.
109. Suwannee River Association, *Minutes*, 1838.
110. Ibid.
111. Ibid., 1839–42.
112. Ochlocknee Association, *Minutes*, 1836.
113. Tucker to *Christian Index*, February 28, 1845.
114. Ochlocknee Association, *Minutes*, 1836.
115. Richland Creek Church, Minutes, February 1840.

Chapter 3. Worship and Discipline

1. Union Church, Minutes, April 1827.
2. Crowley, "Notes," 18.
3. Union Church, Minutes, June 1827, May 1830, June, November 1832, April 1833; Hephzibah Church, Minutes, June 1824; Liberty Church, Minutes, July 1834.
4. Huxford Society, *Pioneers*, 1:39.
5. Parker, *Jones Creek Baptist Church*, 6.
6. Union Church, Minutes, March 1832.
7. Watkins to *Primitive Baptist*, July 13, 1845.
8. Union Church, Minutes, March 1854.
9. Crowley, "Notes," 15–17.
10. P. T. Douglass to *Primitive Baptist*, April 27, 1845.
11. Beebe, "New School Courtesy," in Beebe, *Editorial Articles*, 4:131.
12. Union Church, Minutes, October 1825; Bethel Church, Minutes, August 1826; Hephzibah Church, Minutes, January 1825.
13. Savannah Association, *Minutes*, January 1804.
14. Beard's Creek Church, Minutes, December 1804; Pigeon Creek Church, Minutes, January 1821; Union Church, Minutes, October 1825.
15. Hephzibah Church, Minutes, January 1825.
16. Ochlocknee Association, *Minutes*, 1833.

17. Union Church, Minutes, June, August 1826, June 1827, March, April 1829, August 1831, November 1832, June, September 1833, January, May 1834, May, June 1835, October 1839, January, April 1841, June 1842, September 1843, January 1846.
18. Union Church, Minutes, February 1827.
19. Ibid., March 1827.
20. Ibid., July 1827.
21. Suwannee River Association, *Minutes,* 1840, 1841, 1845, 1852; Crowley, "Notes," 18.
22. Hephzibah Church, Minutes, June 1824, January 1825.
23. Beard's Creek Church, Minutes, April 1832.
24. Union Church, Minutes, March 1828.
25. Ibid., July 1831.
26. Richland Creek Church, Minutes, December 1846.
27. Union Church, Minutes, October 1830.
28. Ibid.
29. Ibid., May 1831.
30. Ibid., April 1832.
31. Ibid., July 1849.
32. Ochlocknee Association, *Minutes,* 1840, quoted in Suwannee River Association, *Minutes,* 1841.
33. Bethlehem Church, Minutes, May 1846.
34. Ibid., November 1834.
35. Beard's Creek Church, Minutes, 23.
36. Hephzibah Church, Minutes, January 1825.
37. Tired Creek Church, Minutes, September 1826.
38. Ibid.
39. Union Church, Minutes, February 1828.
40. Union Church, Minutes, October 1829, August, October 1830; Beard's Creek Church, Minutes, April 1815.
41. Beard's Creek Church, Minutes, June 1838.
42. Brewster, *The Cluster,* 15–18.
43. Upper Black Creek Church, Minutes, August 1823.
44. Parrish, *Parrish,* 71–72.
45. Union Church, Minutes, June 1828, July, October 1829, August 1830.
46. Ibid., August 1829.
47. Ibid., April 1831.
48. Ibid., August 1832.
49. Brannen, William Penn, "Harp of a Thousand Strings," and Anon., "Where the Lion Roareth and the Wang-doodle Mourneth," in Cohen and Dillingham, *Humor of the Old Southwest,* 443–47.
50. Taliaferro, Harden E., "Ham Rachel, of Alabama," in Cohen and Dillingham, *Humor of the Old Southwest,* 136, 141.
51. Crowley, "Notes," 18–19.

52. Kilpatrick, *Hephzibah Association,* 67.
53. Union Church, Minutes, March 1832.
54. Reports in ibid., August 1832, August 1833.
55. Ibid., September, November 1833.
56. Ibid., September 1834.
57. Crowley, "Notes," 20.
58. Stallings to Mitchell.
59. Union Church, Minutes, March 1832.
60. Rorabaugh, *Alcoholic Republic,* 8.
61. Smith, *Georgia Methodists,* 76.
62. Eggleston, *The Hoosier Schoolmaster,* 67.
63. Campbell, *Georgia Baptists,* 242.
64. Union Church, Minutes, October, December 1835, January 1836, March, December 1838, June 1839, May 1841, April 1842.
65. Ibid., October 1842.
66. Crowley, "Notes," 10.
67. Union Church, Minutes, October 1825.
68. Barwick, *Memories,* 57–58.
69. Christian Index, *Baptist Denomination in Georgia,* 89.
70. Quoted in Ibid., 166.
71. Parker, *Jones Creek Baptist Church,* 12.
72. Christian Index, *Baptist Denomination in Georgia,* 166.
73. Tired Creek Church, Minutes, February 1828, April 1829, June 1829, November 1832.
74. Union Church, Minutes, April 1835.
75. Ibid., March 1838.
76. Richland Creek Church, Minutes, May 1848.
77. Bethlehem Church, Minutes, February 1836, June 1838, July 1840.
78. Union Church, Minutes, April 1838.
79. Ibid., January 1840.
80. Ibid., March, May 1840.
81. Ibid., July, October 1841.
82. Surmons, "Experience," 192.
83. Crowley, "Notes," 12.
84. Bryant, *Indian Springs,* 19.
85. Ibid.
86. Tired Creek Church, Minutes, November, December 1836.
87. Parrish, *Parrish,* 72, 112.
88. Beebe, "Proposals," 16.
89. Beard's Creek Church, Minutes, September 1807.
90. Ochlocknee Association, *Minutes,* 1831, quoted in ibid., 1853.
91. Suwannee River Association, *Minutes,* 1852.
92. Pulaski Association, *Minutes,* 1852.
93. Alabaha River Association, "Minutes," 1857.

94. Douglass to *Primitive Baptist,* April 27, 1845.
95. Ochlocknee Association, *Minutes,* 1847.
96. Milfort, *Creek Nation,* 86–87.
97. Harris, *Sut Lovingood,* 88.
98. Covington, *Colquitt County,* 75–80.
99. Union Church, Minutes, December 1838, September 1841, May 1841, June 1843, February 1843, October 1844, April 1849.
100. Tired Creek Church, Minutes, January 1829.
101. Richland Creek Church, Minutes, February–March 1844.
102. Crowley, "Notes," 11.
103. Beard's Creek Church, Minutes, 57.
104. Ibid., 58.
105. Union Church, Minutes, January 1831.
106. Suwannee River Association, *Minutes,* 1839.
107. Tired Creek Church, Minutes, November 1833, September 1847.
108. Union Church, Minutes, June 1833, January 1834, October 1841.
109. Ibid., January 1834.
110. Bethel Church, Minutes, June 1831, cited in Huxford Society, *Pioneers,* 1:135.
111. Union Church, Minutes, November 1841.
112. Surmons, "Experience."
113. Richardson, *Lights and Shadows,* 142.
114. Upper Black Creek Church, Minutes, August 1814.
115. Beard's Creek Church, Minutes, September 1843
116. Ibid., August 1842.
117. Tired Creek Church, Minutes, May, October 1865.
118. Crowley, "Notes," 19–20.

Chapter 4. The Missionary Controversy

1. Prior Lewis to *Primitive Baptist,* December 26, 1842.
2. Crowley, "Notes," 21.
3. Toon, *Hyper-Calvinism,* 131, 150–53.
4. Stanley, *Baptist Missionary Society,* 6–7, 7n.
5. Ibid., 13–14.
6. Mercer, *Georgia Association,* 39–40.
7. Mercer, *Georgia Association,* 40–41; Savannah Association, *Minutes,* 1803.
8. Savannah Association, *Minutes,* November 1804.
9. S[tanaland], "Who are the Primitive Baptists?," 2.
10. Lester, *Georgia Baptist Convention,* 50–53.
11. Armstrong and Armstrong, *The Indomitable Baptists,* 111–19.
12. Allen, *Baptist Annual Register 1833,* 1.
13. Savannah River Association, *Minutes,* 1811.
14. Ibid., 1813.
15. Ibid., 1817.
16. Robert Donaldson to *Primitive Baptist,* June 16, 1842.

17. Kilpatrick, *Hephzibah Centennial,* 28.
18. Ibid., 38–39.
19. Robert Donaldson to *Primitive Baptist,* May 9, 1841.
20. Kilpatrick, *Hephzibah Centennial,* 40–41.
21. Lester, *Georgia Baptist Convention,* 61–63.
22. Kilpatrick, *Hephzibah Centennial,* 43.
23. Ibid.
24. Ibid., 44.
25. Ibid.
26. Ibid.; Donaldson to *Primitive Baptist,* May 9, 1841.
27. Kehukee Association, "Extract," 132–33.
28. Lawrence, "Declaration," 129–30.
29. Ibid., 130.
30. Hassell, "Joshua Lawrence," 312–13.
31. Lawrence, "Declaration," 130.
32. Trott et al., "Address," 2–3, 5.
33. Lawrence, "Declaration," 131.
34. Ibid.
35. Ibid.
36. Robert Donaldson to *Primitive Baptist,* May 9, 1841.
37. Kilpatrick, *Hephzibah Centennial,* 44–45.
38. Allen, *Baptist Annual Register 1833,* 163.
39. Upper Black Creek Church, Minutes, January 1820.
40. Sunbury Association, *Minutes,* 1822.
41. Upper Black Creek Church, Minutes, November 1823.
42. Ibid., February 1824.
43. Ibid., August 1824.
44. Sunbury Association, *Minutes,* 1824.
45. Quoted in Christian Index, *Baptist Denomination in Georgia,* 166.
46. Piedmont Association, Minutes, 1818.
47. Ibid., 1819.
48. Piedmont Association, Minutes, 1822.
49. Ibid.
50. Ibid., 1823.
51. Ibid., 1824.
52. Ibid., 1825.
53. Beard's Creek Church, Minutes, August 1828.
54. Piedmont Association, Minutes, 1829.
55. Beard's Creek Church, Minutes, July 1830.
56. Piedmont Association, Minutes, 1831.
57. Beard's Creek Church, Minutes, May–July 1831.
58. Piedmont Association, Minutes, 1831.
59. Ibid., 1832.
60. Beard's Creek Church, Minutes, March–April 1834.

61. Piedmont Association, Minutes, 1833.
62. McDonald to *Christian Index,* December 22, 1836, 25.
63. Piedmont Association, Minutes, 1828–38.
64. "Minister's Meeting," 799–800.
65. [Conner], "Appointments," 32.
66. Piedmont Association, Minutes, 1828–39.
67. Beard's Creek Church, Minutes, September 1840.
68. Piedmont Association, Minutes, 1825–39.
69. Ochlocknee Association, *Minutes,* 1833.
70. Suwannee River Association, *Minutes,* 1838.
71. Ibid., 1839, 1840.
72. Alabaha River Association, Minutes, 1842.
73. Suwannee River Association, *Minutes,* 1847; Alabaha River Association, Minutes, 1860.
74. Alabaha River Association, Minutes, 1845.
75. Piedmont Association, Minutes, 1845.
76. Alabaha River Association, Minutes, 1843.
77. Ibid., 1846, 1847.
78. Piedmont Association, Minutes, 1847.
79. Trott et al., "Address," 6.
80. Piedmont Association, Minutes, 1847.
81. Ibid., 1848.
82. Wiley Pearce to *Primitive Baptist,* May 25, 1838.
83. *Report of the American Baptist Home Missionary Society,* 21, 28, cited in Joiner, *History of Florida Baptists,* 25.
84. William McElvey to *Primitive Baptist,* May 25, 1838.
85. Wiley Pearce to *Primitive Baptist,* March 1, 1838.
86. Tired Creek Church, Minutes, July, October, September 1828, January, February, April, August, September, November 1830.
87. Richland Creek Church, Minutes, June, July 1835.
88. Elias Hawthorn to *Primitive Baptist,* July 20,1838.
89. Proctor, "Georgia Baptists," 108.
90. Campbell, *Georgia Baptists,* 2d ed., 99–105, 110–11.
91. Mercer, *Ten Letters,* 1–11, 39, cited in Proctor, "Georgia Baptists," 109, 113.
92. Bethel Church, Minutes, November–December 1832, cited in Huxford Society, *Pioneers,* 7:533; Huxford Society, *Pioneers,* 5:164–65.
93. Ochlocknee Association, *Minutes,* 1833.
94. Rosser, *Florida Baptists,* 9–10; Florida Association, *Minutes,* 1880, cited in Rosser, *Florida Baptists,* 9–10.
95. Elias Hawthorn to *Primitive Baptist,* July 22, 1839.
96. Joiner, *History of Florida Baptists,* 22–23.
97. Union Church, Minutes, December 1832, February, April 1833.
98. Joiner, *History of Florida Baptists,* 22–23; *Report of American Baptist Home Missionary Society,* 53, cited in Rosser, *Florida Baptists,* 22–23.

99. Christian Index, *Baptist Denomination in Georgia,* appendix, 313.
100. Ibid., appendix, 36–37.
101. Richland Creek Church, Minutes, July 1835.
102. Christian Index, *Baptist Denomination in Georgia,* appendix, 36–37.
103. Rosser, *Florida Baptists,* 11–12.
104. Bryant, "James McDonald," 71, 74, 77–78, 85.
105. Christian Index, *Baptist Denomination in Georgia,* 374–75.
106. William McElvey to *Primitive Baptist,* August 20, 1839.
107. Elias Hawthorn to *Primitive Baptist,* November 18, 1839.
108. Prior Lewis to *Primitive Baptist,* January 14, 1843.
109. William McElvey to *Primitive Baptist,* December 29, 1839.
110. William McElvey to *Primitive Baptist,* September 20, 1839.
111. Hardy Brooks to *Primitive Baptist,* July 15, 1841.
112. Ochlocknee Association, *Minutes,* 1833.
113. Ochlocknee Association, *Minutes,* 1841.
114. William McElvey to *Primitive Baptist,* November 20, 1841.
115. Ochlocknee Association, *Minutes,* 1842.
116. Ibid., 1844.
117. Suwannee River Association, *Minutes,* 1841; Alabaha River Association, *Minutes,* 1842.
118. Hephzibah Church, Minutes, January 1825.
119. Beard's Creek Church, Minutes, April 1817.
120. Suwannee River Association, *Minutes,* 1839, 1840, 1842.
121. Elias Hawthorn to *Primitive Baptist,* July 22, 1839.
122. Ochlocknee Association, *Minutes,* 1844.
123. Elias Hawthorn to *Primitive Baptist,* July 23, 1838.
124. Elias Hawthorn to *Primitive Baptist,* December 30, 1838.
125. James Alderman to *Primitive Baptist,* March 8, 1839.
126. Daniel O'Neel to *Primitive Baptist,* July 17, 1839; Chloe Hurste to *Primitive Baptist,* December 31, 1840; James Alderman to *Primitive Baptist,* March 8, 1839.
127. Jane A. Stokes in *Primitive Baptist,* December 25, 1843.
128. Hephzibah Church, Minutes, July 1839.
129. James Alderman to *Primitive Baptist,* February 1, 1840.
130. David Callaway to *Primitive Baptist,* February 12, 1839; "List of Agents," *Signs,* 16; Hassell and Hassell, *Church of God,* 935–36.
131. William Moseley to *Primitive Baptist,* February 5, 1840.
132. Hassell and Hassell, *Church of God,* 339.
133. William C. Thomas to *Primitive Baptist,* June 12, 1841.
134. Prior Lewis to *Primitive Baptist,* December 30, 1841.
135. "Ebenezer Association. (Ga.)," 139–40.
136. Ochlocknee Association, *Minutes,* 1836.
137. Elias Hawthorn to *Primitive Baptist,* December 30, 1838.
138. Prior Lewis to *Primitive Baptist,* September 26, 1839.
139. "A Looker On," 1.

140. William McElvey to *Primitive Baptist,* June 15, 1839.
141. H. Thomas to *Primitive Baptist,* January 2, 1842.
142 Suwannee River Association, *Minutes,* 1843.
143. Ibid.
144. Florida Association, *Minutes,* 1846.
145. Hephzibah Church, Minutes, January, August, 1839; James Alderman to *Primitive Baptist,* March 8, 1839.
146. Tired Creek Church, Minutes, September 1839.
147. Union Church, Minutes, September 1840.
148. Elias Hawthorn to *Primitive Baptist,* November 18, 1839.
149. Mercer, "Rather Distressing," 348.
150. Elias Hawthorn to *Primitive Baptist,* September 18, 1840.
151. Ochlocknee Association, *Minutes,* 1842.
152. Ibid., 1842, 1843.
153. Prior Lewis to *Primitive Baptist,* December 30, 1841.
154. "Ochlocknee Primitive—!!," 761.
155. Florida Association, *Minutes,* 1843.
156. D.A.R., *Lowndes County,* 105–6.
157. Florida Baptist Association, *Minutes,* 1843.
158. Elias Hawthorn to *Primitive Baptist,* July 22, 1839.
159. Ochlocknee Association, *Minutes,* 1844.
160. Bethlehem Church, Minutes, September 1840.
161. Suwannee River Association, *Minutes,* 1845.
162. Ochlocknee Association, *Minutes,* 1843; Sunbury Association, *Minutes,* 1821.
163. Mt. Moriah Church, Minutes, June 1844, quoted in Nancy Hagan obituary, 27.
164. Nancy Hagan obituary, 7.
165. John F. Hagan to *Primitive Baptist,* February 12, 1841; John F. Hagan to *Primitive Baptist,* April 7, 1840; Huxford Society, *Pioneers,* 1:113–14.
166. Suwannee River Association, *Minutes,* 1840.
167. Ibid.; Sunbury Association, *Minutes,* 1821.
168. Huxford Society, *Pioneers,* 3:100, 6:312.
169. Union Church, Minutes, February 1832.
170. Huxford Society, *Pioneers,* 3:100.
171. Suwannee River Association, *Minutes,* 1842.
172. Little River Church, Minutes, October 1842, quoted in *Christian Index* 10: 730–31.
173. Suwannee River Association, *Minutes,* 1845.
174. Ibid., 1847.
175. Ochlocknee Association, *Minutes,* 1844; Suwannee River Association, *Minutes,* 1845; Alabaha River Association, Minutes, 1845.
176. Georgia Association, Minutes, 1793.
177. Union Church, Minutes, October 1825.
178. Savannah River Association, *Minutes,* 1806
179. Suwannee River Association, *Minutes,* 1842.
180. Alabaha River Association, Minutes, 1845.

181. Lloyd to *Primitive Baptist,* April 7, 1842.
182. Lloyd to *Primitive Baptist,* April 24, 1847.
183. Crowley, "Notes," 20–21.

Chapter 5. The Civil War Era

1. Suwannee Association, *Minutes,* 1849; Alabaha River Association, Minutes, 1849.
2. Hassell and Hassell, *Church of God,* 787–88.
3. Ibid., 789.
4. Ibid.
5. Ibid., 790.
6. Ibid.
7. *Huxford Genealogical Society Magazine* 12 (December 1985): 344–45.
8. Ibid.
9. Huxford Society, *Pioneers,* 1:159–61.
10. Union Church, Minutes, June 1850, May 1851, March 1853, February 1853, September 1858.
11. Ochlocknee Association, *Minutes,* 1854.
12. Alabaha River Association, Minutes, 1842, 1846.
13. Suwannee River Association, *Minutes,* 1838, 1855.
14. *Signs of the Times* 22 (April 11, 1854): 54.
15. Ibid.
16. Ibid., 56.
17. Ibid., 55–56.
18. *Signs of the Times* 22 (August 1, 1854): 103.
19. *Signs of the Times* 22 (June 15, 1854): 93–94.
20. Suwannee River Association, *Minutes,* 1854.
21. Clark, "Master and Servant," *Primitive Baptist* 24 (August 25, 1860): 243.
22. Ibid., 245.
23. Ibid., 247.
24. Ibid., 249.
25. Ibid., 250.
26. *Primitive Baptist* 24 (October 27, 1860): 1–2; letter of November 28, 1860, in vol. 25 (January 12, 1861): 1–2; letter of January 17, 1861, in vol. 25 (February 10, 1861): 42–43.
27. Ibid., 25 (July 27, 1861): 219–20.
28. Ibid., 25 (January 12, 1861): 12–15.
29. Covington, *Colquitt County,* 24–29.
30. Stallings to Mitchell, January 1, 1876.
31. Huxford Society, *Pioneers,* 1:283–85.
32. Covington, *Colquitt County,* 24–29.
33. Ibid.; Huxford Society, *Pioneers,* 2:253–54.
34. Stallings to Mitchell; Henderson, *Confederate Soldiers of Georgia,* 5:369.

35. *Huxford Genealogical Society Magazine* 18 (September 1991): 224; Pleasant Church, Minutes, June 1899.
36. Hollingsworth, "Experience," 1, 4–8, 10.
37. Bethlehem Church, Minutes, February 1861.
38. Ibid., September 1864.
39. Ibid., January, February 1865.
40. Cedar Creek Church, Minutes, July–September, 1864.
41. Ibid., April–July, 1865.
42. Salem Church, Minutes, February, March 1865, September 1866.
43. Ibid., May 1866.
44. Ibid., September 1864.
45. Union Church, Minutes, May 1863.
46. Griffin, "Papers," 3:71.
47. Ibid., May 1864.
48. Ibid., June 1864.
49. Crowley, "Notes," 22.
50. Pleasant Church, Minutes, June 1899.
51. Ward, "Manning Kirkland Is Killed," 224.
52. Ochlocknee Association, *Minutes,* 1864; Salem Church, Minutea, passim, 1861–65.
53. Henderson, *Confederate Soldiers of Georgia,* 5:369.
54. Stallings to Mitchell; Bethel Church, Minutes, February 1865.
55. Bethlehem Church, Minutes, May 1865; Bethel Church, Minutes, October 1865.
56. Dickison, *Florida,* 57.
57. Suwannee River Association, *Minutes,* 1864.
58. Ibid.; Davis, *Civil War and Reconstruction in Florida,* 305–6.
59. Davis, *Civil War and Reconstruction in Florida,* 259–66.
60. Alabaha River Association, Minutes, 1864.
61. Pulaski Association, *Minutes,* 1864.
62. Huxford Society, *Pioneers,* 1:7, 4:239.
63. Huxford Society, *Pioneers,* 5:261.
64. Tinsley, *Florida Cow Hunter,* 3.
65. Henderson, *Confederate Soldiers of Georgia,* 3:453.
66. Crowley, "Notes," 24.
67. Griffin, "Papers," 3:72.
68. Huxford Society, *Pioneers,* 8: 336–37.
69. Huxford, "Hebron Church." n.p.
70. Huxford Society, *Pioneers,* 8:82.
71. Ibid., 7:56–57.
72. Alabaha River Association, *Minutes,* 1865.
73. Covington, *Colquitt County,* 31–32, 24–37.
74. Huxford Society, *Pioneers,* 3:240.
75. Clements, *Irwin County,* 134.
76. Huxford Society, *Pioneers,* 2:294.

Chapter 6. The Post–Civil War Era

1. Bethlehem Church, Minutes, August 1868, July 1872.
2. Union Church, Minutes, Membership roll.
3. Friendship Church, Minutes, May 1866.
4. Union Church, Minutes, November 1841.
5. Surmons, "Experience," 192.
6. Ibid.
7. Ibid.
8. Ibid.; Union Church, Minutes, November 1841.
9. Union Church, Minutes, September 1895; Surmons, "Experience," 192.
10. Surmons, "Experience," 192; Deed of Gift, Pilgrim's Rest Church.
11. Ochlocknee Association, *Minutes,* 1889; Deed of Gift, Pilgrim's Rest Church.
12. Surmons, "Experience," 192.
13. Ochlocknee Association, *Minutes,* 1889.
14. Union Association [black], *Minutes,* 1906.
15. Griffis, "Big Creek Church," 7.
16. Union Church, Minutes, September 1874; Huxford, "Hebron Church," n.p.
17. Bethlehem Church, Minutes, August 1877, February–April 1883.
18. Friendship Church, Minutes, January, November 1868, April 1869.
19. Ibid., January 1868, February 1869.
20. Ibid., November 1869, January 1870, May 1870, November 1872, April 1873, January 1873, January 1879.
21. R. H. Barwick to *Pilgrim's Banner,* October 31, 1896.
22. Ochlocknee Association, *Minutes,* 1870.
23. Harmony Association, *Minutes,* 1868.
24. Ibid.
25. Savannah Association, *Minutes,* 1802.
26. Hassell and Hassell, *Church of God,* 827.
27. Ochlocknee Association, *Minutes,* 1833.
28. Suwannee River Association, *Minutes,* 1841.
29. Antioch Association, *Minutes,* 1916.
30. Ibid., 1879.
31. Union Association [black], *Minutes,* 1890; Crowley, "Notes," 76.
32. Union Association [black], *Minutes,* 1891.
33. Ibid., 1891, 1906.
34. Ibid., 1925.
35. Ochlocknee Association, *Minutes,* 1883.
36. Crowley, "Notes," 76.
37. Beulah Association, *Minutes,* 1881; Crowley, "Notes," 76–77; *Souvenier Booklet of Wakulla County Primitive Baptist Church Union Meetings,* n.p.
38. Florida Primitive Association, *Minutes,* 1880.
39. McKinney and McKinney, *Black Baptists of Florida,* 268.

40. Ibid., 269, 272.
41. Gilbert, "Historical Sketch," in Mt. Enon Association, *Minutes,* 1898;. Wiggins, *Absolute Mt. Enon Association,* 12–13; Purifoy, "Tour," 231–232.
42. Purifoy, "Tour," 231–32.
43. Piedmont Church, Minutes, May–June, 1868.
44. Stallings,*Timothy William and Susan Newton Stallings,* 12.
45. Crowley, "Notes," 77.
46. Bethlehem Church, Minutes, January 1869.
47. Ibid., March 1869.
48. Ibid., July 1869.
49. Ibid., October 1870; Ochlocknee Association, *Minutes,* 1870.
50. Bethlehem Church, Minutes, July 1870, June 1871, April 1872.
51. Union Association, *Minutes,* 1870.
52. Huxford, "Wayfare Church," n.p.
53. Alabaha River Association, Minutes, 1870.
54. Ibid., 1871.
55. Ibid., 1872.
56. Ibid., 1873.
57. Crowley, "Notes," 24.
58. Huxford Society, *Pioneers,* 5:83.
59. Piedmont Association, Minutes, 1835–37.
60. Alabaha River Association, Minutes, 1842–87; Huxford Society, *Pioneers,* 5:83.
61. Alabaha River Association, Minutes, 1845–87.
62. Broome, *Pierce County,* 201; *Blackshear Georgian,* June 23, 1886, quoted in Broome, *Pierce County,* 55.
63. Huxford Society, *Pioneers,* 4:18.
64. Alabaha River Association, Minutes, 1869.
65. Crowley, "Notes," 24–25; "Richard Bennett," 148.
66. Broome, *Pierce County,* 201–2.
67. Alabaha River Association [Crawford faction], Minutes, 1878–79, 1911.
68. Alabaha River Association [Bennett faction], *Minutes,* 1877.
69. Ibid. [Crawford faction], 1881.
70. Ibid., 1884.
71. Cat Creek Church, Minutes, July 1878.
72. Huxford, "Wayfare Church"; Alabaha River Association [Bennett faction], *Minutes,* 1889.
73. Flint River Primitive Baptist Association, *Minutes,* 1880.
74. San Pedro Association, Minutes, 1884.
75. Wiggins, *Absolute Mt. Enon Association,* 3–5.
76. Wiggins, "James Mosley," in Mt. Enon Association, *Minutes,* 1898.
77. Wiggins, *Absolute Mt. Enon Association,* 7–9.
78. Gilbert, "Historical Sketch."

Chapter 7. The Crawfordites, Jackites, Battleites, and Coonites

1. London Confession, 10:1–3, quoted in Hassell and Hassell, *Church of God,* 676–77.
2. Ochlocknee Association, *Minutes,* 1833.
3. Union Church, Minutes, March 1832, June 1833, June 1836.
4. Suwannee River Association, *Minutes,* 1849.
5. Lloyd, *Primitive Hymns,* 91.
6. Hassell and Hassell, *Church of God,* 258.
7. Gill, *Body of Divinity,* 384.
8. Pulaski Association, *Minutes,* 1855.
9. Hassell and Hassell, *Church of God,* 633–34.
10. Alabaha River Association, Minutes, 1860, 1862.
11. Suwannee River Association, *Minutes,* 1861, 1862, 1869.
12. Alabaha River Association, Minutes, 1862–65.
13. Alabaha River Association [Crawford faction], *Minutes,* 1884.
14. Gibson and Wildes, *W. O. Gibson,* 2.
15. Alabaha River Association, Minutes, 1866, 1868.
16. Pleasant Church, Minutes, July 1869.
17. J. M. Handcock to A. V. Simms, July 6, 1896.
18. Satilla Association, *Minutes,* 1943; Alabaha River Association, *Minutes,* 1869.
19. Vickers, *Explanation,* n.p.
20. Griffin, "Emmaus Church," 3:80, 82, 85; Huxford Society, *Pioneers,* 7:255.
21. Griffin, "Emmaus Church," 3:80–85.
22. Crowley, "Notes," 25.
23. Brushy Creek Union, *Minutes,* 1891.
24. Ward, *Coffee County,* 47.
25. Hebron Convention, *Minutes,* 1881; Satilla Association, *Minutes,* 1889.
26. Crowley, "Notes," 77.
27. Hassell and Hassell, *Church of God,* 894; Beulah Association, *Minutes,* 1874.
28. Stallings to Mitchell.
29. Beulah Association, *Minutes,* 1875.
30. Ibid., 1875, 1885.
31. Harris, *Mercer Association,* 91, 100.
32. Beulah Association, *Minutes,* 1887.
33. West Florida Association, *Minutes,* 1945.
34. Sweet, *Baptists,* 68–69.
35. Parker, "Life," in Irwin, "Principal Writings," 8, 18–19.
36. Parker, "Life," 28–29.
37. Ibid., 12, 30, 31–32, 37–38, 44.
38. Parker, "Life," 20, 32–37.
39. Thompson, *Autobiography,* 114.
40. Parker, "Doctrine of Two Seeds" in Irwin, "Principal Writings," 3, 5–6, 10, 12, 27–28, 33.
41. Ibid., 22–23.

42. Ibid., 16, 30–33.
43. Ibid., 24–25, 34.
44. U.S. Census Office, *Statistics of Churches: 1890,* 208–10.
45. Haynes, *Primitive Baptists,* 204–26; Hassell, *Church of God,* 636–37.
46. Preslar, *Divine Providence,* 178–79.
47. Thompson, *Measuring Rod,* 21, 88, 116–19.
48. Potter, *Labors,* 54, 61–62, 80, 262.
49. Bethel Church, Minutes, May, June, August 1843.
50. Huxford Society, *Pioneers,* 4:268–69.
51. Suwannee River Association, *Minutes,* passim.
52. Cedar Creek Church, Minutes, October 1869.
53. Riley, *Baptists of Alabama,* 62–63.
54. Potter, *Labors and Travels,* 81–82.
55. Suwannee River Association, *Minutes,* 1869; "Dr. Isaac Coon Dead."
56. Huxford, "Isaac Coon," n.p.
57. *Journal of Proceedings,* 5, 20, 21, 33, 34, 35.
58. Huxford, "Isaac Coon," n.p.; detail on his military service is from the Isaac Coon Confederate monument, New Friendship Cemetery, Hahira, Ga.
59. "Dr. Isaac Coon Dead."
60. New Hope Association, *Minutes,* 1887.
61. Suwannee River Association [Coon faction], *Minutes,* 1877.
62. Ibid.
63. Ibid.
64. Ibid.
65. Suwannee River Association [Coon faction], *Minutes,* 1877; Wayfare Church, Minutes, July–October, 1875.
66. Suwannee River Association [Coon faction], *Minutes,* 1877.
67. Huxford, "Hebron Church," n.p.
68. Harmony Church to Antioch Church, December 8, 1876.
69. Bethlehem Church, Minutes, July 1875–November 1876.
70. Harmony to Antioch, December 8, 1876.
71. Harmony Church, Minutes, October 1875, January–November 1876.
72. Ochlocknee Association, *Minutes,* 1876.
73. Ibid., 1879; Antioch Church, Minutes, November 1876, January 1877, November 1877, February 1880.
74. Ochlocknee Association, *Minutes,* 1865.
75. Harmony Church, Minutes, December 1865, July 1866, April 1875.
76. Hassell and Hassell, *Church of God,* 894.
77. Harmony Church, Minutes, April 1875.
78. Suwannee River Association [Coon faction], *Minutes,* 1876, 1877, 1880, 1881.
79. Suwannee River Association, *Minutes,* 1877.
80. Ibid. [Coon faction], *Minutes,* 1876.
81. Ibid., 1877.
82. Lookout Mountain Primitive Baptist Association, *Minutes,* 1889.

83. Suwannee River Association [Coon faction], *Minutes,* 1876, 1877.
84. Potter, *Labors and Travels,* 75–76.
85. Suwannee River Association [Coon faction], *Minutes,* passim.
86. Caney Fork Association, *Minutes,* 1911; Suwannee River Association [Coon faction], *Minutes,* 1911.
87. Suwannee River Association [Coon faction], *Minutes,* 1877, 1881, 1884, 1890, 1916.
88. Ibid., 1893.
89. Ibid., 1895, 1898, 1911, 1919.
90. Cedar Creek Church, Minutes, 1920, 1921.
91. Richland Creek Association, *Minutes,* 1920, 1923, 1924, 1925.
92. Brooks County, Georgia, Deed Book 35, p. 142.
93. Suwannee River Association [Coon faction], *Minutes,* passim.
94. Cedar Creek Church, Minutes, June 1885, March 1898.
95. Suwannee River Association [Coon faction], *Minutes,* 1905.
96. Ibid., passim.
97. Suwannee River Association, *Minutes,* 1864; ibid. [Coon faction], Minutes, 1876, 1890, 1899.
98. Cedar Creek Church, Minutes, passim.
99. Suwannee River Association [Coon faction], *Minutes,* 1887, 1905, 1906, 1912, 1913.
100. Ibid., 1890.
101. Suwannee River Association [Coon faction], *Minutes,* 1890.
102. Harmony to Antioch, December 8, 1876.
103. Antioch Church, Minutes, January 1877.
104. Suwannee River Association [Coon faction], *Minutes,* 1890.
105. Ibid.
106. Lookout Mountain Association, *Minutes,* 1889.
107. Suwannee River Association [Coon faction], *Minutes,* 1890, 1898, 1899, 1900, 1902, 1906.
108. Ibid., 1890; Harmony to Antioch, December 8, 1876.
109. Suwannee River Association [Coon faction], *Minutes,* 1906.
110. Ibid., 1890.
111. Ibid.
112. Ibid.
113. Suwannee River Association [Coon faction], *Minutes,* 1890.
114. Ibid., 1890, 1898.
115. Crowley, "Notes," 22.
116. Suwannee River Association [Coon faction], *Minutes,* 1899, 1905.
117. Bear Creek Association, *Minutes,* 1911.
118. Suwannee River Association [Coon faction], *Minutes,* 1900.
119. Lookout Mountain Association, *Minutes,* 1889.
120. Suwannee River Association [Coon faction], *Minutes,* 1906.
121. Ibid., 1909.

122. Ibid., 1890.
123. Ibid., 1899, 1904.

Chapter 8. The Progressive and Peace Movements

1. Malone, "Piney Woods Farmers," 51–84.
2. Union Association, *Minutes,* 1870, 1879, 1890, 1900; Ochlocknee Association, *Minutes,* 1890, 1898; Simms, "Some Good Meetings," 237–38.
3. Huxford Society, *Pioneers,* 7:365–66; Alabaha Association, *Minutes,* 1889; Union Association, *Minutes,* 1916.
4. U.S. Census Office, *Statistics of Churches: 1890,* 56–57, 201.
5. Harris, *Mercer Association,* 122–23.
6. Simms, "The Rot," 252.
7. Crowley, "Notes," 25.
8. London Confession, 3:1, in Hassell and Hassell, *Church of God,* 670.
9. Gill, *Body of Divinity,* 123.
10. Owen Smith to Gilbert Beebe, December 25, 1850.
11. Simms, "Elder Bartley's Article," 2.
12. Simms, "Associations," 280.
13. Simms, "Flint River Association," 21.
14. Wiggins, *Absolute Mt. Enon Association,* 13–24; Mt. Enon Association, *Minutes,* 1906.
15. Hanks, *The Church of God,* 166.
16. Whitten, *Statement,* n.p.
17. Union Association, *Minutes,* 1893.
18. Ibid., 1894.
19. Ochlocknee Association, *Minutes,* 1833.
20. Ibid.
21. Piedmont Association, Minutes, 1823.
22. I. J. Taylor to Lee Hanks.
23. Ibid.
24. Union Association, *Minutes,* 1897.
25. Aaron Knight monument, Pleasant Cemetery, Berrien Co., Ga.
26. Crowley, "Notes," 25–26.
27. Barwick, *Memories,* 47–50.
28. Harmony Church, Minutes, May 1896.
29. "Resolution," 13–14; "Basis of Agreement," 1–2; Barwick, "That Basis of Agreement Again," 27–29.
30. D.A.R., *Lowndes County,* 105.
31. Harmony Church, Minutes, May 1898.
32. Ibid., September 1899.
33. Ochlocknee Association [Simms-Barwick faction], *Minutes,* 1899.
34. Ibid.; Ochlocknee Association [McCann faction], *Minutes,* 1899.
35. Ochlocknee Association [McCann faction], *Minutes,* 1910.
36. Alabaha River Association [Bennett faction], *Minutes,* 1910, 1911.

37. Ochlocknee Association [Simms-Barwick faction], *Minutes,* 1899.
38. Ibid.
39. Ibid., 1903.
40. Crowley, "Notes," 26.
41. Suwannee River Association, *Minutes,* 1900.
42. Ochlocknee Association [Simms-Barwick faction], *Minutes,* 1900.
43. Cat Creek Church, Minutes, December 1899.
44. Pleasant Church, Minutes, January 1900.
45. Pleasant Grove Church, Minutes, May 1900.
46. D.A.R., *Lowndes County,* 61.
47. Crowley, "Notes," 26–27.
48. Hassell, "Causes of the Division in Southwest Georgia," 104.
49. Pleasant Church, Minutes, June 1899.
50. Crowley, "Notes," 27.
51. T. W. Stallings to A. V. Simms, February 10, 1895.
52. Pleasant Church, Minutes, June 1899.
53. Ibid., November 1900.
54. Simms, "Associations," 280.
55. Crowley, "Notes," 27.
56. Cat Creek Church, Minutes, July 1901.
57. Union Association, *Minutes,* 1901.
58. Ibid.
59. Ibid. [Luke faction], 1903.
60. Ibid. [Old Line faction].
61. Hassell, "Scriptural Impartiality," 184–86; Hassell, "Causes of the Division in Southwest Georgia," 184.
62. Valdosta Church, Minutes, 1900, October 1901, February 1906, July 1907.
63. Crowley, "Notes," 28.
64. Askew, "Hymnals in Southern Baptist Churches," 22.
65. Huxford, *Brooks County,* 296–297.
66. Salem Church, Minutes, May 1909.
67. Crowley, "Notes," 29.
68. Mt. Olive Primitive Baptist Association, *Minutes,* 1910.
69. Ibid.
70. *Minutes of the General Meeting of the Churches of the Mt. Olive Association.*
71. Original Mt. Olive Association, *Minutes,* 1923.
72. Mt. Olive Association [Lewis faction], *Minutes,* 1917; Cat Creek Church, Minutes, January 1906; Wayfare Church, Minutes, March–October 1905.
73. Salem Church, Minutes, June 1913.
74. Ibid., July 1913.
75. Ibid., January–February, December, 1914, June 1915; Mt. Olive Association, *Minutes,* 1920.
76. Salem Church, Minutes, March–April, 1905.
77. *Terms of Agreement.*

78. Salem Church, Minutes, October, December 1926, February, April, May 1927.
79. Crowley, "The Three Faces of Cat Creek," 41–46.
80. Crowley, "Notes," 28–30.
81. Union Association [Peace faction], *Minutes,* 1927; Crowley, "Notes," 29.
82. Original Union Primitive Baptist Association, *Minutes,* 1927.
83. Union Association [Peace faction], *Minutes,* 1927.
84. Original Union Association, *Minutes,* 1930.
85. Ibid. 1928.
86. Crowley, "Notes," 29.
87. Original Union Association, *Minutes,* 1930 ff.

Chapter 9. The Footwashing Controversy and Related Issues

1. Lloyd, *Primitive Hymns,* 205.
2. Blanton, interview, September 6, 1994.
3. Crowley, "Notes," 71.
4. Ibid., 72.
5. Echeconnee Association, *Minutes,* 1872, quoted in Wells, *Condensed History,* 12–13.
6. Thomas Jefferson Bazemore, "Feetwashing," *Gospel Messenger* 1 (October 1878): 14–16.
7. Lee, "Northwest Georgia Primitive Baptists," 9–10.
8. San Pedro Association, *Minutes,* 1926.
9. Original Union Association, *Minutes,* 1931; Pleasant Church should not be confused with Pleasant Grove Church or Mt. Pleasant Church.
10. Original Union Association, *Minutes,* 1934.
11. Crowley, "Notes," 72.
12. Crowley, "Notes," 72–73.
13. Towaliga Association, *Minutes,* 1838, 1854.
14. Wells, *Condensed History,* 13.
15. Ibid., 1861, 1862, 1865, 1866, 1867.
16. Ibid., 1874, 1875.
17. *An Address from Liberty Church.*
18. Towaliga Association, *Minutes,* 1878.
19. Gardner et al, *Georgia Baptist Association,* 157.
20. Towaliga Association, *Minutes,* 1878.
21. Wells, *Condensed History,* 13–14.
22. Towaliga Association, *Minutes,* 1893.
23. Ibid., 1896.
24. Brushy Creek Union, *Minutes,* 1891; Towaliga Association, *Minutes,* 1890.
25. Towaliga Association, *Minutes,* 1893, 1894.
26. Revelations 18:2 AV.
27. Towaliga Association, *Minutes,* 1897.
28. Towaliga Association, *Minutes,* 1899; Kirkland and Kirkland, eds., *Confession of Faith,* 17.

29. Towaliga Association, *Minutes,* 1902.
30. Towaliga Association, *Minutes,* 1910.
31. Wells, *Condensed History,* 14.
32. Towaliga Association, *Minutes,* 1920, 1928.
33. Ibid., 1928–35.
34. Wells, *Condensed History,* 12.
35. Ibid., 16.
36. Ephesus Church Resolutions in Lott's Creek Association, *Minutes,* 1949.
37. Wells, *Condensed History,* 17.
38. Ochlocknee Association, *Minutes,* 1941, 1946; Pilgrim's Rest Association, *Minutes,* 1936; Mt. Enon Association, *Minutes,* 1940–41.
39. Pilgrim's Rest Association, *Minutes,* 1936.
40. Flint River Association, *Minutes,* 1933.
41. Crowley, "Notes," 73.
42. Flint River Association [anti-Towaliga faction] *Minutes,* 1936.
43. Ibid.
44. Ochlocknee Association, *Minutes,* 1935–39.
45. Ibid., 1937.
46. Ibid., 1937–39.
47. Union Association [Peace faction], *Minutes,* 1934.
48. Bennett, interview, September 2, 1994; Union Association [Peace faction], *Minutes,* 1938.
49. Crowley, "Notes," 73–74.
50. Bennett, interview, September 2, 1994.
51. Ibid., May 24, 1991.
52. Cat Creek Church, Minutes, November 1915.
53. Bennett, interview, September 2, 1994.
54. Crowley, "Notes," 74.
55. Ibid.
56. Blanton, interview, September 6, 1994.
57. Crowley, "Notes," 75.
58. Blanton, interview, September 6, 1994.
59. Bennett, interview, September 2, 1994.
60. Blanton, interview, September 6, 1994.
61. Crowley, "Notes," 75.
62. Blanton, interview, September 6, 1994.
63. Crowley, "Notes," 75–76.
64. Bennett, interview, September 2, 1994.
65. Crowley, "Notes," 76.
66. Union Association [Peace faction], *Minutes,* 1937.
67. Cat Creek Church, Minutes, April 1937.
68. Union Association [Peace faction], *Minutes,* 1937; Original Union Association, *Minutes,* 1937.

69. Ibid. [Peace faction], *Minutes,* 1937.
70. Pleasant Church, Minutes, August 1937.
71. Union Association [Peace faction], *Minutes,* 1937.
72. Towaliga Association, *Minutes,* 1941.
73. Ochlocknee Association, *Minutes,* 1939.
74. Bennett, interview, September 2, 1994; Union Association [Peace faction], *Minutes,* 1943.
75. Harris, *Sut Lovingood,* 51.
76. Blanton, interview, September 6, 1994.

Chapter 10. 1945 to the Present

1. Crowley, "Notes," 30–31.
2. Obituary in Original Union Association, *Minutes,* 1994.
3. Original Union Association, *Minutes,* 1945, 1992.
4. Mt. Enon Association, *Minutes,* 1933; Original Mt. Enon Primitive Baptist Association in Order, *Minutes,* 1981.
5. Alabaha River Association [Crawford faction], Minutes, 1941; Alabaha River Association [Crawford faction], *Minutes,* 1941, 1993.
6. Union Association [Peace faction], *Minutes,* 1945, 1993.
7. Ochlocknee Association [Progressive faction], *Minutes,* 1945; Ibid. in *Minutes of Ten Associations.*
8. Huxford Society, *Pioneers,* 3:238, 4:239, 7:270, 8:425.
9. Cat Creek Church, *Minutes,* Original Membership Roll.
10. Crowley, "Notes," 31.
11. Ibid., 31–33.
12. Beard's Creek Church, *Minutes,* September 1814; Crowley, "Notes," 33.
13. Crowley, "Notes," 33.
14. Ibid., 34.
15. Ibid., 35.
16. Ibid.
17. Ibid., 36.
18. Ibid., 36, 37, 39.
19. Ibid., 37.
20. Levi B. Bennett et. al., [Account of His Church Membership].
21. Crowley, "Notes," 37.
22. Hassell and Hassell, *Church of God,* 826.
23. Huxford Society, *Pioneers,* 1:159.
24. Crowley, "Notes," 38.
25. Ibid., 37–39.
26. Ibid., 40.
27. Wells, *Condensed History,* 17.
28. Crowley, "Notes," 40; Union Association [Peace faction], *Minutes,* 1955.
29. Flint River Association [anti-Towaliga faction], *Minutes,* 1955.

30. Original Ochlocknee Association, *Minutes,* 1953, 1957.
31. Cat Creek Church [Old Line faction], Minutes, August 1927, December 1954; Original Union Association, *Minutes,* 1959.
32. Mercer, *Georgia Association,* 131.
33. Suwannee River Association, *Minutes,* 1847.
34. Beebe, "Marriage," 140.
35. Huxford Society, *Pioneers,* 8:173–74.
36. Empire Church, Minutes, May 1896, September 1899, cited in Huxford, "Empire Church, " 18, 19.
37. Alabaha River Association [Bennett faction], *Minutes,* 1932, cited in Alabaha River Association *Minutes,* 1937.
38. Crowley, "Notes," 40–41.
39. Crowley, "Notes," 41–43.
40. Blanton, interview, July 24, 1991.
41. Union Association [Peace faction], *Minutes,* 1972.
42. Suwannee River Association [Peace faction], *Minutes,* 1969, 1984.
43. Union Association [Peace faction], *Minutes,* 1968, 1977; San Pedro Association, *Minutes,* 1969, 1977.
44. Crowley, "Notes," 43–44.
45. *First North Florida Fellowship Meeting,* 1972; *Nineteenth North Florida Fellowship Meeting of Primitive Baptist Churches,* 1990.
46. Crowley, "Notes," 44.
47. Ibid.
48. Bennett, interview, September 2, 1994.
49. Dickerson, interview, September 14, 1994.
50. Middlebrooks, "Future View of America," 10–11.
51. Crowley, "Notes," 45.
52. Bennett, interview, September 2, 1994.
53. Blanton, interview, September 6, 1994.
54. Crowley, "Notes," 45.
55. Pilgrim's Rest Association [anti-Towaligan faction], *Minutes,* 1947.
56. Ibid., 1948.
57. Cat Creek Church [Independent faction], Minutes, February 1985; Dickerson, interview, September 14, 1994.
58. Pilgrim's Rest Predestinarian, *Minutes,* 1952.
59. Pilgrim's Rest Association [Main faction], Ministers' Meeting.
60. Jones et. al., "Statement on Good Works."
61. Blanton, interview, July 24, 1991.
62. Original Ochlocknee Association, *Minutes,* 1953.
63. Blanton, interview, July 24, 1991.
64. Crowley, "Notes," 46.
65. Ibid., 47.
66. Haynes, *Primitive Baptists,* 267–75.
67. Crowley, "Notes," 48; *Holy Spirit Conference with Charles Carrin.*

68. Beulah Association, *Minutes,* 1990.
69. Crowley, "Notes," 49, 50.
70. Ibid., 51.
71. Ibid., 52.
72. Ibid., 53.
73. Quoted in obituary in Original Union Association, *Minutes,* 1994.
74. Crowley, "Notes," 53–54.
75. Dickerson, interview, September 14, 1994.
76. Bennett, interview, September 2, 1994.
77. Crowley, "Notes," 55.
78. Ibid., 56.
79. Ibid., 57–58; Crowley, "The Three Faces of Cat Creek," 41–46.
80. Crowley, "Notes," 59.
81. Crowley, "The Three Faces of Cat Creek," 45–46.
82. Alabaha River Association [Crawford faction], Minutes, 1921, 1952, 1960, 1968; Satilla River Association, *Minutes,* 1977.
83. "Declaration of Pleasant Grove."
84. Alabaha River Association [Fowler faction], *Minutes,* 1948; Suwannee River Association [McCall faction], *Minutes,* 1953.
85. Union Association [Peace faction], *Minutes,* 1968; Suwannee River Association [Peace faction], *Minutes,* 1961.
86. Suwannee River Association [Harris faction], *Minutes,* 1977.
87. Original Union Association, *Minutes,* 1977–82.
88. "Church Directory," *Gospel Appeal* 30 (February 1996): back cover.
89. Union Association [Peace faction], *Minutes,* 1977; Fred Bethea, "Brethren Separated."
90. New Hope, Poplar Springs, and Mt. Zion Churches to the Lott's Creek Association, in Original Flint River Association, *Minutes,* 1993.
91. Suwannee River Association, *Minutes,* 1985.
92. Original Union Association, *Minutes,* 1995; Alabaha River Association [Bennett faction], *Minutes,* 1995.
93. Pleasant Union Association, *Minutes,* 1967; Crowley, "Notes," 61.
94. Original Union Association, *Minutes,* 1956.
95. Ibid., 63–64.
96. Ibid., 65–66; West Florida Association, *Minutes,* 1945.
97. Old West Florida Association, *Minutes,* 1988; Crowley, "Notes," 66.
98. Union Association [black], *Minutes,* 1973, 1990.
99. Crowley, "Notes," 67.
100. Pulaski Association, *Minutes,* 1994.
101. Crowley, "Notes," 68–69.
102. Ibid., 70–71.
103. Boen et. al., *Under the Shadow of the Almighty,* 7–13.
104. Crowley, "Notes," 69.

BIBLIOGRAPHY

"A Looker On." Letter, Madison Co., Fla., November 15, 1844. *Christian Index* 13 (January 10, 1845): 1.

Aaron Knight monument. Pleasant Cemetery, Berrien Co., Ga.

Abrahamson, Warren G., and David C. Harnett. "Pine Flatwoods and Dry Prairies." In Ronald J. Myers and John J. Ewel. *Ecosystems of Florida,* with introduction by Marjorie H. Carr. Orlando: University of Central Florida, 1990.

Alabaha River Primitive Baptist Association, Georgia-Florida [Crawford faction after 1871]. Minutes. TMs. in possession of John G. Crowley, Hahira, Ga.

———. [Bennett faction]. *Minutes.*

———. [Crawford faction]. *Minutes.*

———. [Fowler faction]. *Minutes.*

Alderman, James. Letter, Gadsden Co., Fla., March 8, 1839. *Primitive Baptist* (Tarboro, N.C.) 4 (April 13, 1839): 108.

———. Letter, February 1, 1840. *Primitive Baptist* 5 (April 11, 1840): 165.

Allen, I. M. *The United States Baptist Annual Register and Almanac 1833.* Philadelphia: Baptist General Tract Society, 1833. Microfilm.

An Address of Explanation from Liberty Church to Her Sister Churches and Friends at Large. n.p., n.d.

Analytical Repository 1 (September–October 1802): 124.

Antioch Church, Minutes, Ms. in MacArthur Collection, Ramah Primitive Baptist Church, Buena Vista, Ga.

Antioch Primitive Baptist Association, Georgia. *Minutes.*

Armstrong, O. K., and Marjorie Armstrong. *The Indomitable Baptists.* Garden City, N.Y.: Doubleday, 1967.

Askew, Harry L. "Use and Influence of Hymnals in Southern Baptist Churches up to 1915." *Baptist History and Heritage* 21 (July 1986): 22.

Asplund, John. *The Universal Register of the Baptist Denomination in North America for the Years 1790, 1791, 1792, 1793, and Part of 1794.* Boston: J. W. Folsom, 1794. Reprint, The Baptist Tradition, Edwin S. Gaustad, series ed., New York: Arno Press, 1980.

Barwick, R[obert] H. Letter, Brooks Co., Ga., October 31, 1896. *Pilgrim's Banner* (Valdosta, Ga.) 3 (November 15, 1896): 118.

———. *Memories.* Barnesville, Ga.: Published by the author, 1942.

———. "That Basis of Agreement Again." *Pilgrim's Banner* 5 (May 1898): 27–29.

"Basis of Agreement." *Pilgrim's Banner* 5 (January 1, 1898): 1–2.

Bazemore, Thomas Jefferson. "Feetwashing." *Gospel Messenger.* October 1878, 14–16.

Bear Creek Predestinarian Baptist Association, Arkansas. *Minutes.*

Beard's Creek Primitive Baptist Church, Tattnall Co., Ga. Minutes. TMs. Photocopy in possession of John G. Crowley, Hahira, Ga.

Beebe, Gilbert. "Editorial." *Signs of the Times* (22 April 11, 1854): 54.

———. "Marriage." *Signs of the Times* 8 (September 15, 1840): 140.

———. "New School Courtesy." [September 11, 1858.] In *A Compilation of Editorial Articles Copied from the "Signs of the Times" Embracing a Period of Forty-Nine Years 1832–1881, in Which Is Reflected the Doctrine and Order of the Old School, or Primitive Baptists, Written by Gilbert Beebe, Editor.* 4 vols. Salisbury, Md.: Signs of the Times, Inc., 1982.

———. "Proposals for Publishing a Semi-Monthly Paper, Called the 'Signs of the Times,' by an Association of Brethren." *Signs of the Times* 1 (November 28, 1832): 16.

Benedict, David. *Fifty Years among the Baptists.* New York: Sheldon and Co., 1860. Quoted in Lee Hanks, *The Church of God.* Atlanta: Lee Hanks, c. 1920. Reprint, Atwood, Tenn.: Christian Baptist Publishing Co., 1982.

———. *A General History of the Baptist Denomination in America and Other Parts of the World.* 2 vols. Boston: David Benedict, 1813. Microfilm.

Bennett, Levi, et al. [Account of His Church Membership]. Ms. annotated by another hand. Photocopy in possession of John G. Crowley, Hahira, Ga.

Bennett, Lucius. Interviews by the author. May 24, 1991, and September 2, 1994, Adel, Ga.

Bethea, Fred. "Brethren Separated." TMs. in possession of John G. Crowley, Hahira, Ga.

Bethel Primitive Baptist Church, Brooks Co., Ga. Minutes. Ms. Photocopy in Odom Genealogical Library, Moultrie, Ga.

Bethlehem Primitive Baptist Church, Brooks Co., Ga. Minutes. Ms. Photocopy in possession of John G. Crowley, Hahira, Ga..

Beulah Primitive Baptist Association, Georgia-Florida. *Minutes.*

Blackshear Georgian. June 23, 1886. Quoted in Dean Broome, comp. *History of Pierce County, Georgia.* Blackshear, Ga.: n.p., 1973.

Blanton, Elder Fred. Interview by author. July 24, 1991. Valdosta, Ga.

Blanton, Elder Fred. Interview by author. September 6, 1994. Valdosta, Ga.

Boen, Freddy, W. R. Daniels, L. Jeff Harris, and Gus Harter. *Under the Shadow of the Almighty: God's Work in the Phillipines.* n.p.: Eureka Primitive Baptist Church, 1995.

Book and Bible List. *Old Faith Contender* 56 October-December 1978: 125–27.

Brewster, C. Ray. *The Cluster of Jesse Mercer.* Macon, Ga.: Renaissance Press, 1983.

Brooks, Hardy. Letter, Nassau Co., Fla., July 15, 1841. *Primitive Baptist* 6 (August 14, 1841): 231–32.

Brooks County, Georgia, Deed Book 35.

Broome, Dean, comp. *History of Pierce County, Georgia.* Blackshear, Ga.: n.p., 1973.

Brushy Creek Union Primitive Baptist Association, Georgia. *Minutes.*

Bryant, James C. *Indian Springs: The Story of a Pioneer Church in Leon County, Florida.* Tallahassee: Florida State University, 1971.

———. "James McDonald: Missionary to East Florida." *Viewpoints: Georgia Baptist History* 10 (1986): 71–85.

Callaway, David. Letter, Madison Co., Fla., February 12, 1839. *Primitive Baptist* 6 (March 23, 1839): 96.

Campbell, J. H. *Georgia Baptists: Historical and Biographical.* Richmond: H. K. Ellyson, 1847. 2d ed., Macon, Ga.: J. W. Burke and Co., 1874.

Caney Fork Predestinarian Baptist Association, Tennessee. *Minutes.*

Cat Creek Primitive Baptist Church, Lowndes Co., Ga. Minutes. Ms. in possession of church.

——— [Old Line faction]. Minutes. Ms. in possession of church.

Cedar Creek Primitive Baptist Church, Baker Co., Fla. Minutes. Ms. in possession of John G. Crowley, Hahira, Ga.

Christian Index. *History of the Baptist Denomination in Georgia.* Atlanta: James P. Harrison and Co., 1881.

"Church Directory." *Gospel Appeal* 30 (February 1996): back cover.

Clark, John. "Discourse of Elder John Clark, upon the Subject of 'The Relation of Master and Servant." *Primitive Baptist* 24 (August 25, 1860): 243.

Clements, J. B. *History of Irwin County.* Atlanta: Foote and Davies, 1932.

Cohen, Hennig, and William B. Dillingham, eds. *Humor of the Old Southwest.* 3rd edition. Athens: University of Georgia Press, 1994.

[Conner, Wilson.] "Appointments for Preaching." *Christian Index* 5 (January 12, 1837): 32.

Coon, Elder Isaac. "Synopsis of Doctrinal Points." In Suwannee River Primitive Baptist Association [Coon faction], Florida. *Minutes,* 1890.

Coulter, E. Merton. *A History of Georgia.* 2d. ed. Chapel Hill: University of North Carolina, 1960.

Covington, W. A. *History of Colquitt County.* Atlanta: Foote and Davies, n.d.

Crowley, John. "Notes on the Primitive Baptist Church in South Georgia and Florida and Other Topics Related to That Region." Ms. in possession of John G. Crowley, Hahira, Ga.

———. "The Three Faces of Cat Creek: A Study of a Primitive Baptist 'Split Church.'" *Piney Woods Journal of History* 1 (1989–90): 41–48.

Davis, William Watson. *The Civil War and Reconstruction in Florida.* New York: n.p., 1913.

"Declaration of Pleasant Grove Church [Colquitt Co., Ga.] and Amendment to the Declaration." September 7, 1963. TMs. in possession of John G. Crowley, Hahira, Ga.

Deed of Gift from J. G. McCall to David Daniels, H. S. Sermons, et al., Trustees of Pilgrim's Rest Primitive Baptist Church (Colored). August 6, 1900. In Brooks Co., Ga., Deed Book O. 75.

"Detailed Report of General Brisbane." In Richard Keily. *A Brief and Statistical Sketch of Georgia.* London: 1849. Quoted in George B. Crawford, "Cotton, Land, and Sustenance: Towards the Limits of Abundance in Late Antebellum Georgia," *Georgia Historical Quarterly* 72 (Summer 1988).

Dickerson, Elder Bob. Interview by author. September 14, 1994. Valdosta, Ga.

Dickison, J. J. *Florida.* Vol. 16: *Confederate Military History, Extended Edition, in Sixteen Volumes, Written by Distinguished Men of the South,* ed. Clement A. Evans. Confederate Publishing Co., 1899. Reprint, Wilmington, N.C.: Broadfoot Publishing Co., 1989.

Donaldson, Robert. Letter, Bulloch Co., Ga., May 9, 1841. *Primitive Baptist* 6 (June 26, 1841): 133–34.

———. Letter, June 16, 1842. *Primitive Baptist* 7 (June 25, 1842): 215.

Douglas, P. T. Letter, Bainbridge, Ga., April 27, 1845. *Primitive Baptist* 10 (July 20, 1845): 218–19.

"Dr. Isaac Coon Dead." *Valdosta (Ga.) Times,* 17 October, 1891: 5.

"Ebenezer Association. (Ga.)." *Primitive Baptist* 2 (May 13, 1837): 139–40.

Echeconnee Primitive Baptist Association, Georgia. *Minutes.* Quoted in Charles F. Wells, *Condensed History of Baptists, Mainly Georgia Primitive Baptists: Facts, Records, Divisions, Also Interesting Features.* Macon, Ga.: Published by the author, [1962].

Edwards, Morgan. *Tour of Morgan Edwards of Pennsylvania to the American Baptists in North Carolina in 1772–1773.* Quoted in George Washington Paschal, *History of North Carolina Baptists.* 2 vols. Raleigh, N.C.: General Board of the North Carolina Baptist State Convention, 1930.

Eggleston, Edward. *The Hoosier Schoolmaster.* 1871. American Century Series. New York: Hill and Wang, 1957.

Ephesus Church Letter and Resolutions. In Lott's Creek Primitive Baptist Association, Georgia. *Minutes,* 1949.

The First North Florida Fellowship Meeting, October 27–29, 1972.

Flint River Primitive Baptist Association, Georgia. *Minutes.*

Flint River Primitive Baptist Association [anti-Towaliga faction], Georgia. *Minutes.*

Florida Baptist Association, Georgia-Florida. *Minutes.*

Florida Primitive Baptist Orthodox Zion Association. *Minutes.*

Friendship Primitive Baptist Church, Lowndes Co., Ga. Minutes. Ms. in possession of Cat Creek Primitive Baptist Church, Lowndes Co., Ga.

Furman, Wood, comp. *A History of the Charleston Association of Baptist Churches in the State of South Carolina With an Appendix Containing the Principal Circular Letters to the Churches.* Charleston, S.C.: n.p., 1811. Microfiche.

Gannon, Michael V. *The Cross in the Sand: The Early Catholic Church in Florida 1513–1870.* Gainesville: University of Florida Press, 1965.

Gardner, Robert G., Charles O. Walker, J. R. Huddlestun, and Waldo P. Harris. *A History of the Georgia Baptist Association, 1784–1984.* Atlanta: Georgia Baptist Historical Society, 1988.

General James Jackson Chapter, D.A.R. *History of Lowndes County, Georgia.* 1942. Reprint, Spartanburg, S.C.: Reprint Company, 1978.

Georgia Baptist Association. Minutes. Ms. in special collections, Mercer University Library, Macon, Ga.

Georgia Baptist Association. *Minutes.*

Gibson, Lamar, and Sandy Wildes, eds. *Rambling Meditations of W .O. Gibson.* N.p. n.d.

Gilbert, M. L. "Historical Sketch: A Synopsis of the History of the Primitive Baptists That Have Grown out of Mt. Enon, the First Church of That Faith and Order in South Florida." In Mt. Enon Primitive Baptist Association, *Minutes,* 1898.

Gill, John. *A Body of Doctrinal and Practical Divinity; Or, a System of Practical Truths Deduced from the Sacred Scriptures.* 1771. Reprints, London: Button and Son, and Whittingham and Arliss, 1815; Streamwood, Ill.: Primitive Baptist Library, 1977.

Gillette, A. D., ed. *Minutes of the Philadelphia Baptist Association, from [sc]A.D.[sc] 1707 to [sc]A.D.[sc] 1807; Being the First One Hundred Years of Its Existence.* Phildelphia: American Baptist Publication Society, 1851. Reprint, Otisville, Mich.: Baptist Book Trust, 1976.

Griffin, W. Henry, comp. "Emmaus Church (Flat Creek): A Review of Her History." In "The Griffin Papers: Being a Collection of Family Histories and Data and Information about Early Berrien County." 3 vols. TMs. in Nashville, Ga., Public Library.

Griffis, Ivey. "A History of Big Creek Primitive Baptist Church." 1972. TMs. in Huxford Genealogical Library, Homerville, Ga.

Hagan, John F. Letter, Jefferson Co., Fla., April 7, 1840. *Primitive Baptist* 5 (June 27, 1840): 186.

———. Letter, February 12, 1841. *Primitive Baptist* 6 (March 27, 1841): 127.

Hagan, Nancy. Obituary. *Christian Index* 15 (January 1, 1847): 7.

Hall, Basil. *Travels in North America in the Years 1827 and 1828.* 3 vols. Edinburgh: Ballantyne and Company, 1829.

Handcock, J. M. Letter, Berrien Co., Ga., July 6, 1896. *Pilgrim's Banner* 3 (November 15, 1896): 264.

Hanks, Lee. *The Church of God.* Atlanta: By the author, c. 1920. Reprint, Atwood, Tenn.: Christian Baptist Publishing Company, 1982.

Harmony Primitive Baptist Church, Brooks Co., Ga. Minutes. Ms. Photocopy in Odom Genealogical Library, Moultrie, Ga.

Harmony Primitive Baptist Church, Brooks Co., Ga., to Antioch Primitive Baptist Church, Thomas Co., Ga., December 8, 1876. MacArthur Collection, Ramah Primitive Baptist Church, Buena Vista, Ga.

Harris, George Washington. *Sut Lovingood's Yarns.* 1867. Reprint, ed. M. Thomas Inge, Memphis: St. Luke's Press, 1987.

Harris, Robert H. *Compendious History of the Mercer Baptist Association.* N.p. n.d.

Hassell, C. B. "Biography of Elder Joshua Lawrence." *Primitive Baptist* 8 (October 28, 1843): 312–13.

Hassell, Cushing Biggs, and Sylvester Hassell. *History of the Church of God, from the Creation to [sc]A.D.[sc] 1885; Including Especially the History of the Kehukee Primitive*

Baptist Association. Middletown, N.Y.: Gilbert Beebe's Sons, 1886. Reprint, Conley, Ga.: Old School Hymnal Co., 1973.

Hassell, Sylvester. "The Causes of the Division in Southwest Georgia." *Gospel Messenger* 26 (March 1904): 104.

———. "Scriptural Impartiality." *Gospel Messenger* 26 (March 1904): 184–86.

Hawthorn, Elias. Letter, Decatur Co., Ga., July 20, 1838. *Primitive Baptist* 3 (August 25, 1838): 253–54.

———. Letter, July 23, 1838. *Primitive Baptist* 3 (September 8, 1838): 270.

———. Letter, December 30, 1838. *Primitive Baptist* 5 (March 9, 1838): 68.

———. Letter, July 22, 1839. *Primitive Baptist* 4 (September 14, 1839): 260.

———. Letter, November 18, 1839. *Primitive Baptist* 4 (December 14, 1839): 350.

Hawthorn, William. Letter, Decatur Co., Ga., May 20, 1839. *Primitive Baptist* 4 (June 8, 1839): 174.

Haynes, Julietta. *A History of the Primitive Baptists*. Ph.D. Diss., University of Texas, 1959. Ann Arbor: University Microfilms International, 1989.

Hebron Primitive Baptist Convention, Coffee Co., Ga. *Minutes*.

Henderson, Lillian, comp. *Roster of the Confederate Soldiers of Georgia 1861–1865*. 5 vols. Hapeville, Ga.: Longino and Porter, n.d.

Hephzibah Primitive Baptist Church, Gadsden Co., Fla. Minutes. Ms. in possession of Piedmont Primitive Baptist Church, Grady Co., Ga.

Hephzibah Baptist Association, Georgia. *Minutes*.

Hervey, James, to John Gill. Quoted in n.a., "A Brief Memoir of the Life, Labours, and Character of the Reverend and Learned John Gill, D.D." London: 1839. In John Gill, *A Body of Doctrinal and Practical Divinity*. Reprint, Atlanta: Turner Lassetter, 1959.

Hickox, David. Letter, Pierce Co., Ga., May 21, 1861. *Primitive Baptist*. 25 (July 27, 1861): 219.

Hollingsworth, William. "My Experience and Call to the Ministry." 1910. TMs. Photocopy in possession of John G. Crowley, Hahira, Ga. Copied by Wayne Faircloth from original ms. in possession of Laura Walden, Elder Hollingsworth's daughter, Mobile, Ala.

Holy Spirit Conference with International Evangelist Charles Carrin. Flyer for May 1–4, 1994, meeting at Grace Chapel, Mandarin, Fla.

Hooker, Richard J., ed. *The Carolina Backcountry on the Eve of the Revolution: The Journal and Other Writings of Charles Woodmason, Anglican Itinerant*. Chapel Hill, N.C.: University of North Carolina Press, 1953.

Hopewell Primitive Baptist Association, Alabama. *Minutes*.

Hurste, Chloe. Letter, Jefferson Co., Fla., December 31, 1840. *Primitive Baptist* 6 (February 13, 1841): 39.

Hutto, Isaac D. "Experience." *Pilgrim's Banner* 4 (July 15, 1897): 5.

Huxford, Folks. "Fleming Bates." Ms. in Huxford Genealogical Society Library, Homerville, Ga.

———. *The History of Brooks County*, Georgia 1858–1948. Quitman, Ga.: n.p., 1948.

———. "Isaac Coon." Ms. in Huxford Genealogical Society Library, Homerville, Ga.

———. "Minutes of Empire Baptist Church, Lanier Co., Ga." *Huxford Genealogical Quarterly* 20 (March 1993): 18, 19.

———. "Prospect Primitive Baptist Church, Hamilton Co., Fla." *Huxford Genealogical Society Magazine* 12 (December 1985): 344–45.

———. "Records of Hebron Primitive Baptist Church, Hamilton County, Florida, Constituted February 20, 1858." TMs. in Huxford Genealogical Society Library, Homerville, Ga.

———. "Records of Wayfare Church [Echols Co., Ga.]." TMs. in Huxford Genealogical Society Library, Homerville, Ga.

Huxford Genealogical Society. *Pioneers of Wiregrass Georgia.* 8 vols. Various places: Various publishers, 1951–88.

Isaac Coon Confederate monument. New Friendship Cemetery, Hahira, Ga.

Jackson, George Pullen. "The Story of the Sacred Harp." In B. F. White and E. J. King, *The Sacred Harp, Facsimile of the Third Edition, 1859, Including as a Historical Introduction, 'The Story of the Sacred Harp' by George Pullen Jackson.* Nashville: Broadman Press, 1968.

Johnson, Jerah, and Joseph A. Perdigao. "The Pioneers of Old Lowndes County: A Case Study of Settlers on the Antebellum Southern Frontier." *Piney Woods Journal of History* 1 (1989–90): 1–19.

Johnson, Michael P. "A New Look at the Popular Vote for Delegates to the Georgia Secession Convention." *Georgia Historical Quarterly* 56 (Summer 1972): 259–75.

Jones, Frank S. *History of Decatur County, Georgia.* 1971. Reprint, Spartanburg, S.C.: Reprint Company, 1980.

Jones, S. P., C. Cromer Crawford, A. D. Cook, and C. T. Morris. "Statement on Good Works." TMs. in possession of John G. Crowley, Hahira, Ga.

Journal of the Proceedings of the People of Florida, Begun and Held at the Capitol in the City of Tallahassee, on Thursday, January 3, 1861. 1861. Reprint, Jacksonville, Fla.: H. and W. B. Drew Co., 1928.

Kehukee Primitive Baptist Association, North Carolina. "Extract from the Minutes of the Kehukee Association, Held at Kehukee meeting house, in 1827." *Primitive Baptist* 7 (May 14, 1842): 132–33.

Kilpatrick, W. L. *The Hephzibah Baptist Centennial 1794–1894.* Augusta, Ga.: Richards and Shaver, 1894.

Kirkland, J. V., and R. S. Kirkland, eds. *A Comprehensive Confession of Faith Put Forth by the Ministers and Messengers Representing Upwards of One Hundred Congregations of Baptists in England and Wales While Convened in London, July 3–11, 1689, Republished by the Phildelphia Association of Baptists, September 25, 1742, Unanimously Approved and Republished with Explanatory Footnotes and a General Address by the National Convention of Primitive Baptists, While in Session at Fulton, Ky., November 14–18, 1900, with an Address Put Forth by the Ministerial Meeting at Oakland City, Ind., Appended.* Fulton, Ky.: By the editors, [1900].

Lambert, Byron. *The Rise of the Anti-Mission Baptists: Sources and Leaders, 1800–1840.*

Ph.D. Diss., University of Chicago, 1957. Reprint, The Baptist Tradition, New York: Arno Press, 1980.

Lawrence, Joshua. "Declaration of the Reformed Baptist Churches in the State of North Carolina [1827]." *Primitive Baptist* 7 (May 14, 1842): 129–31.

Lee, Jerry. "Separation and Crystallization of Northwest Georgia Primitive Baptists." Synopsis of a Research Paper on the on the "Old School" or "Primitive" Baptist Movement in Northwest Georgia delivered at Shorter College, Rome, Ga., during the 1973 session of the Georgia Baptist Historical Society. TMs. Photocopy in possession of John G. Crowley, Hahira, Ga.

Leland, John. "A Letter of Valediction, on Leaving Virginia, in 1791." In L. F. Greene, ed., *The Writings of Elder John Leland, Including Some Events in His Life, Written by Himself, With Additional Sketches.* New York: G. W. Wood, 1845. Reprint, Religion in America, Edwin S. Gaustad, series ed., New York: Arno Press and the New York Times, 1969.

———. "Virginia Chronicle." 1790. In L. F. Greene, ed., *Writings of Elder John Leland.*

Lester, James Adams. *A History of the Georgia Baptist Convention 1822–1972.* Nashville: Executive Committee of the Baptist Convention of the State of Georgia, 1972.

Lewis, Prior. Letter, Thomas Co., Ga., September 26, 1839. *Primitive Baptist* 4 (November 23, 1839): 345.

———. Letter, December 29, 1839. *Primitive Baptist* 5 (February 8, 1840): 46.

———. Letter, December 30, 1841. *Primitive Baptist* 7 (February 12, 1842): 47

———. Letter, December 26, 1842. *Primitive Baptist* 8 (January 14, 1843): 14–15.

Liberty Primitive Baptist Church, Liberty Co., Fla. Minutes. Ms. in possession of Piedmont Primitive Baptist Church, Grady Co., Ga.

"List of Agents." *Signs of the Times* 18 (January 15, 1850): 16.

Little River Baptist Church, Lowndes Co., Ga. Minutes. October 15, 1842. In *Christian Index* 10 (December 2, 1842): 761.

Lloyd, Benjamin. Letter, Wetumpka, Ala., April 7, 1842. *Primitive Baptist* 7 (April 23, 1842): 119–20.

———. Letter, April 24, 1847. *Primitive Baptist* 11 (July 31, 1847): 303–4.

Lloyd, Benjamin, comp. *Primitive Hymns.* 1858. Reprint, Rocky Mount, N.C.: Primitive Hymns Corporation, 1971.

London Baptist Confession of 1689. In Hassell and Hassell. *Church of God.*

Lookout Mountain Primitive Baptist Association, Georgia. *Minutes.*

Lott's Creek Primitive Baptist Association, Georgia. *Minutes.*

MacDonald, James. Letter, Darien, Ga., December 22, 1836. *Christian Index* 5 (January 12, 1837): 25.

Mallary, Charles Dutton. *Memoirs of Elder Edmund Botsford* Charleston: W. Riley, 1832.

———. *Memoirs of Elder Jesse Mercer.* New York: John Gray, 1844. Quoted in James Mosteller, *Kiokee Church.*

Malone, Ann Patton. "Piney Woods Farmers of South Georgia, 1850–1900: Jeffersonian Yeomen in an Age of Expanding Commercialism." *Agricultural History* 60 (Fall 1986): 51–84.

Mayfield, Marjorie Maxwell. *Calvary, Georgia Heritage 1828–1976.* Cairo, Ga.: Marjorie Mayfield and Marilee Butler, 1976.

McCrary, Asa, to Burwell Temple, Thomas Co., Ga., September 17, 1860. *Primitive Baptist* 24 (October 27, 1860): 1.

———. Letter, November 28, 1860. *Primitive Baptist* 25 (January 12, 1861): 1.

———. Letter, January 17, 1861. *Primitive Baptist* 25 (February 10, 1861): 42.

McElvey, William. Letter, Decatur Co., Ga., May 25, 1838. *Primitive Baptist* 3 (June 23, 1838): 188.

———. Letter, June 15, 1839. *Primitive Baptist* 4 (July 27, 1839): 221.

———. Letter, August 20, 1839. *Primitive Baptist* 4 (October 12, 1839): 302.

———. Letter, September 20, 1839. *Primitive Baptist* 5 (June 11, 1840): 13.

———. Letter, November 20, 1840. *Primitive Baptist* 6 (March 13, 1841): 68–69.

McKinney, George Patterson, and Richard I. McKinney. *History of the Black Baptists of Florida, 1850–1985.* Miami: Florida Memorial Press, 1987.

McQueen, A. S., and Hamp Mizell. *History of the Okefenokee Swamp.* 1926. Reprint, Folkston, Ga.: n.p., 1949.

McWhiney, Grady. *Cracker Culture: Celtic Ways in the Old South.* Prologue by Forrest McDonald. Tuscaloosa: University of Alabama Press, 1988.

Mercer, Jesse. *History of the Georgia Baptist Association, Compiled at the Request of that Body.* Washington. Ga.: n.p., 1838. Reprint (with an introduction by Waldo P. Harris, and appendix, "Early Baptist Churches in Georgia," by Robert G. Gardner, and an index by Anne F. Gardener and Robert F. Gardner), Washington, Ga.: Georgia Baptist Association Executive Committee, 1970.

———. "Rather Distressing." *Christian Index* (November 28, 1839). Quoted in Elias Hawthorn letter, September 18, 1840, *Primitive Baptist* 5 (October 5, 1840): 348.

———. *Ten Letters Addressed to the Rev. Cyrus White in Reference to His Scriptural View of the Atonement.* Washington, Ga.: 1830. Cited in Emerson Proctor. "Georgia Baptists: Organization and Division 1772–1840." M.A. Thesis, Georgia Southern College, 1969.

Middlebrooks, Samuel A. "A Future View of America" with editorial comments by Elder T. R. Crawford. *Goodwill* 23 (May 1964): 10–11.

Milfort, Louis Leclerc. *My Ten Years Sojourn in the Creek Nation.* 1802; 1959. Reprint (translated and edited with and introduction by Ben C. McCrary), Savannah: Beehive Press, 1972.

Minutes of the General Meeting of the Churches of the Mt. Olive Association, Held with Concord Church, Berrien County, Georgia, December 29, 1916.

"Minutes of the Minister's Meeting Held at Eatonton, Ga." *Christian Index* 5 (December 14, 1837): 799–800.

Moseley, William. Letter, Bear Creek, Ga., February 5, 1840. *Primitive Baptist* 5 (February 5, 1840): 63.

Mosteller, James. *A History of the Kiokee Baptist Church in Georgia.* Ann Arbor: Edwards Brothers, 1952. Reprint, Washington, Ga.: Wilkes Publishing Company, 1972.

Mt. Enon Primitive Baptist Association, Florida. *Minutes.*

Mt. Moriah Primitive Baptist Church, Jefferson Co., Fla. Minutes. Quoted in Nancy Hagan Obituary. *Christian Index* 15 (January 1, 1847): 7.

Mt. Olive Primitive Baptist Association, Georgia. *Minutes*

———. [Lewis faction]. *Minutes.*

Myers, Ronald L. "Scrub and High Pine." In Ronald J. Myers and John J. Ewel, *Ecosystems of Florida,* with introduction by Marjorie H. Carr. Orlando: University of Central Florida, 1990.

New Hope Predestinarian Baptist Association, Illinois. *Minutes.*

New Hope [Grady Co., Ga.], Poplar Springs [Grady Co., Ga.], and Mt. Zion [Thomas Co., Ga.] Churches to the Lott's Creek Primitive Baptist Association, October 10, 1987. In Original Old Line Flint River Primitive Baptist Association. *Minutes.*

Ninde, Edward S. *The Story of the American Hymn.* New York: Abingdon Press, 1921. Reprint, New York: AMS Press, 1975.

The Nineteenth North Florida Fellowship Meeting of Primitive Baptist Churches, September 28, 29, 30, 1990.

Ochlocknee Baptist Association Corresponding Letter. In *Southern Spy* (Bainbridge, Ga.), October 20. 1829.

"Ochlocknee Primitive—!!" *Christian Index* 10 (December 2, 1842): 761.

Ochlocknee Primitive Baptist Association, Georgia. *Minutes.*

———. [McCann faction]. *Minutes.*

———. In *Minutes of Ten Primitive Baptist Associations.* [Valdosta, Ga.: Multimedia Ministries, 1993].

———. [Simms-Barwick faction]. *Minutes.*

Old West Florida Primitive Baptist Association. *Minutes.*

O'Neel, Daniel. Letter, Fowlton, Ga., July 17, 1839. *Primitive Baptist* 4 (October 12, 1839): 299.

Original Mt. Enon Primitive Baptist Association in Order. *Minutes.*

Original Mt. Olive Old School Baptist Association, Georgia. *Minutes.*

Original Ochlocknee Primitive Baptist Association, Georgia. *Minutes*

Original Union Primitive Baptist Association, Georgia. *Minutes.*

Parker, Daniel. "A Brief Account of the Life, Experience, Labours, Privations, Struggles, Persecutions, Sufferings, Victories of Elder Daniel Parker." In "The Principal Writings of Elder Daniel Parker," ed. Ben H. Irwin. TMs. Photocopy in possession of John G. Crowley, Hahira, Ga.

———. "The Doctrine of the Two Seeds." In "The Principal Writings."

Parker, Elmer Orris. *A History of Jones Creek Baptist Church, Long County, Georgia 1810–1985.* Greenville, S.C.: Jones Creek Baptist Church, 1985.

Paisley, Clifton. *The Red Hills of Florida.* Tuscaloosa: University of Alabama Press, 1989.

Parrish, June Jackson. *Parrish: A Compilation of the Available Records Covering Direct Descendants of Four Parrish Brothers: Henry, Joel, Ansel, and Absalom, Sons of Henry Parrish (1740) and Grandsons of Joel Parrish (1700), Also Descendants of Henry Jackson Parrish, Son of Hezekiah, a Brother of the Four Brothers Named, Grandson of Henry.* Adel, Ga.: By the author, 1948.

Paschal, George Washington. *History of North Carolina Baptists.* 2 vols. Raleigh, N.C.: General Board of the North Carolina Baptist State Convention, 1930.

Peacock, Isham. Obituary. *Christian Index* 18 (June 14, 1851): 95.

Pearce, Wiley. Letter, Decatur Co., Ga., March 1, 1838. *Christian Index* 3 (March 24, 1838): 85.

Perry, Joel W. *History of Early County.* 1871. Cited in Frank S. Jones, *History of Decatur County, Georgia.* 1971. Reprint, Spartanburg, S.C.: Reprint Company, 1980.

Phillip's Mill Baptist Church to the Georgia Association, 1787, written by Silas Mercer. In Jesse Mercer, *History of the Georgia Baptist Association.*

Piedmont Baptist Association, Georgia-Florida. Minutes. Ms. Photocopy in possession of John G. Crowley, Hahira, Ga.

Piedmont Primitive Baptist Church, Grady Co., Ga. Minutes. Ms. in possession of the church.

Pierce, John J. *Birds of a Feather: The Origins of the Southern Peacocks.* n.p. 1984.

Pigeon Creek Primitive Baptist Church, Nassau Co., Fla. Minutes. TMs. Photocopy in possession of John G. Crowley, Hahira, Ga.

Pilgrim's Rest Primitive Baptist Association, Florida. Minutes.

Pilgrim's Rest Primitive Baptist Association Ministers' Meeting, Ft. Pierce, Florida, May 28, 1965.

Pilgrim's Rest Primitive Baptist Association of Old Line Predestinarian Faith and Order. *Minutes.*

Pleasant Grove Primitive Baptist Church, Berrien Co., Ga. Minutes. Ms. in possession of the church.

Pleasant Primitive Baptist Church, Berrien County, Ga. Minutes. Ms. Photocopy in Odom Genealogical Library, Moultrie, Ga.

Pleasant Union Primitive Baptist Association. *Minutes.*

Potter, Lemuel. *Labors and Travels of Elder Lemuel Potter, as an Old School Baptist Minister, for Thirty Years, With a Brief Sketch of His Earlier Life, Christian Experience, and Call to the Ministry, Together With His Doctrinal Sentiments on Some Vital Points* (Evansville, Ind.: For the author, 1894).

Preslar, Hosea. *Thoughts on Divine Providence, or a Sketch of God's Care Over and Dealings with His People: Together with a Concise View of the Causes and Effects of the Late War in the United States.* Cincinnati: By the author, 1867. Reprint, Streamwood, Ill.: Primitive Baptist Library, 1977.

Proctor, Emerson. "Georgia Baptists: Organization and Division 1772–1840." M.A. Thesis, Georgia Southern College, 1969.

Pulaski Primitive Baptist Association, Georgia. *Minutes.*

Purefoy, George W. *A History of the Sandy Creek Association from its Organization in [sc]A.D.[sc] 1758, to [sc]A.D.[sc] 1858.* New York: Sheldon and Co., 1859.

Purifoy, J. H. "Elder Purifoy's Tour." *Gospel Messenger* 11 (June–July 1889): 231–32.

Rambo, Gene. "The 1820 Land Lottery in Georgia." *Piney Woods Journal of History* 1 (1989–90): 20–40.

Report of the American Baptist Home Missionary Society, 1838. Quoted in Earl Joiner, *History of Florida Baptists.* Jacksonville, Fla.: Convention Press, 1972.

Report of the American Baptist Home Missionary Society. 1844. Cited in Joiner, *History of Florida Baptists.*

"Resolution." *Pilgrim's Banner* 4 (November 15, 1897): 13–14.

"Resolutions of Delaware and Baltimore Associations." *Signs of the Times* 22 (June 15, 1854): 93.

Revolutionary War Pension File W8513 (Isham and Lydia Peacock).

"Richard Bennett." *Huxford Genealogical Society Magazine* 21 (June 1994): 148.

Richardson, Simon Peter. *Lights and Shadows of Intinerant Life: An Autobiography . . . .* Dallas: Publishing House Methodist Episcopal Church South, 1900.

Richland Creek Predestinarian Baptist Association, Tennessee. *Minutes.*

Richland Creek Primitive Baptist Church, Grady Co., Ga. Minutes. Ms. in possession of Tired Creek Church, Grady Co., Ga.

Riley, B. F. *History of the Baptists of Alabama from the Time of Their First Occupation of Alabama in 1808, until 1894: Being a Detailed Record of Denominational Events in the State during the Stirring Period of Eighty-Six Years, and Furnishing Biographical Sketches of Those Who Have Been Conspicuous in the Annals of the Denomination, Besides Much Other Incidental Matter Relative to the Secular History of Alabama.* Birmingham: Alabama Baptist Historical Society, 1895.

Rippon, John. *Selection of Hymns from the Best Authors, Intended to be an Appendix to Dr. Watts's Psalms and Hymns.* New York: William Durrell, 1792. Microfiche.

Rorabaugh, William. *The Alcoholic Republic: An American Tradition.* New York: Oxford University Press, 1979.

Rosser, John Leonidas. *A History of Florida Baptists.* Nashville: Broadman Press, 1949.

Salem Primitive Baptist Church, Cook Co., Ga. Minutes. Ms. Photocopy in Odom Genealogical Library, Moultrie, Ga.

San Pedro Primitive Baptist Association. Minutes. Ms. in possession of Lawrence Holden, Perry, Fla.

San Pedro Primitive Baptist Association, Florida. *Minutes.*

Satilla Primitive Baptist Association, Georgia. *Minutes.*

Satilla River Primitive Baptist Association, Georgia. *Minutes.*

Savannah Baptist Association, Georgia–South Carolina, *Minutes.*

Savannah River Baptist Association, Georgia–South Carolina, *Minutes*

Shelton, Jane Twitty. *Pines and Pioneers: A History of Lowndes County, Georgia, 1825–1900.* Atlanta: Cherokee Publishing Co., 1976.

Sherwood, Adiel. Letter. 1870. Quoted in Julia L. Sherwood. *Memoirs of Adiel Sherwood, D.D.* Philadelphia: Grant and Faires, 1884. Quoted in James Adams Lester. *A History of the Georgia Baptist Convention 1822–1972.* Nashville: Executive Committee of the Baptist Convention of the State of Georgia, 1972.

———. *Memoirs.* Quoted in Christian Index, *History of the Baptist Denomination in Georgia.* Atlanta: James P. Harrison and Co., 1881.

Shurden, Walter B. *Associationalism among Baptists in America, 1707–1814.* Ph.D. Diss., New Orleans Baptist Theological Seminary, 1967. Reprint, The Baptist Tradition, New York: Arno Press, 1980.

Simms, A. V. "Associations." *Pilgrim's Banner* 1 (November 15, 1894): 280.

———. "Elder Bartley's Article." *Pilgrim's Banner* 3 (November 1, 1896): 252.
———. "Flint River Association." *Pilgrim's Banner* 3 (November 15, 1896): 264.
———. "Some Good Meetings." *Pilgrim's Banner* 1 (October 15, 1894): 237–38.
———. "The Rot." *Pilgrim's Banner* 1 (November 1, 1894): 252.
Smith, George C. *The History of Georgia Methodism from 1786 to 1886.* Atlanta: A. B. Caldwell, 1913.
Smith, Owen. Letter, Lowndes Co., Ga., December 25, 1850, to Gilbert Beebe, New Vernon, N.Y. *Signs of the Times* 19 (February 1, 1851): 22.
Southern Spy (Bainbridge, Ga.), June 30, 1829.
Souvenir Booklet of Wakulla County Primitive Baptist Church Union Meetings. n.p., 1984.
Stallings, Roscoe. *Ancestors and Descendants of Timothy William and Susan Newton Stallings.* n.p., 1982.
Stallings, T. W. Letter, Cecil, Ga., February 10, 1895, to A. V. Simms, Valdosta, Ga. *Pilgrim's Banner* 2 (February 15, 1895): 46.
———. Letter, Lowndes Co., Ga., January 1, 1876, to W. M. Mitchell, Opelika, Ala. In "Voices of the Past," *Signs of the Times.* 146 (July 1978): 161–65.
S[tanaland], R. T. "Who Are the Primitive Baptists?" *Christian Index* 13 (January 17, 1845): 2.
Stanley, Brian. *The History of the Baptist Missionary Society.* Edinburgh: T. and T. Clark, 1992.
Stokes, Jane A. Letter, Milton, Fla., December 25, 1843. *Primitive Baptist* 9 (January 27, 1844): 31.
Sunbury Baptist Association, Georgia. *Minutes.*
Surmons, Dinah. "Experience of a Colored Woman." *Pilgrim's Banner* 3 (September 15, 1896): 192.
Suwannee River Primitive Baptist Association, Florida. *Minutes*
———. [Coon faction]. *Minutes.*
———. [Harris faction]. *Minutes.*
———. [McCall faction]. *Minutes.*
———. [Peace faction]. *Minutes.*
Sweet, William Warren. *Religion on the American Frontier.* Vol. 1: *The Baptists 1783–1830: A Collection of Source Material.* New York: Cooper Square Publishers, 1964.
Taylor, I. J. Letter, Texas, to Lee Hanks, Georgia. *Pilgrim's Banner* 4 (September 1, 1897): 7–12.
Temple, Burwell. "Editorial." *Primitive Baptist* 25 (January 12, 1861): 12.
Terms of Agreement Between Spring Hill and Concord Primitive Baptist Churches in Settling Their Differences of 26 Years Standing and Letters of Correspondence Between Empire and Spring Hill Churches Concerning the Settlement Between Concord and Spring Hill. n.p. 1927.
Thomas, H. Letter, Decatur Co., Ga., January 2, 1842. *Pilgrim's Banner* 7 (May 28, 1842): 130–31.
Thomas, William C. Letter, Fowlton, Ga., October 25, 1840. *Primitive Baptist* 6 (June 12, 1841): 165.

Thompson, Gregg M. *The Measuring Rod: Or, the Principles and Practice of the Primitive Baptists. Stated and Defended against Modern Arianism, Two-Seedism, &c. With an Appendix in Which the Writer Has Met and Refuted the Many False Charges Made upon Him by Elders T. P. Dudley, G. Beebe, & W. C. Cleaveland.* Nashville: By the Author, 1860.

Thompson, Wilson. *The Autobiography of Elder Wilson Thompson, His Life, Travels, and Ministerial Labors.* 1867. Reprint, Conley, Ga.: Old School Hymnal Co., 1978.

Tinsley, Jim Bob. *Florida Cow Hunter: The Life and Times of Bone Mizell.* Orlando: University of Central Florida Press, 1990.

Tired Creek Primitive Baptist Church, Grady Co., Ga. Minutes. Ms. in possession of the church.

Toon, Peter. *The Emergence of Hyper-Calvinism in English Nonconformity.* London: Olive Tree, 1967.

Towaliga Primitive Baptist Association, Georgia. *Minutes.*

Trott, Samuel, John Healy, Thomas Poteet, Thomas Barton, Gilbert Beebe, et al. "Address to the Particular Baptist Churches of the 'Old School' in the United States. [The Black Rock Address]." *Signs of the Times* 1 (November 28, 1832): 1.

Tucker, John. Letter, Newnansville, Fla., February 25, 1845. *Christian Index* 12 (March 21, 1845): 1.

Union Primitive Baptist Church, Lanier Co., Ga. Minutes. Ms. in Huxford Genealogical Society Library, Homerville, Ga.

Union Primitive Baptist Association, Georgia. *Minutes.*

———. [black]. *Minutes.*

———. [Luke faction]. *Minutes.*

———. [Old Line faction]. *Minutes.*

———. [Peace faction]. *Minutes.*

Upper Black Creek Primitive Baptist Church, Bulloch Co., Ga. Minutes. Ms. in special collections, Mercer University Library, Macon, Ga. Microfilm.

U.S. Census Office. *Report on Statistics of Churches in the United States at the Eleventh Census: 1890.*

Valdosta [Ga.] Primitive Baptist Church. Minutes. Ms. in possession of the church.

Vickers, John. *An Explanation of the Split between the Hardshell Baptists and the Primitive Baptists.* N.p., n.d.

Ward, Warren P. "Ward's Column: Manning Kirkland Is Killed." *Huxford Genealogical Magazine* 8 (September 1991): 224.

———. *Ward's History of Coffee County.* 1930. Reprint, Spartanburg, S.C.: Reprint Co., 1978.

"Warwick Baptist Association vs. Clerical Arrogance." *Signs of the Times* (22 August 1, 1854): 103.

Watkins, Hartwell. Letter, Jefferson Co., Fla., July 13, 1845, to Ely Holland, N.C. *Primitive Baptist* 10 (August 23, 1845): 255.

Wayfare Primitive Baptist Church, Echols Co., Ga. Minutes. Ms. in possession of the church.

Wells, Charles F. *Condensed History of Baptists, Mainly Georgia Primitive Baptists: Facts, Records, Divisions, Also Interesting Features.* Macon, Ga.: By the author, [1962].

West Florida Primitive Baptist Association. *Minutes.*

Whitten, Samuel F. *Statement.* N.p., 1895.

Wiggins, E. I. *History of the Absolute Mt. Enon Association.* N.p., n.d. Reprint, Mt. Enon Cemetery Memorial, 1975.

Wiggins, W. L. "Elder James Moseley." In Mt. Enon Primitive Baptist Association, Florida. *Minutes.*

Yarborough, Slayden. "The Origin of Baptist Associations among the English Particular Baptists." *Baptist History and Heritage* 23 (April 1988): 14–24.

INDEX

John G. Crowley is assistant professor of history at Valdosta State University, Valdosta, Georgia. He specializes in American social history, with interests in religion and southern culture.

CPSIA information can be obtained
at www.ICGtesting.com
Printed in the USA
BVOW08s2009151116
467956BV00001B/11/P